HIGH
PERFORMANCE
HABITS

How Extraordinary
People Become That Way

BRENDON BURCHARD

HAY HOUSE, INC.
Carlsbad, California • New York
London • Sydney • Johannesburg
Vancouver • New Delhi

For permissions requests, speaking inquiries, and bulk order purchase options, e-mail support@Brendon.com.

Published and distributed in the United States by Hay House, Inc.: www.hayhouse. com® • *Published and distributed in Australia by* Hay House Australia Pty., Ltd.: www .hayhouse.com.au • *Published and distributed in the United Kingdom by* Hay House UK, Ltd.: www.hayhouse.co.uk • *Published and distributed in the Republic of South Africa by* Hay House SA (Pty.), Ltd.: www.hayhouse.co.za • *Distributed in Canada by* Raincoast Books: www.raincoast.com • *Published in India by* Hay House Publishers India: www.hayhouse.co.in. For international rights requests, e-mail support@Brendon.com

Cover design and illustrations: Brendon Burchard
Interior design: Brendon Burchard and Riann Bender
Author photo: Maggie Kirkland, © 2017 The Burchard Group
Author illustration on page 349: Nancy Januzzi

Except from *The Charge* on page 334 appears with permission of Simon & Schuster.

Cataloging-in-Publication data is on file with the Library of Congress.

Hardcover ISBN: 978-1-4019-5285-3
10 9 8 7 6 5 4 3 2 1
1st edition, September 2017

Printed in the United States of America

Dedicated to my sunshine, Denise,
the most extraordinary person I know.

CONTENTS

INTRODUCTION

"Excellence is an art won by training and habituation.
We do not act rightly because we have virtue or excellence,
but we rather have those because we have acted rightly.
We are what we repeatedly do.
Excellence, then, is not an act but a habit."

—Aristotle

"Why are you so terrified to want more?"

A large oak desk separates me from Lynn. She pulls back in her chair and stares out the window for a moment. We're on the forty-second floor, nearly eye level with the morning mist, looking out over the ocean.

Even before I ask the question, I know she won't like it.

Lynn is one of those people you could describe as highly effective. She's focused and gets stuff done. She exhibits strengths for critical thinking and leading others. She's received three big promotions in five years. People admire her. They say she's on her way, that she's got the "it" factor.

"Terrified" is not how most would describe her. But I know.

She glances back at me and starts to reply: "Well, I wouldn't say that I'm . . ."

I lean in and shake my head.

She catches herself and nods, smoothing her already smooth brown hair. She knows she can't get away with a fake story right now.

"Okay," Lynn says. "Maybe you're right. I'm scared to go to the next level."

I ask why.

"Because I'm barely surviving this one."

#

This book is about how people become extraordinary, and why others block themselves from that possibility. It will show clearly and unmistakably why some excel, others fail, and far too many never even try.

As a high performance coach, I've worked with a lot of people like Lynn. Achievers fight long and hard to succeed, propelling themselves forward by grit and hustle. And then, at some point they could never have anticipated, they plateau, lose passion, or burn out. To outside observers, they may appear steady and calm as they plod ahead. But deep inside, achievers often feel that they are thrashing about, lost in a sea of priorities and opportunities. They feel unsure what to focus on or how to confidently replicate or scale their success. They've come far in life yet still have no standard operating principles for sustaining success. Even though they're capable, many live in constant fear that they will fall behind or catastrophically fail to handle the demands of the next level of success. Why the fear and hardship? And why do some people break free from this reality, keep rising higher, and enjoy the vibrant well-being and abundant long-term success that so many envy or consider out of reach?

To understand the phenomenon, this book pulls together twenty years of research, ten years of insights gained from elite-level performance coaching, and a vast data set on high performers worldwide gathered through surveys, structured interviews, and professional assessment tools. It will reveal what it takes to become not just an *achiever* but a *high performer*—someone who creates ever-increasing levels of both well-being and external success over the long term.

During the journey, I will expose many of the prevailing myths about "success," including why grit, willpower, practice, and your "natural" strengths and talents are not enough to take you to the next level in a world that demands you add value, lead others, and manage competing priorities and complex projects. To reach high performance, you have to consider more than your individual passions and efforts, and you'll have to go well beyond what you like, prefer, or naturally do well, because, to be frank, the world cares less about your strengths and personality than about your service and meaningful contributions to others.

By the end of this book, you will never again wonder what it really takes to succeed when starting a new project at work or pursuing a bold new dream. You will be empowered with a set of reliable habits that research has shown to work with a broad range of personalities, and in a variety of situations, to create extraordinary long-term results. You'll feel a new sense of vital energy and confidence from knowing where to focus your energies and how to serve most effectively. You'll understand how to keep growing after you've enjoyed initial success. If you're ever thrown into a situation where you must work or compete with others at the highest levels of achievement, you'll know *exactly* how to think and what to do.

This isn't to say you will be superhuman, or need to be. You have flaws; we all do. Yet at the end of this book, you'll say to yourself, "I finally know *exactly* how to be consistently at my best. I'm confident in my ability to figure things out, and fully capable of overcoming adversity on the path of success, for the rest of my life." You will have a standard mental operating system and proven set of habits that reliably lead to long-term success across many different situations, and across multiple domains of life. In my own work as a high performance coach, I've seen these habits transform the effectiveness of people from all walks of life—from Fortune 50 CEOs to entertainers, from Olympians to everyday parents, from world-class experts to high school students. If you've ever wanted a serious field-tested and science-backed path to improving your life, you have found it, here in this book.

Armed with the information you'll learn in the pages ahead, you will live a life in which your full potential is in play, you have a vital sense of well-being, you are capable of leading others to excellence, and you are deeply fulfilled. Assuming you bring full intention and discipline to deploying the high performance habits, you're about to enter a very transformational period of your life and career. You're about to become even more extraordinary.

WHY THIS BOOK? WHY NOW?

I've been blessed to train millions of people worldwide on personal and professional development, and I can report that it's a palpable feeling everywhere right now: People are tremendously uncertain about how to get ahead and which decisions are right for them, their families, and their careers. People want to scale up, but they're wiped out. They're working so hard, but they're just not breaking through. They are driven, but they don't always know exactly what they want. They desire to go for their dreams, yet they're afraid they'll be judged crazy or fail if they try.

Add to that the unrelenting tasks, the self-doubt, the unwanted obligations, the overwhelming choices and responsibilities—it's enough to exhaust anyone. For too many, there is a sense that things will never get better and they'll always be swimming in a churning sea of distractions and disappointments. If that sounds dire, it is. People are hopeful and ready to make a change, but lacking direction and the right habits they risk living unexciting, disconnected, unful-filling lives.

Of course, many people are living happy, wonderful lives. But consistency is a problem. They may feel capable—even feel that they hit "peak performance" once in a while—but there's always that steep cliff on the other side. And so people are tired of the ups and downs of peak performance. They're wondering how to reach heightened and *sustained* growth and success. They don't need just new tricks to get into better states and moods; they need real skills and methods for holistically advancing their lives and careers.

That's not an easy order. Though everyone says they want to advance in every area of their lives, many, like Lynn, are deeply concerned that pursuing their dreams will cause collateral damage—wrecked relationships, financial ruin, social ridicule, unbearable stress. At some point, perhaps, we all worry about such things. Isn't it true that you already know how to get stuff done, yet sometimes you limit your vision for the future because you're *already* so busy, so stressed, so overextended?

It's not that you're incapable of performing better. You know that sometimes you *crush it* on one project at work, but struggle on another, similar one. You know that you can be a star in one social setting, but not in another. You know how to motivate yourself, but sometimes you hate yourself at the end of the day for having completed nothing but a three-season binge on Netflix.

Perhaps, too, you've noticed other people advancing more quickly than you. Maybe you've seen one of your peers just waltz with grace from project to project, succeeding each time no matter what gets thrown in their way. It's as if you can put them in any context, any team, any company, any industry, and they'll just *win*.

Who are these people, and what's their secret? They are high performers, and their secret is their habits. The good news is you can become one of them, and you can leverage those same habits whatever your background, personality, weaknesses, or field of endeavor. With the right training and habits, anyone can become a high performer, and I can prove it. That's why I wrote this book for you.

THE BASELINE MOVED

Many of us feel a gap between our ordinary lives and the extraordinary lives we wish to have. Fifty years ago, perhaps, it was easier to navigate the world and get ahead. The baseline for success was more straightforward: "Work hard. Play by the rules. Keep your head down. Don't ask too many questions. Follow the leader. Take time to master something that will keep you around here."

Then, twenty years ago, the baseline began to shift. "Work hard. Break the rules. Keep your head up—optimists win. Ask questions of the experts. You are a leader. Hurry up and figure it out."

Today, for many, the baseline feels distant, blurred, almost unknowable. Gone are the days when our work was predictable and the expectations of those around us were "fixed." Change accelerated. Now everything feels chaotic. Your boss, lover, or customer always wants something new, *now*. Your work isn't as simple or siloed as it used to be. And if it is, the odds are a computer or a robot will soon replace you. To compound the stress, now *everything* is connected, so if you mess up one thing, it messes up an entire network of other things. Mistakes are no longer private affairs. They are public and global.

It's a new world. Certainty is down, yet expectations are up. Instead of mantras about working hard, following the rules, keeping your head down or up, we have an unspoken but widely accepted norm: "Pretend you're not working as hard, so your friends are impressed with your leisurely posts and photos at breakfast, but yes, work hard. Don't wait for instruction, because there are no rules. Try to keep your head on, because it's a madhouse here. Ask questions, but don't expect anyone to know the answers. There are no leaders, because we all lead, so just find your groove for right now and add value. *You'll never figure anything out—just keep adapting, because tomorrow everything changes again.*"

This isn't just unsettling. Getting ahead amid the chaos feels like trying to run under ten feet of murky water. You can't see where you're going. You're flailing about, but there's no progress. You're looking for help, an edge, a lifeline, *anything*, but you're not finding any air or any stairs out. You had good intentions and a strong work ethic, but you don't even know where to apply them. You have people counting on you, but you're not sure which direction to point.

Even if you don't feel as if you are drowning, you might sense that you are plateauing. Or maybe you have the sinking feeling that you're about to be left behind. Sure, you've gotten ahead so far by sheer passion, guts, and hard work. You've climbed a few mountains. But the next questions are throwing you off: *Where to now? How to go higher? Why are others climbing more quickly than I am? When, if ever, can I relax and set down some roots? Does it always have to feel like such a grind? Am I really living my best life?*

What you need is a reliable set of practices for unleashing your greatest abilities. Study high performers and you will see that they have systems built into their days that drive their success. Systems are what separate the pro from the novice, and science from armchair philosophy. Without systems, you cannot test hypothesis, track progress, or repeatedly deliver exceptional results. In personal and professional development, these systems and procedures are, ultimately, *habits*. But which ones work?

WHAT'S NOT WORKING

When we try to deal with the difficult demands of today, what advice do we receive? The same thing we've been told for hundreds of years, perhaps with a few feel-good twists:

- Work hard.
- Be passionate.
- Focus on your strengths.
- Practice a lot.
- Stick to it.
- Be grateful.

No doubt, this is popular, positive, *useful* advice. It's solid and it's timeless. You can't go wrong with this philosophy. And it certainly makes one hell of a commencement speech.

But is this advice *adequate?*

Do you know any hardworking people who have *all* these things going for them, yet they're *still* not even close to the level of success and fulfillment they want in life?

Isn't it true that there are billions of hard workers on the bottom of the pile? Don't you know plenty of passionate people in your hometown who have plateaued? Haven't you met plenty of people who know their strengths but still struggle with clarity, don't have a clue what to do when a new project starts, and keep getting surpassed by people with lesser strengths?

Maybe all these people should practice more, right? Put in their ten thousand hours? But lots of practices happen and championships are still lost. Maybe it's their attitude? Maybe they should just be more grateful and mindful? Yet there are plenty of folks gratefully persevering themselves into dead-end jobs and relationships.

What gives?

MY SEARCH FOR A BETTER WAY

I was one of those people. As a young man, I was the one drowning. When I was nineteen, I had become despondent and suicidal after a breakup with the first woman I ever loved. It was a very dark time. Ironically, what pulled me through the emotional wreckage at that point of my life was a car accident. My friend was driving when we flipped off the highway going about eighty-five miles per hour. We both ended up bloody and terrified but alive. The incident changed my life, giving me what I call "mortality motivation."

I've written about my accident in my previous books, so I'll just share what I learned: Life is precious beyond words, and when you get a second chance—and every morning, every decision, can be that second chance—take a moment to define who you really are and what you really want. I realized I didn't want to take my life; I wanted to *live.* My heart had been broken, yes, but I still wanted to *love.* I felt I was given a second chance, so I wanted to make it *matter,* to make a difference. *Live. Love. Matter.* That became my mantra. That's when I decided to change. That's when I started looking for answers to live a more charged, connected, and contributing life.

I did the things you would expect: I read all the self-help books. I took psychology classes. I listened to the motivational audio programs. I went to the personal development seminars, and I followed the formula they all espoused: I worked hard. I was passionate. I focused on my strengths. I practiced. I stuck to it. I was grateful on the journey.

And you know what? *It worked.*

The advice changed my life. Over a period of years, I ended up with a good job, a good girlfriend, a good set of friends, and a decent place to live. I had much to be grateful for.

But then, even while practicing all that basic good advice, I plateaued. For six or seven years, life didn't really advance that much for me. It was maddening. There's something frustrating about working hard, being passionate and grateful, and still not advancing, still not feeling it. There's also something depleting about it all: excelling sometimes but feeling exhausted too often; having grit and getting paid but not feeling rewarded; being motivated but not creating real momentum; engaging with others but not really connecting; adding value but not making a dent. That's not a vision of the life we desire.

Slowly, I realized that I'd had some success, though I couldn't say *why.* I wasn't as disciplined as I wanted to be, I was far from world-class, and I wasn't contributing at the level I desired, either. I wanted an exacting plan for what I needed to do every day, and in every new situation, so I could learn faster, contribute better, and, yes, also enjoy the journey more.

I realized that the problem with the old formula for success—work hard; be passionate; focus on your strengths; practice a lot; stick to it; be grateful—is that so much of it is geared toward *individual* results and *initial* success. These things get you in the game and keep you in the game. But what happens *after* you've gotten those first wins? What happens after you have earned those grades, found some passion, gotten that job or started that dream, developed some expertise, saved some money, fallen in love, built some momentum? What helps when you want to become world-class, to *lead*, to create lasting impact beyond yourself? How can you generate the confidence you need to reach the *next* level of success? How can you joyfully *sustain success* over the long term? How can you inspire and empower others to do the same?

Answering such questions became my personal obsession and, ultimately, my profession.

HIGH PERFORMANCE LESSONS

This book is the culmination of the intervening twenty years as I have sought answers to three fundamental questions:

1. Why do some individuals and teams succeed *more quickly* than others and *sustain* that success over the long term?

2. Of those who pull it off, why are some *miserable* and others *happy* on their journey?

3. What motivates people to reach for higher levels of success in the first place, and what kinds of habits, training, and support help them improve faster?

My work and research into these questions—what have become known as high performance studies—have led me to interview, coach, or train many of the world's most successful and happiest people, from CEOs to celebrities, from high-level entrepreneurs to entertainers such as Oprah and Usher, from parents to professionals in dozens of industries, to more than 1.6 million students from 195 countries around the world who have taken my online courses or video series.

The adventure has taken me into tension-filled boardrooms and Super Bowl locker rooms, onto Olympic tracks, up in private helicopters with billionaires, and to dinner tables around the world, where I've talked with my students, research participants, and everyday people striving to improve their lives.

This work helped me create the world's most popular online course on high performance, the most widely read newsletter related to the topic, and the largest data set on high performers' self-reported personal characteristics. It also led to the founding of the High Performance Institute, where a team of scholars and I conduct research on how high performers think, behave, influence others, and win. We've created the world's only validated high performance assessment as well as the first professional certification program in the field: Certified High Performance Coaching™. We have now been blessed to train, coach, and measure more high performers than any other organization in the world, and I personally certify over two hundred elite-level high performance coaches per year.

The insights from all these efforts fill this book. The research not only spans twenty years of my own personal development and self-experimentation, but also includes data from coaching interventions with thousands of clients, detailed before-and-after assessments from thousands of live-workshop attendees, structured interviews with hundreds of people at the top of their fields, insights gleaned from academic literature reviews, and hundreds of thousands of codified comments from my students and from my free online training videos, which have received over 100,000,000 views.

From this vast data set and two decades of experience, I've found habits that have been tested and proved in both personal and professional contexts. Here's what I've learned:

With the right habits, anyone can dramatically increase results and become a high performer in almost any field of endeavor.

High performance is not strongly correlated with age, education, income, race, nationality, or gender. This means that many of the excuses we use to explain why we can't succeed are simply wrong. High performance is not achieved by a specific kind of *person*, but rather by a specific set of *practices*, which I call *high performance habits*. Anyone can learn them, regardless of experience, strengths, personality, or position. People who are struggling to make new progress can use this book to revitalize their lives, get ahead, and fulfill their potential. And those who are already successful can use this to get to the next level.

Not all habits are created equal.

It turns out that there are bad, good, better, and best habits for realizing your full potential in your life and career. It matters which practices in your life come first and how they are arranged to create effective habits. If there's anything special about the work of my team of researchers, it's that we've cracked the code, figuring out *which habits matter most* and how you can set up practices that strengthen and sustain these habits. Yes, you can start a gratitude journal and that will make you happier, but is it enough to propel you toward real progress in every area of your life? Yes, you can start a new morning routine, but will that be enough to significantly improve your overall performance and happiness? (The answer is no, by the way). So where to focus? We've found that six deliberate habits move the needle most in helping you reach high performance across multiple domains of your life. We've also learned that there are habits for tactically getting ahead, and strategic habits for enjoying life. You'll learn both.

Achievement is not your problem—alignment is.

If you're reading these words, then the odds are that achievement is not the issue. You already know how to set goals, make checklists, knock off to-dos. You care about excelling in your chosen field. But odds are, you're experiencing your fair share of stress and overwhelm. You can deliver, sure, but you'll learn something every achiever must discover: Just because people want to put things on your plate because you're good doesn't mean you should let them. *What's achievable is not always what's important.* You have a lot of things you *can* do. So the central question shifts from "How do I achieve more?" to "How would I like to *live?*" This book is an escape plan from the soul-killing singular pursuit of external success for no other reason than achievement for achievement's sake. It's about realigning your thoughts and behaviors so that you can experience growth, well-being, and fulfillment as you strive.

Certainty is the enemy of growth and high performance.

Too many people want certainty amid the chaos of this world. But certainty is the fool's dream and, thus, the charlatan's selling point. Certainty ultimately blinds you, sets false or fixed limits, and creates "automatic" habits that become predictable bad thinking and openings for your competitors to surpass you. The person who is certain is most closed to learning, most vulnerable to dogma, and most likely to be blindsided and overtaken by innovators. You'll learn that high performers outgrow their youthful need for certainty and replace it with curiosity and genuine self-confidence.

Technology won't save us.

We've been sold this alluring vision of a world where new gadgets will make us smarter, faster, and better. But many of us are beginning to see behind the hype. Tools cannot replace wisdom. You can have all the gadgets in the world and dive deep into the "quantified self" movement, where every step, second of sleep, beat of your heart, and moment of your day is tracked, scored, gamified. But a lot of people are connected and tracking and remain alone and troubled. Too many are checking in to all the apps and stats and still losing touch with their real ambitions and soul. Amid all the excitement about technology improving our lives, it turns out that what does the job better than anything else are simple human habits of high performance.

WHAT IS HIGH PERFORMANCE?

For our purposes in this book, high performance refers to *succeeding beyond standard norms, consistently over the long term.*

However success is defined in any given field of endeavor, a high performer—be it a person, team, company, or culture—simply does *better for longer periods.* But high performance isn't just about neverending improvement. Mere improvement does not always result in high performance. Lots of people are improving but not necessarily crushing it—they're inching forward, but so is everyone else. Lots of people make progress but not real impact. High performers break the norms. They're consistently exceeding the standard expectations and results.

High performance is also very different from mere expertise development. The quest isn't just to learn a new skill or language, or become a chess master, a world-class pianist, or a CEO. A high performer in any field isn't just good at a singular task or skill—she or he has learned adjacent competencies to complement a particular expertise. They are not a one-hit wonder. They have multiple skill sets that allow them to succeed over the long term and—importantly—lead others. They practice meta-habits that enable them to excel in multiple areas of their lives. A Super Bowl–winning quarterback doesn't just know how to throw a ball. He has had to master mental toughness, nutrition, self-discipline, team leadership, strength and conditioning, contract negotiations, brand building, and so on. Someone who reaches high performance in any career must have competence in many of the areas that touch that career.

In our definition of *high performance*, "consistently" followed by "over the long term" may seem redundant. But the two are, in fact, different. For example, high performers don't "end up" successful at the very last minute of a decade's efforts. They don't come crashing across the finish line of success. They're *steady*. They regularly beat expectations. There is a consistency to their efforts that eludes their peers. That's why, when you look at them post-success, you come to realize they are *not* surprise winners.

As you will learn, meeting this definition of "succeeding beyond standard norms consistently over the long term" requires habits that protect your well-being, maintain positive relationships, and ensure that you serve others as you climb. *You simply can't beat the norms if you've driven yourself into the ground.* As it turns out, high performers' sustained success is due in large part to their healthy approach to living. It's not just about achievement in a profession or in just one area of interest. It's about creating a *high performance life*, in which you experience an ongoing feeling of full engagement, joy, and confidence that comes from being your best self.

That's why the high performance approach extends beyond such popular concepts as "focus on your strengths" and "just put in your ten thousand hours." Lots of people have amazing personal strengths, but they destroy their health in their quest for success and, thus, can't maintain high performance. Lots of people obsessively practice or put in the hours to such a degree that they destroy the relationships they need to support their continuing growth. They push away the coach who was helping them progress; they ruin a relationship, and the emotional fallout knocks them off their game; they upset their investors, and suddenly there's no money coming in to keep growing.

> **I care that you succeed *and* have a healthy life**
> **full of positive emotions and relationships.**

High performance, as I define it and as the data confirms, is not about getting ahead at all costs. It's about forming habits that help you both *excel in* and *enrich* the full spectrum of your life.

Organizations, too, move in and out of high performance. Today more than ever, organizations worldwide struggle to stay consistently out front. Many senior leaders are fighting disengaged or underperforming organizational cultures. They desperately want to take on bold visions and push their people harder, but they already realize that their people are burning out. That's why executives will love this book: They'll be thrilled to learn that their organizations can be healthy and high performing. In fact, the latter requires the former. The habits in this book work just as well for teams as for individuals.

To those individual high achievers and leaders who want to help their organizations excel: Trust that you can reach the next level of success more sanely, swiftly, and confidently than last time. There is indeed a better way to live and lead, and the good news is that it's not a mystery. The high performance habits in this book are precise, actionable, repeatable, scalable, and sustainable.

WHAT WE KNOW ABOUT HIGH PERFORMERS

What do we know about the people who succeed beyond standard measures consistently over the long term?

High performers are more successful than their peers, yet they are less stressed.

The myth that we have to grin and bear more burdens and anxiety as we become more successful simply isn't true (as long as we have the right life habits). You can live an extraordinary life that is far different from the battle that most people endure as they fight for survival or experience achievement only by bluster or burnout. This isn't to say high performers don't ever feel stress—they do—but they cope better, stay more resilient, and experience less severe performance dips related to fatigue, distraction, and overwhelm.

High performers love challenges and are more confident that they will achieve their goals despite adversity.

Too many people avoid any sense of hardship in their lives. They fear they can't handle it or that they'll be judged or rejected. But high performers are different. It's not that they lack any self-doubt at all. It's that they look forward to trying new things and they believe in their abilities to figure things out. They don't shrink from challenge and that not only helps them progress in life but it inspires those around them.

High performers are healthier than their peers.

They eat better. They work out more. The top 5 percent of high performers are 40 percent more likely to exercise three times per week. Everyone wants health, but they may think they have to trade it for success. They're wrong. In survey after survey, we find high performers to be more energized—mentally, emotionally, and physically—than their peers.

High performers are happy.

We all want to be happy. But many people are unhappy achievers. They get a lot done but don't feel fulfilled. Not so for high performers. It turns out that every single habit of high performance we've discovered, even if practiced without the others, increases overall life happiness. Taken together, the six habits you'll learn here won't just get you to excellence, they'll make you happier—and the data proves it. The positive emotions of engagement, joy, and confidence that define the high performer's emotional state can be *yours*.

High performers are admired.

Their peers look up to them, even though the high performers are outperforming them. Why? Because to become a high performer, ego takes a backseat to service. High performers have mastered the art of influencing others in such a way that others feel respected, valued, and appreciated—and more likely to become high performers themselves.

High performers get better grades and reach higher positions of success.

High performance is statistically correlated with GPA. In one study of two hundred collegiate athletes, we found that the higher their score on the High Performance Indicator—an assessment tool for measuring high performance potential—the higher their GPA. High performers are also more likely to be CEOs and senior executives. Why? Because their habits help them lead others and climb organizational charts.

High performers work passionately regardless of traditional rewards.

High performance does not correlate with compensation. This means that what you get paid doesn't affect your odds or your ability to perform at a high level. High performers work hard not because of money but because of something called *necessity*, which you will soon learn about. They are not in it for the trophies or accolades or bonuses; they're in it for the meaning. That's why, in surveys, high performers almost always indicate that they feel well rewarded regardless of income level. They also rarely feel their work is "thankless" or that others don't appreciate how hard they work. It's not because their work is unique or always their dream job. Instead, it's that they approach their work in a more purposeful manner, which helps them feel more engaged, competent, and satisfied.

High performers are assertive (for the right reasons).

They jump into experiences and express themselves, not to "conquer" or even to compete. They are assertive because of a habit of courage in sharing new ideas, engaging in complex conversations, expressing their real thoughts and dreams, and standing up for themselves. The data also shows that they speak up for others and champion other people's ideas more often. That is to say, they're perfectly queued to be direct and inclusive leaders.

High performers see and serve beyond their strengths.

There's a myth that our innate "strengths" are what we all should be focusing on. But the time for navel-gazing is long since over. We must see beyond what comes naturally to us, and develop into what we must be in order to grow, serve, and lead. High performers get that. They're less into "finding their strengths" and more into "adaptive service"—exploring what needs fixing and growing into the person who can fix it. The question they ask is less often "Who am I and what am I good at?" and more often "What is required to be of service here, and how can I grow into that or lead others to deliver that?" High performers do *not* report working on their strengths any more than other people do, so that focus isn't what gives them the edge.

High performers are uniquely productive—they've mastered prolific quality output.

No matter the field, they produce more quality output that matters in their field. It's not that they get more done, per se; lots of their peers might do more tasks. It's that high performers get more things done that are *highly valued* in their primary field of interest. They remember that the main thing is to keep the main thing the main thing. That focus and effort to create only output that will be meaningful helps them excel.

High performers are adaptive servant leaders.

What separates my work on high performance from the hype around world-class experts is that I'm not seeking out lone experts or individual outliers. High performers don't think, live, or practice in a vacuum. They're influencing people and adding tremendous value to those around them, not just trying to win spelling bees or chess matches. They tend to be leaders who can adapt to challenging circumstances and guide others to their own successes and contributions. In this capacity, high performers can go from project to project and succeed, over and over. It's as if you could put them in any context, any team, any company, any industry, and they would win—not because they're geniuses or lone wolves, but because they positively influence others to rise. **They don't just develop *skill*; they develop *people*.**

I'm aware that reading a list like this can make a high performer sound like an infallible wonder-worker. But that's not it at all. The list above is a good general description of high performers, but of course, there is plenty of room for individual differences and variability. Some high performers, for example, may not be as healthy as others even though they generate more productive output. Some may be happy and healthy but are not as admired. In other words, these descriptions are not 100 percent accurate for 100 percent of individuals. But the odds are that over time, their habits detailed in this book lead to the listed benefits, and to extraordinary lives.

If any of the descriptions above don't sound like you yet, don't worry—high performers aren't "born that way." Having trained over one million people on this topic, I can share that there are no superhumans in the mix. High performers are not fundamentally different from you or anyone else because of some special talent, signature strength, genetic miracle, or fixed personality makeup. High performance isn't a natural strength; it's the result of a specific set of deliberate habits. You can learn these habits and reach high performance in nearly any endeavor you choose. And we can measure it and prove it.

THE HABITS OF HIGH PERFORMANCE

If anything defines my research and training approach, it's that certain habits give a competitive advantage, turning an average performer into a high performer. High performers have simply mastered—either on purpose or by accident through necessity—six habits that matter *most* in reaching and sustaining long-term success.

We call these six habits the HP6. They have to do with clarity, energy, necessity, productivity, influence, and courage. They reflect what high performers actually *do* continually—from goal to goal, from project to project, from team to team, from person to person. Each of the habits is learnable, improvable, and deployable across all contexts of life. You can start using these habits today, and they will make you better. We'll cover each habit in the chapters ahead and give you practices to develop them.

Before we get into the HP6, though, let's talk habits. As traditionally conceived, habits are created when we do something so many times that it becomes almost automatic. Do a simple action that's easy to remember, do it repeatedly, and get rewarded for it, and you start to develop a habit that will soon become second nature. For example, after doing it a few times, it's easy to tie your shoes, drive a car, type on a keyboard. You can now do those things without much thought. You've done them so many times, they became *automatic* routines.

This book is *not* about that sort of habit. I'm not interested in teaching you simplistic routine behaviors that can be done with little or no conscious thought. I want you *fully aware* as you fight big battles, strive for the mountaintops, and lead others. That's because the habits that really matter in improving performance are *not* unconscious. They don't necessarily become automatic or easier with time, because the world gets more complex as you seek greater success. Thus, you need to be mindful of your footing as you climb higher.

This means that the high performance habits you'll learn in this book are *deliberate habits*. These must be consciously chosen, willed into existence, and continually revisited to strengthen your character and increase your odds of success.

Deliberate habits usually won't come easily. You have to practice them with real mental focus, especially in changing environments. Every time you feel stuck, every time you start a new project, every time you measure your progress, every time you try to lead others, you must deliberately think about the high performance habits. You'll have to use them as a checklist, just as a pilot uses a preflight checklist before every takeoff.

I believe this is a good thing, too. I don't want my clients getting ahead unconsciously, reactively, or compulsively. I want them to *know* what they do to win, and do it with full intention and purpose. That way, they are captains of their own fate, not slaves to their impulses. I want you in charge, conscious, and clear about what you're doing, so you can see your performance get better and better—and so you can help others get better, too.

It's going to take a lot of work to deploy the high performance habits you're about to learn, but don't shy from the effort.

**When you knock on the door of opportunity,
do not be surprised that it is Work who answers.**

Some will say I could have given easier habits and I would probably sell more books. But in improving your life, *ease* is not the point; *growth* is the point. And the data is clear that these six habits will make a significant difference for you even though they do require consistent attention and effort. If our aim is high performance, then you and I will have to work to implement and develop these habits in every context of our lives—for the rest of our lives.

Just as athletes never quit training, high performers never stop consciously conditioning and strengthening their habits.

Real success—holistic, long-term success—doesn't come from doing what's natural, certain, convenient, or automatic. Often, the journey to greatness begins the moment our preferences for comfort and certainty are overruled by a greater purpose that requires challenge and contribution.

The skills and strengths you have now are probably insufficient to get you to the next level of success, so it's absurd to think you won't have to work on your weaknesses, develop new strengths, try new habits, stretch beyond what you think your limits or gifts are. That's why I'm not here to sell you the easy solution of just focusing on what is already easy for you.

Just so we're clear: There's a lot of work ahead.

PERMISSION GRANTED

Beyond habits, what else holds most people back? I've found that many people simply feel undeserving or unready to rise to the next level. They question their value or await some external validation—promotion, certification, award—before they can start playing a bigger game. This is wrong, of course. You deserve extraordinary success just as much as anyone. And you don't need anyone's permission to start living life on your own terms. You just need a plan. And I promise you it's in this book.

Sometimes, people haven't sought greater success in their lives because they're surrounded by people who say, "Why can't you just be happy with what you have?" Those who say this don't understand high performers. You can be wildly happy with what you have, and still strive to grow and contribute. So don't ever let anyone discourage you from your ambition for a better life. Don't minimize yourself or your dreams for any reason. *It's okay that you want more.* Don't fear your new ambitions. Just understand how to reach for them with more focus, elegance, and satisfaction than you did last time. Just follow the path outlined in this book.

The next chapter will reveal six high performance habits, the HP6, and give you more detail about how they were discerned. Knowing the science behind these findings will help you understand the nuance and power of this approach. Then we'll jump right into each of the six habits. Each habit has its own chapter, which will teach you three new practices to help you establish the overall habit. Finally, I'll warn you about the traps that can cause you to plateau or fail, and I'll leave you with the number one thing needed to maintain your progress.

As your guide, I will inspire new thinking, challenge you along the way, and help you become more mindful of what *really* matters. If, at times, I seem overzealous, forgive me. I've just spent a decade coaching extraordinary people, and I know the incredible results that await you. Unlike a podcaster or academic, I'm only compensated for getting measurable results, and I've done it for individuals and teams from all walks of life and all over the world. I've seen what's possible for you, and it enlivens my entire soul as I write this sentence. My tremendous passion for sharing these ideas comes from seeing my students and the data prove these methods over and over again. So yes, you'll have to forgive my exuberance at times. I truly geek out about this work. But if you'll allow me to do that, you might also allow me to ask the tough questions and suggest actions that may seem tedious or make you a little uncomfortable. If I were sitting next to you, I'd ask permission to push you and challenge you and demand that you give your all. Since you chose this book, I have no doubt that you're ready for the journey.

I should also share what you *won't* find in the pages ahead. I've worked hard to keep this book as practical as possible, favoring *strategies* that you can apply to improve your life over *stories* about people you don't know and academic details that you probably don't care about. I don't pretend that this book is a complete work of human psychology or achievement science; it is an attempt to filter twenty years of insights into a practical road map for you. In a work of such scope, there will inevitably be generalizations and open questions, and I've done my best to call them out.

Narrowing this book to practical habits was difficult. The first draft was 1,498 pages, and I had to make some hard choices on what to cut. To make the decisions, I followed the advice I shared earlier, which so many high performers have taught me:

**To succeed, always remember that the main thing is
to keep the main thing the main thing.**

In this book, the "main thing" is to teach you the habits that will make you extraordinary. It is to help you understand the habits conceptually and also be able to practice them confidently.

So I cut some entertaining, thought-provoking material—profiles of historical figures or contemporary leaders, fascinating stories about lab experiments—because those things were better suited for my blog or podcast than for this book. I made this choice so the book would be more of a user manual than a collection of case studies or academic notes. I will share vignettes about working with high performers, as well as a lot of our broad research findings, but for the most part, I'll focus on what *you* should actually *do* to reach the next level of success. If you would like even more human stories or case studies, check out my blog or podcast via Brendon.com. If you want a more academic approach and a deeper look into our methodology, visit HighPerformanceInstitute.com.

Here, I'll focus on making this book useful and timeless so that no matter how often you return to it throughout your life, the instruction will still be relevant and exacting. Because our students always ask how these topics apply to me as a public figure, I will share some personal examples. But even those are ultimately illustrations of what I've learned from high performers. Since what matters most in improving your performance are six specific habits, I won't spend time telling you about some high performers' diets, childhoods, favorite books, morning routines, or favorite apps—all those things are highly variable, and we haven't found any of those things to be strongly correlated with high performance. So I'll leave those types of lifestyle discussions to podcasters and journalists who ask fascinating people fascinating questions. This book is different because it's about performance, not personality or intrigue. It's not a book of profiles; it's a book of proven *practices*.[1] Here, it's about *you*. It's about how to think, and the habits that you need to begin deliberately implementing in your life. Now, let's get to work.

WHAT TO DO RIGHT NOW

You're busy, I know. You have lots to do today. Perhaps I've piqued your curiosity, and you truly are committed to improving your life right now. But I also know there's a risk that your interest won't translate to immediate action. So I have two suggestions you can do right now, to break through *today.*

1. Take the assessment at HighPerformanceIndicator.com.

Don't worry, it's *free* and it takes just five to seven minutes to complete. You have five to seven minutes. You'll get scores across the six categories that correlate with high performance. You'll learn where you're not doing well and where you are. This assessment will help you predict whether, on your current trajectory, you are likely to achieve any long-term goals or dreams. Once you take your assessment and receive your scores, you'll get course recommendations and other free resources. You're welcome to share that link or your results with your peers or team. Feel free to compare how you score with others, but be sure to come back to this book and learn how to get better.

2. Read the next two chapters today.

Yes, today. Now. It won't take long. If you'll just jump in and commit to reading the next two chapters, you will learn the factors that make the statistical difference in helping you succeed over the long term, no matter what you do. You'll come away with measurable ways to improve, and you'll never again wonder what matters most in achieving lasting success.

High performance can be yours. An extraordinary life awaits. Just turn the page.

BEYOND NATURAL:
THE QUEST FOR HIGH PERFORMANCE

"Don't bother just to be better than
your contemporaries or predecessors.
Try to be better than yourself."

—William Faulkner

An e-mail that changed my life:

Brendon,

I am an INTJ on the Myers-Briggs Type Indicator. This tells you absolutely nothing about me or my ability to succeed. Not now. Not over the next few years.

My top two strengths on the StrengthsFinder are "Developer" and "Achiever." This also tells you absolutely nothing about my ability to get things done or attain any specific outcomes.

On the Kolbe, I score highest as a Quick Start. This means nothing because over time I've had to deal with real life and improve at the other modes I suck at like Fact Finder, Follow Thru, and Implementor.

I prefer blue over green.

I'm more like a lion than a chimp.

I'm gritty but too often lazy. I identify more with a circle than a square. I eat mostly a Mediterranean diet but like hamburgers. I like being around people, for a while, but often I long to escape into solitude with a pot of tea and a thick book. I shop weekly at Whole Foods, but many of my lunchtimes are spent at a cheap Mexican place.

Nothing about *any* of this can tell you anything, at all, about my capabilities, my odds of success, or my future performance.

So please, man, stop trying to bucket me into a "type" or assume that my "strengths" or background give me any edge whatsoever. Labeling people sucks, regardless of how it's done. I hear you that these assessments are for exploring and learning about myself, not labeling me or directing me per se.

But look, we know my supposed "strengths" and they're *still* not helping me get ahead. My natural tendencies don't do the job. As a leader, I have to be honest—sometimes it's just not about who *I* am, what *I* prefer, or what *I'm* naturally good at. It's about me rising to serve a mission, not the mission bowing down to match my limited strengths.

I know you like to ask about my background, too. You know I'm from the Midwest but now live in California. My mom raised me and my sister by herself. She was a hair stylist in the mornings and a hostess at a buffet at night. Dad quit on her and us when I was 14. I got average grades. I was only bullied once or twice. I loved to play golf in college. In about a five-year period after college, I went through two pretty bad relationships. I was fired once. But I found some good friends, too, and I gradually acquired confidence. I sort of stumbled into the work I do now, but it's great.

This background, too, tells you *nothing* about my potential. It gives no definitive clues or path to get ahead today.

So, I'm just being honest, Brendon. I know you like personality assessments and to ask about my background. But if everyone has a past and a story, then certainly a person's past or story is not what gives them an edge.

I guess I am saying that I can do the navel-gazing just fine on my own. I hired you to tell me what to *do* to get to the next level.

I need to know what to *do*, Brendon. What practices work *regardless* of personality?

Don't say who high performers *are.* Tell me what they *do* at a granular level, across projects, that can be replicated. That level of detail. That's the gold.

Find it for me, and you have a client for life.

Otherwise, it's time to part ways.

#

I received this e-mail from Tom, a coaching client, early in my career. To say the least, it took me by surprise. Tom was a kind person and a successful executive. He was collaborative and always willing to try new things.[1] An e-mail like this, putting our working relationship on notice unless I found "the gold," was unusual from him. The follow-up conversation I had with him was even more direct. He was exasperated.

Tom wanted *results*. But I wasn't sure how we could get them.

This was a decade ago. Back then, when I was just a run-of-the-mill "life coach," it was common to do four things to figure out how to help someone improve their performance.

It often began with asking the client questions about what he or she wanted, and what "limiting beliefs" got in the way. You also interviewed them about the past, trying to spot any events that might be influencing current behaviors.

Second, you used assessment tools to help determine personality styles, patterns, and preferences. The goal was to help people better understand themselves and any behaviors that might help them succeed. Popular tools included Myers-Briggs, the Clifton Strengths-Finder, the Kolbe A™ Index, and the DiSC® Test. Often, the life coach would hire experts or consultants certified in these tools, to help administer them.

Third, the coach would sift through performance reviews from work and talk to the people around the client, using 360-degree assessments to figure out how others perceived them and what others wanted from them. You'd talk to the people they lived and worked with.

Fourth, you'd evaluate their actual *output*. You'd look at their past results to see what stood out, what processes helped them create good work, how they most loved to make an impact.

So in this tradition, I did all these things. Because Tom liked tangible data and reports, we spent a lot of time taking and then discussing the assessments. We worked with several high-level consultants who were experts in the various tools. We had binders full of information.

Then, over a span of two years, despite knowing my client's traits, talents, scores, and background, I watched him continually *fail*.

I felt terrible. I couldn't figure out why he wasn't achieving the results he wanted. That was about the time he sent the e-mail.

THE LAB

Fast-forward a decade from Tom's e-mail, and I'm now blessed to have one of the largest personal and professional development "labs"— which is how we think of my global audience and platforms—in the world. As of this writing, that audience includes over *ten million* followers across our Facebook pages; two million–plus newsletter subscribers; one and a half million students who have completed my video series or online courses; thousands of attendees at our multiday live high performance seminars; millions of book and blog readers on the topics of motivation, psychology, and life change; and over half a million YouTube subscribers. This audience has now helped my personal development videos exceed 100,000,000 views online—and all without a single cat video.

What's unique about the audience is that they come to us solely for personal development advice and training, which gives us an illuminating view into what people are struggling with, what they say they want in life, and what helps them change. At the High Performance Institute, we use this large public following to take surveys, conduct interviews, mine data from student behavior and comments, and study before-and-after results from online training courses and one-to-one performance-based coaching sessions. Every time we want to understand something about human behavior and high performance, we go to our lab for insights.

Much of what we've learned from these large audiences and data sets sounds like common sense. In becoming successful, hard work, passion, practice, resilience, and people skills are often more important than IQ, raw talent, or where you're from. Nothing here should be surprising, since this knowledge dovetails with contemporary research on success and world-class performance. Read any of the latest social science (and I've provided plenty of endnotes in case you want to read the studies for yourself), and you'll see that success in general, in almost any endeavor, is made possible by malleable factors—things you can change and improve with effort. For example:

- the mindset you choose to adopt[2]

- the focus you give to your passions, and the persistence you pursue them with[3]

- the amount of practice you dedicate yourself to[4]

- the way you understand and treat others[5]

- the discipline and constancy with which you strive for your goals[6]

- the way you bounce back from losses[7]

- the amount of physical exercise you do to keep your brain and body fit and your overall well-being cared for[8]

What has emerged in our work and in the scientific and academic literature is that success is achieved not by *a specific type of person* but rather by people from all walks of life who *enact a specific set of practices*. The question that inspired this book was "What, exactly, are the most effective practices?"

FINDING WHAT MATTERS

"Motivation is what gets you started.
Habit is what keeps you going."

—Jim Rohn

Over the past several years, we've zeroed in on what moves the needle most in helping people achieve long-term success. And we've found what Tom knew intuitively: High performers *do* things differently from the way others do, and their practices can be replicated across projects (and almost any situation) regardless of your personality, past, or preferences. In fact, we've found that there are six deliberate habits that made most of the difference in performance outcomes across domains. Even your greatest strengths or natural abilities are moot without these habits to support them.

To uncover which habits mattered most, we used relevant concepts from the academic literature, data from our global lab, and insights from over three thousand high performance coaching sessions. We then marshaled all these inputs to create structured interview questions that we could ask high performers.

We identified high performers through standard social science practices, such as survey identification and objective performance measures (e.g., academic performance, athletic performance, objective business and financial outcomes, etc.). For example, we asked people how strongly they agreed with statements such as the following:

- Most of my peers would consider me a high performer.

- Over the past few years, I've generally maintained a high level of success.

- If "high performance" is defined as succeeding at what you do over the long term, compared to most people, I identify as a high performer.

- In my primary field of interest, I've had success for a longer time than most of my peers.

For those who strongly identified with these statements, we then conducted one-on-one interviews with them (and often their peers). We also took additional surveys asking the self-reported high performers questions such as:

- When you start a new project, what do you consciously and consistently do to set yourself up to win?

- What personal and professional routines help you stay focused, energized, creative, productive, and effective? (We asked about each trait in turn.)

- What habits have you started and discarded, and what habits have you kept that *always* seem to work?

- What recurring thoughts or affirmations do you purposefully say to yourself, to perform your best when you (a) go into new situations, (b) respond to adversity or disappointment, and (c) help others?

- If you had to discern three things that make you successful, and you knew you could deploy only those three again in your next major project, what would those three things be?

- When you prepare for a meeting (or match, performance, scene, conversation) that really matters, how do you go about (a) your preparation, and (b) your practices?

- If you took on a major new team project tomorrow, what, exactly, would you say and do to set your team up for success?

- Which habits get you quick wins, and which are longer-term practices that make you stand out?

- When you're under the pressure of a near-term deadline, how do you maintain or protect your well-being?

- What do you habitually tell yourself when you experience self-doubt or disappointment or feel that you're failing?

- What makes you confident, and how do you "turn on" confidence when you need it?

- How do you approach dealing with other people in your life who (a) support you, (b) don't support you, and (c) you want to support you but who don't?

- What practices keep you happy and healthy as you strive for bigger goals?

These questions and dozens more like them helped us begin narrowing down the factors and habits that high performers reported as making the greatest difference in their success. Clear themes emerged, and an initial list of almost two dozen high performance habits was created.

Next, we rolled out surveys to the general public, with questions similar to those we asked the self-reported high performers. After studying which habits best differentiated high performers from those in our general surveys, we narrowed the list even more. Finally, we pared it down to the habits that were deliberate, observable, malleable, trainable, and, most important, effective across domains. That is, we wanted habits that would help someone become successful not just in one domain of expertise but across multiple topic areas, activities, and industries. We wanted habits that anyone, anywhere, in any field of endeavor, could apply over and over again to measurably improve performance.

Ultimately, just six habits made the grade. We call these final six the high performance habits, or HP6.

Once we identified the HP6, we worked to conduct additional literature reviews and validity tests. We created the High Performance Indicator (HPI), based on the six habits as well as other proven success measures. We tested the HPI pilot with over 30,000 people from 195 countries and quantitatively proved its validity, reliability, and usefulness.[9] We found that not only do the six habits *combine* to correlate with high performance, but *each* habit correlates with high performance on its own. And together they correlate with other important life outcomes, such as general happiness, better health, and positive relationships.

The HP6 will help you succeed whether you are a student, entrepreneur, manager, CEO, athlete, or stay-at-home parent. Whether you are already successful or not, these habits will help you reach the next level.

While dozens of other factors can affect your long-term success—luck, timing, social support, or sudden creative breakthroughs, to name a few—the HP6 *are under your control* and improve your performance more than anything else we've measured.

If you want to reach higher levels of performance in anything you do, you must *consistently* do the following:

1. *Seek clarity* on who you want to be, how you want to interact with others, what you want, and what will bring you the greatest meaning. As every project or major initiative begins, you ask questions such as "What kind of person do I want to be while I'm doing this?" "How should I treat others?" "What are my intentions and objectives?" "What can I focus on that will bring me a sense of connection and fulfillment?" High performers ask these types of questions not only at the beginning of an endeavor but consistently throughout. They don't just "get clarity" once and

develop a mission statement that lasts the test of time; they consistently seek clarity again and again as times change and as they take on new projects or enter new social situations. This kind of routine self-monitoring is one of the hallmarks of their success.

2. *Generate energy* so that you can maintain focus, effort, and well-being. To stay on your A game, you'll need to actively care for your mental stamina, physical energy, and positive emotions in very specific ways.

3. *Raise the necessity* for exceptional performance. This means actively tapping into the reasons you *absolutely must* perform well. This necessity is based on a mix of your internal standards (e.g., your identity, beliefs, values, or expectations for excellence) and external demands (e.g., social obligations, competition, public commitments, deadlines). It's about always knowing your *why* and stoking that fire all the time so you feel the needed drive or pressure to get at it.

4. *Increase productivity* in your primary field of interest. Specifically, focus on *prolific quality output* (PQO) in the area in which you want to be known and to drive impact. You'll also have to minimize distractions (including opportunities) that steal your attention from creating PQO.

5. *Develop influence* with those around you. It will make you better at getting people to believe in and support your efforts and ambitions. Unless you consciously develop a positive support network, major achievements over the long haul are all but impossible.

6. *Demonstrate courage* by expressing your ideas, taking bold action, and standing up for yourself and others, even in the face of fear, uncertainty, threat, or changing conditions. Courage is not an occasional act, but a trait of choice and will.

HIGH PERFORMANCE HABITS

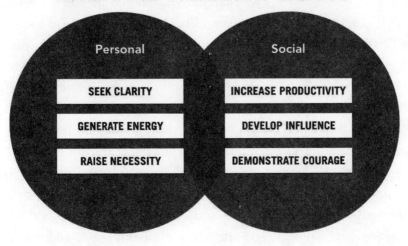

Seek clarity. Generate energy. Raise necessity. Increase productivity. Develop Influence. Demonstrate Courage. These are the six habits that you need to adopt if you are to reach high performance in any situation. In the hundreds of personal efforts and social behaviors that we've observed, these habits move the needle the most in dramatically improving performance.

In the next six chapters, we'll address the extraordinary power unlocked by developing these habits.

STRENGTHS ALONE ARE NEVER ENOUGH

You may have noticed that nowhere in this list does it say to focus on your innate gifts, talents, blessings, past, or strengths. That's because no matter how great a personality you have, how many supposed innate strengths you possess, how much money you have, how beautiful you are, how creative you are, what talents you've cultivated, or how brilliantly you've succeeded in the past—none of these things would mean much on their own. They wouldn't matter if you didn't know what you wanted and how to go get it (clarity), felt too wiped out to perform (energy), didn't have a sense of drive or any pressure to get things done (necessity), couldn't focus and create the outputs that matter most (productivity), lacked the people skills to get others to believe in you or support you (influence), or failed to take risks or speak up for yourself and others (courage). Without the HP6, even the most gifted person would be lost, tired, unmotivated, unproductive, alone, or fearful.

Effectiveness in life does not come from focusing on what is automatic, easy, or natural for us. Rather, it is the result of how we consciously strive to meet life's harder challenges, grow beyond our comforts, and deliberately work to overcome our biases and preferences, so that we may understand, love, serve, and lead others.

When I make this argument, people often balk due to the popularity of the "strengths" movement. Personally, I'm a fan of any tools that help people learn more about themselves. I also greatly admire Gallup, the organization that has led the strengths-based revolution. But I don't recommend that people use the strengths assumption to lead others or to seek the next level of success in their own lives. The strengths movement is based on the idea that we have "innate" strengths—talents that we are born with. It assumes we are "naturally" good at some things from birth, and that we might as well focus on those things. Without question, that's a feel-good formula, and it's certainly better than obsessing about our weaknesses all the time.

My main reservation about the strengths movement is that in a complex and rapidly changing world, reaching the top doesn't come naturally to *anyone*. Regardless of what you are naturally good at, to rise higher you must go beyond what came naturally to you at birth or in your teen years, right? That's why the *innate* argument doesn't hold up so well. To reach exceptional performance and win over the long term, you will be required to develop *well beyond* what is easy or natural to you, because the real world is full of uncertainty and ever-increasing demands for growth. Your "natural" birth strengths will not be enough. As Tom said in the e-mail to me at the beginning of this chapter, "It's about me rising to serve a mission, not the mission bowing down to match my limited strengths." If you have great ambitions to contribute extraordinary things, you'll have to grow and stretch far beyond what's natural to you. To rise to high performance, you'll have to work on the weaknesses, develop entirely new skill sets beyond what you find easy or what you "like to do." It should be common sense: If you really want to make your mark, you'll have to grow more to give more, and that won't feel easy or natural.

In the end, even if you don't agree with my thinking process here, knowing your personality type or supposed innate strengths just isn't all that useful in helping you achieve your next big goal in uncertain environments. Knowing your label or strength and just trying to be "more of that" is like telling a bear that's trying to get honey out of a nest high on an unexplored cliff, "Just try being more of a bear."

To my friends and colleagues running companies: Let's stop spending all this money on expensive strength and personality assessments in vain attempts to categorize people, and instead focus on training our people in proven habits that anyone can use to up their performance.

The good news is, no one "innately" lacks any of the high performance habits. High performers are not lucky stiffs loaded with a great big bag of strengths at birth. They simply deploy the habits we've discussed, and do it more consistently than their peers. That's it. *That's the difference.*

So it doesn't matter whether you are an extrovert or an introvert, an INTJ or an ESFP, a Christian or an atheist, a Spaniard or a Singaporean, an artist or an engineer, a manager or a CEO, an achiever or an analyzer, a mom or a Martian—the six high performance habits each have the power to make a dramatic impact on the areas that matter most to you. Together, they have the power to revolutionize your performance across every meaningful domain in your life. You are not supposed to be innately good at the HP6. You have to work at them all the time. Whenever you hope to succeed at a new goal, project, or dream, you have to bust out the HP6. Every time you find yourself performing below your full potential, bring the HP6 to bear. If you ever wonder why you're failing at something, just go take the HPI and identify which habits you're scoring low in. Then improve that area and you'll be back on track.

This deliberate focus is an important distinction, especially because it frees us from the myth that success comes more "naturally" to some than to others. Looking across my decade serving so many elite-level achievers as well as all our surveys and professional assessments, we just haven't seen high performance consistently correlate strongly with personality, IQ, innate talent, creativity, years of experience, gender, race, culture, or compensation.[10] In the past two decades of research in neuroscience and positive psychology, researchers have begun to notice the same and flip the old model on its head. What we do with what we have tends to be far more important than what we have in the first place. What you're innately good at is less important than how you choose to see the world, develop yourself, lead others, and remain persistent through difficulty.

We all know someone who has all the cards stacked in their favor—blessed upbringing, great personality, creative mind—but who still doesn't get off the couch or succeed. Lots of people are highly paid but not high performing. Anyone in an organization who has had their team take a strengths assessment can surely attest that plenty of their peers know their strengths, and even do work related to their strengths, but *still* fail to deliver great work. And in any given great company culture, there are always high performers and low performers. Why? Because high performance is not about a specific *type* of person. It's not about winning the genetic lottery, how long you've worked, the shade of your skin, how many people are supporting you, or what you're getting paid. It's about your performance habits—which *you* have complete control over.

This finding is worth hammering home, because too many people use these factors to explain their poor performance. Just think how often you hear things such as:

- "I just don't have the *personality* to get ahead. I'm just not [extroverted, intuitive, charismatic, open, conscientious]."

- "I'm just not the smartest person in the room."

- "I'm just not naturally gifted like they are. I wasn't born good at that. I don't have the right mix of strengths."

- "I'm not a right-brained person."

- "I don't have enough experience."

- "I'm a [woman, black man, Latino, middle-aged white guy, immigrant], and that's why I'm not succeeding."

- "My company culture doesn't support me."

- "I'd be a lot better if they paid me what I'm really worth."

It's time we all recognized these reasons for what they are: lame excuses for suboptimal performance, especially over the long term.

This is not to say intrinsic factors don't matter *at all*. There is strong evidence that they are important, especially in childhood development, and many of these factors can dramatically influence your mood, behavior, choices, health, and relationships as an adult. (If you'd like a more academic treatment of why those factors are important but matter less for long-term success than most people imagine, please visit our published articles at HighPerformanceInstitute.com/research.)

Leaders should take note: Focusing on any of the factors I mentioned in that list won't get you very far in helping your people improve performance. Those factors are just not that easy to define, manage, or improve. For example, imagine you're working on a project with a few teammates. You have one person in particular who is not performing well. Imagine how ridiculous it would be for you to walk over to that person and say:

> "If you could just improve your personality for us . . ."
>
> "If you could just up your IQ for us . . ."
>
> "If you could just change how you were innately gifted . . ."
>
> "If you could just be more right-brained . . ."
>
> "If you could just have five more years' experience under your belt here . . ."
>
> "If you could just be more [Asian, black, white, male, female] . . ."
>
> "If you could just improve the culture here real quick . . ."
>
> "If you could just pay yourself the perfect amount to be more productive . . ."

You get the point. **These are simply not useful categories to focus on.**

The bottom line is that if you're going to focus on *anything* to improve your or your team's performance, start with the HP6.

A RISING TIDE LIFTS ALL BOATS— ONE HABIT LIFTS ALL OTHERS

We like to think of the HP6 as "meta-habits" because they make all other good habits in life fall into place. By seeking clarity, you develop a habit of asking questions, looking within, observing your behaviors, assessing whether you're on track. By generating energy, you'll be better rested, you'll eat healthier, you'll exercise more. And so on.

What's fascinating about our research into the HP6 is that each improvement in any one area improves the others. This means that if you increase clarity, you'll likely see improvement in energy, necessity, productivity, courage, and influence. Our analysis also suggests that even though people who score high on one habit tend to score high on the others, each habit is giving them a little extra edge in increasing their overall high performance score. Improve just one of these habits, and you improve your performance.

Another fascinating thing we learned is that *all* the HP6 predict overall happiness, meaning the higher your score in *any* habit, the greater the odds you'll report being happy in life. Taken together, then, the HP6 are a powerful predictor of not just whether you're a high performer but also whether you'll be *happy*.

IS THERE A HIGH PERFORMANCE "STATE OF MIND"?

"Ecstasy is a full, deep involvement in life."

—John Lovell

People often ask me whether there is a specific "state" that will enable them to succeed over the long term. Well, by definition, emotional and mental states don't endure. They're fleeting. Moods stick around longer, and habits hold the longest, which is why we focus there.

But I think what people are really getting at is, "How will I *feel* when I've hit high performance? What does it feel like, so I can reverse-engineer that?"

The question can be answered by the data. In a keyword analysis of public survey data on over thirty thousand high performing respondents, it's pretty clear: When people talk about how they feel in high performance, they report feeling *full engagement*, *joy*, and *confidence* (in that order).

> **This means they tend to be fully
> immersed in what they are doing,
> they *enjoy* what they're doing, and they have
> confidence in their ability to figure things out.**

Rounding out the top five were *purposefulness* and *flow*, as in "I feel like I'm in flow." ("In the zone" was not an option in our surveys because it's a phrase rather than a word, but it was the most common written-in descriptor.) *Determination*, *focus*, *intention*, *deliberateness*, and *conscientiousness* rounded out the top concepts people used to describe what being in high performance felt like.

Knowing this, you might as well start with the end in mind. Start bringing your full attention to the moments of your life. Start bringing more joy. Start bringing more confidence. These things will not only make you feel better, they'll also help you perform better. Still, the same caveat applies to states as to strengths: Without effective habits, they're just not enough.

TESTING THE HP6

The HP6 gave me a proven game plan for succeeding at my projects in life. Now they are a standard operating system for entering any new situation. I've been using them in my professional career, and the results have been astounding and quite public.

Beyond myself, the habits and concepts in this book have measurably improved the lives of tens of thousands of our students. These students take the HPI before and after our online programs, live training events, and coaching experiences. They love seeing *demonstrable data* that they are improving their lives. We regularly see our students significantly increase their overall high performance scores (and overall life happiness). We've also used the HPI in organizations to help them pinpoint where their employees and teams should focus their development.

Further, we've seen remarkable results through client coaching interventions. Over three-thousand hour-long coaching sessions led by independent Certified High Performance Coaches™ reveal that people can dramatically change their behaviors and reach higher performance in many areas of their lives in *weeks*, not years.

This isn't to say that high performance habits are a silver bullet for all life's challenges. Over the past decade as a high performance coach and researcher, I have sought plenty of disconfirming evidence for the HP6, and I'll happily share that here. In seeking disconfirming evidence, we have looked for people who are *not* high performing despite practicing the habits in this book. Are there individuals in the world who actively seek clarity, generate energy, raise necessity, increase productivity, develop influence, and demonstrate courage who are in fact underperformers, or even *failures*? I have never seen that to be the case, but common sense says there is bound to be an exception somewhere. Can someone lack one of the habits and still become successful? For example, can someone be a wild success yet still lack clarity? Absolutely. Can someone lack courage and still be a success? You bet they can. But remember, we aren't talking about *initial* success here. We're talking about the *long term*. Odds are, if you lack any of the HP6 for too long, your high performance scores (and happiness scores) will drop. You simply wouldn't be as effective or as extraordinary as you could be.

Some critics will say that our descriptions of high performance habits, or statements used in the HPI, are too vague or open to interpretation. That, of course, is always a risk when describing human behavior. If we say that someone "has grit," "is creative," "is an extrovert," or "struggles to maintain focus," one could always argue that such descriptions are vague or generalized. But that doesn't mean we shouldn't attempt to define them, measure them, or educate people about them. Studying human psychology is an imprecise endeavor, but it's worth the work if it helps us learn what makes someone high performing. All we can do is use the validated yet inexact tools available and continue homing in on how to describe and correlate the statements and habits that are true for high performers. And that's what we've been doing.

In addition to actively seeking to disconfirm our own assumptions, we have sought to overcome self-reporting biases by checking to see that what people reported in our initial surveys was true in their real lives. We did this by randomly interviewing them, comparing objective performance measures, and seeking peer feedback. For the most part, we've found that people share their honest responses in this field, because they want to accurately assess where they are and discover where they can improve. We've also included reverse statements and scoring in many of our surveys, to see whether responses held true.

Like any researcher, I'm always open to new evidence, and I look at findings, including those in this book, as merely another messy step in the long march of understanding humans and how they work. I'll remind you, I am not a psychologist, psychiatrist, neuroscientist, biologist, or any other title I'm aware of that ends in "-ist." I am a professional high performance coach and trainer who is paid for results, not discussion or theory. And this, inevitably, biases me toward what I've seen work. And while I feel blessed to have become the world's highest compensated and most followed on this topic, I am without question as fallible as any writer or practitioner trying to take on a topic of such scope and complexity. I have a lot more to learn about high performance. There's plenty that this entire field does not yet know and that needs to be explored. What effects do mental illnesses, childhood experiences, and socioeconomic and neurobiological factors have on forming and sustaining these habits? Which of the habits move the needle most in specific industries, careers, or educational levels?

Throughout this book, I openly invite you to ask your own questions as well as question my assertions. In our published articles, I have openly called for further testing of our ideas, and I'd love to hear your feedback, too. Every day, my team and I try to learn more and finer distinctions about this subject. I'll be studying it for life. I'd love to hear what works for you and what doesn't. And whether or not you agree with what you'll find in the pages ahead, I merely suggest you keep what works for you and discard the rest.

TEST IT FOR YOURSELF

Will the HP6 get as dramatic results for you as we've seen in our research, training, and coaching? I would love to test them with you. That's why, once again, I invite you to be the judge of how effective these habits are. In case you haven't yet gotten around to following my advice in the previous chapter, before you read further, take the HPI. It takes only a few minutes, and it's free online at HighPerformanceIndicator.com. It will give you a score on each of the six habits, and no, it won't "label" you. Take the survey. Do it now. And be sure to enter your e-mail so I can send you another link to take the assessment again in seven to ten weeks. (Between now and then, read this book and watch the videos you'll receive after you take the assessment, so that you have the tools needed to improve.) You'll know by your own responses to the assessment in a few weeks just how much this work can begin to change your life.

One thing is abundantly clear from our findings: You should never wait to pursue a dream or add value out of fear that you lack the "right stuff." High performance happens because of what you deliberately think and do on a routine basis in order to excel and serve at higher levels. It is this quest to challenge yourself to develop good habits that will make you feel enlivened and help you realize your full potential.

In Montana, where I grew up, we had this saying: "The time to have the map is before you enter the woods." Someday soon, you'll enter an uncertain situation where your performance really matters. Before that day, read this book and begin the six high performance habits. This is your map, and it will lead you through the thicket of life to your highest levels of success. In the next chapter, we put an X on that map. We get clarity about who you are and where you want to go *at this stage* of your life.

SECTION ONE

PERSONAL HABITS

HIGH PERFORMANCE HABITS

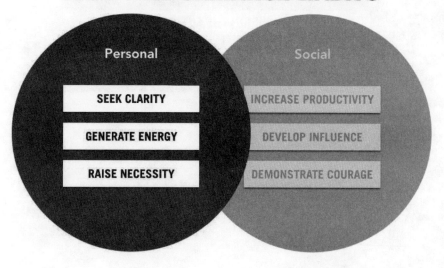

HIGH PERFORMANCE HABIT #1
SEEK CLARITY

"If you don't have clarity of ideas,
you're just communicating sheer sound."

—Yo-Yo Ma

ENVISION THE FUTURE FOUR

DETERMINE THE FEELING YOU'RE AFTER

DEFINE WHAT'S MEANINGFUL

Kate, the woman sitting in front of me, crying, "has it all."

She manages thousands of employees at one of the top companies in her industry. She's an admired leader with dozens of years' experience. Because her company is wildly profitable, her high six-figure salary is almost double the average for her position. But she never lets that go to her head. Her bragging is limited to talking up her team. She's proud of how hard they work and support one another.

No matter what Kate is talking about, you can tell she's genuinely interested in *you*. She has an indescribable grace about her. Whenever I see her walk into a room, I think of the saying "There are two types of people. One walks into the room and announces, 'Here I am!' The other walks in and says, 'Oh, there you are!'"

Kate is raising three children. Her mother died from cancer when Kate was fifteen, so she puts a high value on being present with her kids.

Recently, she got another promotion, so her husband, Mike, quit his job to be home with the kids. They're happy they have more time together.

Kate has hired me as her coach, and in order for us to get to know each other better, she invited me to their house in the suburbs for a barbecue. Within a few minutes of arriving at her home that sunny afternoon, I found myself with four of her friends, chatting over glasses of wine in the kitchen. I asked how they knew Kate and how they would describe her. They called her "an awesome human being," "a giver," "someone you want to be like," and "a success that makes us all look lazy." One friend said Kate was involved in everything yet always there for you. Another said she was always impressed by how Kate could do it all and still manage to fit into her Lulu Lemons. When another said, "I don't know *how* she does it all," the other three women nodded and mm-hmmmed like a church congregation.

Shortly after, Kate asked me to sit and chat in her home office. Floor-to-ceiling windows lit the space, and French doors opened to the deck, where I could see Mike working the grill.

Kate seemed in good spirits. And then I commented on how her friends admired her.

Suddenly, her voice cracked. She said she appreciated their compliments; then her eyes welled up. She looked away, and with her gaze went her presence.

As I often do in these situations, I respond with humor. I ask, "What did I miss? Do you secretly hate one of those women?"

"What?" She looks confused, but as she realizes I was joking, she snaps back. "Oh." She laughs. "No, no. I'm just emotional right now."

"I see that. What's up?"

She looks out the window to her husband and friends on the patio. She tries to compose herself, sitting more upright, wiping her tears with the edge of her hand. "It means a lot to me that my friends said nice things, Brendon. I'm glad you're meeting them and Mike." Her voice cracks again, and the tears keep coming. Then she looks away again, toward the ground, and shakes her head. "I'm sorry, my life is just a hot mess right now."

"A mess?" I ask.

She nods, wipes the tears away, and sits up again. "I know. It's silly. 'Oh, poor me,' right? The lady with the good job and good family isn't happy. It sounds like a daytime drama. And I know you're not here to do a therapy session. It's just that when you feel really blessed and people look up to you, it's hard to complain. That's why I asked you here. I'm struggling even if no one sees it. I don't want you or anyone to feel sorry for me. And I don't want you to tell me I'm *not* a mess—that's what my friends do. It's good for me to let this out. Things are good, but something's not right."

"Tell me."

She takes a deep breath. "Have you ever felt like you're just going through the motions, for maybe just too long?"

I think to myself, *Is there a proper length of time anyone should live life just going through the motions?* But I don't say that, because she asked if *I* have ever felt that. When people are struggling with their emotions, they often externalize the situation and ask questions about other people instead of owning it.

"Is that what *you* are feeling, Kate? As if you've been just going through the motions?"

"I guess so."

I lean in. "How do you explain those two things: going through the motions and feeling like a mess?"

She pauses. "I don't know exactly. That's why I wanted your perspective. I've just got so many things going on. I feel like I'm always reinventing the wheel and never catching up. So that makes me feel like a mess in some ways. And yet, I'm good at what I do, so I can handle it all. So I feel like I'm just going through the motions, and all the chaos has become almost . . . routine. There's a lot going on, but I'm not drowning. I'm just sort of frustrated and restless at the same time. Does that make sense?"

"It does. How have you been dealing with those feelings?"

Kate looks unsure and glances out the window. "That's the thing. I don't know if I've dealt with it all. I'm doing everything you're supposed to do, you know? They say be present and love your family. I try.

Every day, I try to be good for the kids and Mike. They say be effective. I have the to-do lists, the plans, and the checklists to make it happen. I get stuff done. They say be passionate at work. I am. They say be persistent and resilient. I have been. I've risen through so much gender discrimination in my career. I've come a long way and I'm happy and no one has to feel sorry for me. But I just don't know, Brendon . . ."

"Yes, I think you *do* know. Tell me."

She pulls back in her chair. Her shoulders slump, and she takes a sip of wine as more tears break out.

"In all this running around and trying to do everything, I'm just starting to feel a little disconnected from it. Sort of . . . *lost.*"

I nod and wait for what almost always comes next.

"I just don't know what I want anymore."

#

I bet you know a lot of people like Kate. She's hardworking, smart, capable, caring. Like a lot of achievers, she has a list of goals, and she accomplishes most of them. But the truth is she doesn't know what will bring the vibrancy back into her life.

Without an immediate change in habits, she'll be in trouble. This doesn't mean she will crash and burn. When achievers struggle in real life, it's not like on TV. There's no huge existential dilemma or midlife crisis that causes them to quit everything in an instant, burning their business or relationships to the ground in one sudden manic weekend of insanity.

That's not what achievers do. When they're struggling, especially when they are unsure what they want, they tend to march on like good soldiers. They don't want to mess things up. They're afraid to make sudden changes because the reality is that things are *good.* They don't want to walk away from everything they've worked so hard for. They don't want to go backward or lose momentum or be overtaken by their coworkers or competitors.

They know in their gut that there is another level, a different quality of life. But they feel deep uncertainty over changing what is already working. Improving a bad thing is easy for the achiever. But messing with a good thing? That's terrifying.

Uncertain what they really want, achievers often choose just to keep at it. But at some point, if they don't get *very clear* about who they are and what they want *at this stage of their life*, things start to unravel.

At the beginning, the decline in their performance is subtle. They start to feel that something is off, so they don't bring as much intent to their efforts. They back off just a bit. That's not to say they feel their life is lacking. "I have a lot to be grateful for," they will say. But the issue is not about something external they should feel grateful for—it's that something inside doesn't feel right. Like Kate, they're frustrated or restless *even though life is good.*

They begin to worry, "Maybe I haven't found my real thing"— even though they've given so much of their lives to that very "thing."

When the office lights turn out at the end of the night or when they finally get a moment of silence after weeks of pushing hard, their internal chatter starts scratching at their reality:

- *Is all the complexity I've created in my life even worth it?*

- *Is this the right direction for my family and me at this stage of our lives?*

- *If I just took a break, maybe a few months to learn something new or try a new direction, would I miss out or get passed up?*

- *Things are good, so if I try something new will everyone think I'm crazy? Am I just being stupid or ungrateful?*

- *I'm already stretched pretty thin. Can I really give any more right now?*

- *Am I really good enough to play at the next level?*

- *Why am I starting to feel so distracted?*

- *Why do my relationships feel sort of blah?*

- *Why am I not more confident at this point in my life?*

When these questions go unanswered for too long, an unraveling begins. Someone like Kate starts looking at all the mountains she has summited in life, and fears she has climbed too many of the wrong ones. She learns that what is achievable isn't always what is important.

Soon, day-to-day motivation wanes. They begin feeling restrained or unfulfilled. They start focusing on protecting their successes versus progressing. Nothing seems thrilling anymore.

But no one really notices at first, because an achiever is *still good*. Sure, the passion isn't at the level it used to be, but at least everyone at home and at work is fairly happy (or maybe just unaware).

This is the situation Kate has found herself in. No one knew she was "a hot mess," but she couldn't escape the feeling.

Ultimately, the dissatisfaction spreads into relationships at home or at work, and others notice. The stress of disappointment imparts a hard edge that upsets loved ones or coworkers. The person misses meetings and calls. They turn work in late. The contribution of good ideas falls off. Calls don't get returned. It's obvious to both the achiever and the people around her that she has started just going through the motions. The excitement, joy, and confidence are gone, and with them goes the performance.

If this sounds familiar to you personally, then this chapter is your chance to reset. And if any of this sounds overdramatic, it's probably because you haven't hit that wall yet. Let's make sure you never do.

CLARITY BASICS

"The feeling is clear and indisputable. As if you suddenly sense the whole of nature and suddenly say: Yes, this is true."

—Fyodor Dostoyevsky

This chapter is about finding clarity in your life. It's about how you think about tomorrow and what you do to stay connected with what matters today. The essential habit of *seeking clarity* helps high performers keep engaged, growing, and fulfilled over the long haul.

Our research shows that compared with their peers, high performers have more clarity on who they are, what they want, how to get it, and what they find meaningful and fulfilling. We've found that if you can increase someone's clarity, you up their overall high performance score.

Whether you have a high degree of clarity in life or not, don't fret, because you can learn to develop it. Clarity is not a personality trait that some are blessed to "have" and others are not. Just as a power plant doesn't "have" energy—it transforms energy—you don't "have" any specific reality. You generate your reality. In this same line of thinking, you don't "have" clarity; you generate it.

So don't hope for a flash of inspiration to reveal what you want next. You generate clarity by asking questions, researching, trying new things, sorting through life's opportunities, and sniffing out what's right for you. It's not as though you walk outside one day and the Piano of Purpose falls on your head and all things become clear. *Clarity is the child of careful thought and mindful experimentation.* It comes from asking yourself questions continually and further refining your perspective on life.

Clarity research tells us that successful people know the answers to certain fundamental questions: Who am I? (What do I value? What are my strengths and weaknesses?) What are my goals? What's my plan? These questions may seem basic, but you would be surprised how much knowing the answers can affect your life.

Clarity on who you are is associated with overall self-esteem. This means that how positive you feel about yourself is tied to how well you *know* yourself. On the flip side, lack of clarity is strongly associated with neuroticism and negative emotions.[1] That's why self-awareness is so key to initial success. You have to know who you are, what you value, what your strengths and weaknesses are, and where you want to go. This kind of knowledge makes you feel better about yourself and about life.

Next, you need to have unambiguous and challenging goals. Decades of research show that having specific and difficult goals increases performance, whether those goals are created by you or assigned to you. Clear "stretch" goals energize us and lead to greater enjoyment, productivity, profitability, and satisfaction in our work.[2] Choosing stretch goals in each area of your life makes a good starting place for high performance.

You should also give yourself deadlines for your goals, or you won't follow through. Studies show that having a specific plan attached to your goals—knowing when and where you will do something—can *more than double* the likelihood of achieving a challenging goal.[3] Having a clear plan is as important as motivation and willpower. It also helps you see past distractions and inoculates you against negative moods— the more clarity you have, the more likely you are to get stuff done even on the days you feel lazy or tired.[4] When you see the steps right there in front of you, it's hard to ignore them.

Our research further validates all this. In one survey, we asked over twenty thousand people to read the following statements and rate themselves on a scale of 1 through 5, with 1 being "strongly disagree" and 5 being "strongly agree":

- I know who I am. I'm clear about my values, strengths, and weaknesses.

- I know what I want. I'm clear about my goals and passions.

- I know how to get what I want. I have a plan to achieve my dreams.

The higher the scores on questions such as these, the better the overall high performance scores. Data from the High Performance Indicator also shows that higher clarity scores are significantly associated with greater confidence, overall happiness, and assertiveness. Subjects with greater clarity also tend to report that they are performing with more excellence than their peers and feel they are making a greater difference. For students, the higher the scores on clarity, the higher their GPA. This means young people who have more clarity on their values, goals, and path ahead tend to have a higher GPA.

Most of this sounds like common sense, of course. "Know who you are and what you want" isn't exactly cutting-edge advice. Still, it bears examination: Are you clear about these things? If not, start there. It can be as simple as journaling about these topics. For now, though, let's focus on the promise of the book: the more advanced concepts that will move the needle in your performance. To get there, let's consider what you would tell someone like Kate, who already knows who she is, and has set and achieved challenging goals for decades.

NEXT-LEVEL CLARITY IS ABOUT THE FUTURE

"I looked over and I've seen the promised land."
—Martin Luther King, Jr.

Most recently in my career, I've wondered whether high performers have a particular worldview on clarity—about themselves, what they want, and how to get it. I wondered what, if anything, they were *clearer about* than most people.

To find out, I analyzed the comments of high performance students, called on achievement researchers, and spoke with Certified High Performance Coaches™ about what gives their clients an edge. I also conducted structured interviews focused solely on the topic of clarity, with nearly a hundred people who reported in our surveys as being high performers. I asked them questions such as:

- Which things are you absolutely clear about that help you perform better than your peers?

- What do you focus on to stay clear about what matters most?

- What *aren't* you clear about, and how does that affect your performance?

- What do you do when you are feeling uncertain or undirected?

- If you had to explain to someone you were mentoring what it is that makes you successful, what would you say?

- What else do you know about yourself—beyond your values and strengths and plans—that makes you successful?

In almost every basic question of who they were or what they wanted, the highest performers had a great ability to *focus on the future* and divine how they would achieve excellence. They didn't just know who they were; indeed, they rarely focused on their present personality or preferences. Instead, they consistently thought about *who they wanted to be* and how to become that. They didn't just know their strengths today; they knew what broader skill sets they would have to master in coming months and years to serve with excellence at the next level. They didn't just have clear plans to achieve their goals this quarter; they had lists of future projects that would lead them to a bigger dream. They didn't think just about how they could get what they personally wanted this month; they obsessed with the same focus about how to help others get what they wanted in their overall lives and careers.

This "future focus" went well beyond what they wanted to become or how they would achieve what they and others wanted. They could also describe with great clarity how they wanted to *feel* in upcoming endeavors, and they knew specifically what conditions could destroy their enthusiasm, sense of satisfaction, and growth.

Out of this research, we discovered specific habits that help create this kind of next-level clarity.

PRACTICE ONE

ENVISION THE FUTURE FOUR

*"Dream lofty dreams, and as you dream, so you shall become.
Your vision is the promise of what you shall one day be;
your ideal is the prophecy of what you shall at last unveil."*

—James Allen

High performers are clear on their intentions for themselves, their social world, their skills, and their service to others. I call these areas self, social, skills, and service, or the Future Four.

Self

"Know thyself" is the timeless advice inscribed on the Temple of Delphi in Greece over 2,400 years ago. But there's a difference between "*know* thyself" and "*imagine* thyself." High performers know themselves, but they don't get stuck there.[5] They are more focused on sculpting themselves into stronger and more capable people. That's another big difference: *introspection* versus *intention*.

We've found that high performers can articulate their future self with greater ease than others. Tactically, this means they tend to have a faster and more thoughtful, confident response when I ask them, "If you could describe your ideal self in the future, the person you are trying to become, how would you describe that self?"

In reviewing recordings from my interviews, it's clear that high performers have thought about this more than others. Their descriptions came sooner, with the coherent part—the part after the "hmm's" and "good question"—clocking in an average of seven to nine seconds faster. Their responses were less meandering than the others'. When I asked people to describe their future best self in just three words, high performers also replied faster and in a more confident tone.[6]

Trying to imagine ourselves in the future with great clarity is hard work for anyone. That's why most people tend to do it only once per year—that's right, on New Year's Eve. But high performers spend a lot of time thinking about their best self and the ideal they're trying to grow into. In interviews with my ten highest-scoring and ten lowest-scoring clients on the HPI, I found that the highest-performing clients report thinking about their ideal future self and engaging in activities related to that almost sixty minutes more *per week* than the lowest-scoring clients. For example, if you see yourself as a great communicator in the future, you would not only be more likely to imagine scenarios of yourself speaking with others, but also spend more time doing so. You're actively doing things that exhibit a future characteristic you desire.

This isn't to say that high performers are more introspective than anyone else. Lots of people journal every week and could be said to be self-aware without being high performing. For example, lots of people think of themselves constantly, but much of that thinking is just negative ruminations. So what makes the difference is that high performers imagine a positive version of themselves in the future, and then they *actively engage* in trying to be that. This part about actively engaging is important. They aren't waiting to demonstrate a characteristic next week or next month. They are living into their best self *now*.

You get the point, so let's encapsulate this advice with some simple things you can do: Be more intentional about who you want to become. Have vision beyond your current circumstances. Imagine your best future self, and start acting like that person today.

This doesn't have to be complicated. When I was nineteen years old and struggling to bounce back from a car accident, three one-word commands helped turn my life around. These commands, as you may know, were inspired by the lessons I had learned about life when I faced my own mortality. They are simple and concise: *LIVE. LOVE. MATTER.*

These three words became my clarity checkpoint in life. Every night, lying in bed just before dozing off, I would ask myself, "Did I live fully today? Did I love? Did I matter?" I've asked those questions of myself every night for over twenty years. The truth is, I don't always go to bed with a resounding "Yes!" to all three questions. I have bad days, just like anyone else. But the nights that I can say yes to those questions—when I feel clear and on track—are the nights I sleep best. That simple practice has given me more clarity than anything else I've done in life. Today, I still wear a bracelet engraved with those three words. I don't need the bracelet. I don't need to continue asking the questions. But I do because it keeps me clear and on track.

This is similar to the work I had to do with Kate. Her identity-formation practices had stagnated.

She hadn't thought about a better version of herself for a long time, because she was already doing so well.

So in one coaching session, I asked her to describe herself in various situations of her life over the past few weeks: upon coming home, while playing with her kids, when making a presentation at work, during interactions with friends, while out on a date with Mike. Then I asked her to do it again, this time describing herself in those same situations as if she were an even better future version of herself. She began to realize that who she had been in the past several weeks was not who she really imagined herself being in the upcoming years. That should be a wakeup call for anyone.

Next, I asked her to identify three aspirational words that would describe her future self. She came up with *alive, playful*, and *grateful*.

None of her descriptions or words sounded like merely "going through the motions," which was how she had felt recently. This activity was also simple but eye-opening for her. Sometimes, it's the simple thought processes that help us reset our focus. Kate was generally confident, but the issue was she had stopped envisioning a future Kate to grow into. That's what was hurting her: *no vision, no enthusiasm.* So I had her put her three aspirational words into her phone as an alarm label that went off three times per day. This means that as Kate went about her day, an alarm would go off and she'd see her words on her phone to remind her who she was and could become.

Now it's your turn.

1. Describe how you've perceived yourself in the following situations over the past several months—with your significant other, at work, with the kids or team, in social situations with strangers.

2. Now ask, "Is that who I really see myself being in the future?" How would my future self look, feel, and behave differently in those situations?

3. If you could describe yourself in just three aspirational words—words that would sum up who you are at your best in the future—what would those words be? Why are those words meaningful to you? Once you find your words, put them in your phone as an alarm label that goes off several times per day.

Social

High performers also have clear intentions about how they want to treat other people. They have high situational awareness and social intelligence, which help them succeed and lead.[7] In every situation that matters, they know who they want to be and *how they want to interact with others.*

If this sounds like common sense, let's find out whether it's common practice in your life:

- Before you went into your last meeting, did you think about how you wanted to interact with each person in the meeting?

- Before your last phone call, did you think about the tone you would choose to use with the other person?

- On your last night out with your partner or friends, did you set an intention for the energy you wanted to create?

- When you were dealing with that last conflict, did you think about your values and how you wanted to come across to the other person when you talked to them?

- Do you actively think about how to be a better listener, how to generate positive emotions with others, how you can be a good role model?

Questions of this kind may help you look within and gauge your level of intention.

I've found that high performers also regularly ask themselves a few primary questions right before interacting with people. They ask questions like these:

- How can I be a good person or leader in this upcoming situation?

- What will the other person(s) need?

- What kind of mood and tone do I want to set?

Here are more interesting findings. When asked to choose words that describe their best interactions with others, high performers most often responded with words such as *thoughtful, appreciative, respectful, open, honest, empathetic, loving, caring, kind, present,* and *fair.* When asked to choose three words that best define how they would like to be treated by others, high performers most valued being respected and appreciated.

The issue of respect, specifically, comes up a lot in conversations with high performers. They want to be respected and they want to demonstrate respect with others. And this matters to them in all areas of their life, including at home. A field study of two hundred couples in the United States who were married forty years or longer—and *still* reported being happy—found that the couple's number one value and strength was respect.[8] The four worst behaviors that lead to divorce—criticalness, defensiveness, contempt, and stonewalling—often feel so offensive precisely because they smack of devaluing or disrespect.[9]

What is apparent across all high performers is that they
anticipate positive social interactions
and they strive consciously and consistently to create them.

It's a universal finding. When it comes to their interactions with others, they don't just go on autopilot. They're intentional, and that improves their performance.

In looking to the future, it's clear they've thought about the big picture of their social life, too. They've thought about how they want to be remembered—they think about their character and legacy. High performers are looking out there, beyond today, beyond the meeting, beyond the month's to-dos and obligations. They're *consistently* wondering, "How do I want those I love and serve to remember me?"

Working with Kate, it was always clear that she tremendously valued and loved her family. Yet she sensed she was often juggling so many things that she wasn't as present with them as she wanted to be. She once said, "I feel like they deserve more from me, but I don't know if I have that much more to give." Do you know what the issue with that is? *When you are constantly juggling and feel depleted, you don't think about the future.* You're just trying to survive today, and so you start to lose your clear intention for your interactions with your family and teams tomorrow.

This is a common struggle with achievers. They want to be better lovers and parents but feel stretched too thin. Their mistake is the same one Kate was making. She kept thinking that more *time* was what she needed to be a good mom or wife. *One day,* she thought, *I'll finally get to be the mom I want to be with my kids, and the wife I hope to be.* But you and I both know that "one day" really means "never." To help Kate change and improve her relationships, I had her imagine in advance her interactions with people and then live into those intentions each day. She didn't need more time or to wait one more day. It wasn't about quantity, but about quality. So I asked Kate to try this activity, which I recommend you try, too:

a. Write down each person's name in your immediate family and team.

b. Imagine that in twenty years each person is describing *why* they love and respect you. If each person could say just three words to summarize the interactions they had with you in life, what would you want those three words to be?

c. Next time you're with each of those people, approach your time with them as an opportunity to demonstrate those three qualities. Have those words as the goal and start living into those qualities. Challenge yourself to be that person *now.* This will bring life back into your relationships.

I said it to Kate all the time: It's almost impossible just to "go through the motions" when you have clear and compelling intentions.

Skills

Next, we found that high performers are very clear about the skill sets they need to develop now to win in the future. They don't draw a blank when you ask them, "What three skills are you currently working to develop so you'll be more successful next year?"

When I'm brought in to work with Fortune 500 senior executives, I have them open their calendars and talk me through their upcoming days, weeks, and months. It turns out that executives who score higher on the HPI tend to have more blocks of time already scheduled for learning than do their peers with lower scores. There's an hour blocked out here for taking an online training, another there for executive coaching, another for reading, and yet another for a mastery-oriented hobby (piano, language learning, cooking class, and so on). They've built a curriculum for themselves and are actively engaged in learning. What's clearly linking all these blocks of scheduled time is the desire to develop specific skill sets. The online training is about how to code or manage finances better; the executive coaching is focused on developing listening skills; the reading focuses on a specific skill they've been trying to master, such as strategy, listening in meetings, or story development; the hobby is something they take seriously—they aren't doing it just for pleasure, per se, but to actively develop mastery.

Here's the big distinction: High performers are also working on skills that focus on what I call their *primary field of interest* (PFI). They aren't scattershot learners. They've homed in on their passionate interests, and they set up activities or routines to develop skill in those areas. If they love music, they laser in on what kind of music they want to learn, and then study it. Their PFI is *specific*. They don't just say "music" and then try to learn all forms of music—playing guitar, joining an orchestra, singing with a band. They choose, say, a five-string guitar, find a master teacher, and make time for practice sessions that focus more on *skill building* than on *casual exploration*. In other words, they know their passions and set up time to dial in the skills that will turn those passions into proficiencies. *This means high performers approach their learning not as generalists but as specialists.*

Since by now you have some familiarity with my work, I'll use my career as an example. I began as a change-management analyst for a global consulting company. I was right out of grad school. In my first six months on the job, I approached my work the way most of my peers did: as a generalist. I was trying to learn everything about the company, my clients, the world. That's what you do when you're a novice.

But soon I realized that many of the partners had specific areas of expertise. And if I was going to stand out among the other eighty thousand–plus employees, I'd better develop a skill set fast. So I chose leadership, which was also my area of focus in grad school. Specifically, I wanted to develop the skill of knowing how to build curriculum for leaders and their teams. *Leadership was my PFI; curriculum-building was the skill.* I requested or created relevant projects. My career skyrocketed.

When I left corporate America to become a full-time writer and trainer, I made similar decisions. I made my PFI personal development. But so had many thousands of other writers, bloggers, speakers, and trainers. How would I stand out? I realized that the skill most of these folks lacked wasn't related to their topic, but rather to their marketing of the topic. I was in the same boat. Personal development was always a passion, and I already spent most of my personal reading time studying psychology, neuroscience, sociology, and behavioral economics. I was fascinated by those subjects. So I didn't need *more* focus there. I needed more focus on building my brand. So I made a *huge* shift: I made *marketing* my PFI.

This was a monumental decision for me because I had absolutely no talent, skills, strengths, or background in marketing. But I recognized it as the key that would unlock the door to success in my new career. So I started drilling down into skill sets. I didn't focus on every skill related to marketing, as a generalist would do, just as I hadn't focused on everything related to leadership in general at my corporate gig. Instead, I zeroed in on e-mail marketing and video production. I took online courses on these topics, and I went to seminars. I hired a coach. My calendar was full of building those two skills. For eighteen months, I focused almost exclusively on learning and trying new things related to e-mail marketing and making videos. Specifically, I learned to capture e-mails and send those subscribers weekly newsletters that linked to a featured video training on my blog. I also learned how to put all my videos in an online members' area and charge people money to access them.

Eighteen months later, I found I had succeeded as an early pioneer in online education. Thousands of people were signing up for my online courses, some of which cost over a thousand dollars. Many people in my industry thought it was some sort of magic act or assumed that I was some kind of online genius. But neither was true. I had simply looked to the future, identified what it would take to win in the industry in coming years, and then realigned my activities to develop the skills I needed to succeed. The lesson was simple but powerful:

> **Look to the future.**
> **Identify key skills.**
> **Obsessively develop those skills.**

This sounds easy, but in a world where we are so distracted and reactive, it has become a lost art. We just forget to develop our own curriculum in life—even those of us at the highest levels. I remember I once had the blessing of being brought in to speak to Oprah and her executive team. The aha moment was this idea that high performers build their own curriculum. I remember being surprised that after I finished the training, of all the things I had said, the team posted this one quote from me to summarize our session: "If you leave your growth to randomness, you'll always live in the land of mediocrity."

I hope the takeaway is clear: No matter your current level of performance, clarifying your PFI and the skills you need to master for your next level of success *must be a priority*.

Reconnecting with your passion and setting up structure to develop more skills related to it is a game changer. It's just one thing Kate did to burst through her feelings of just going through the motions. We spent time talking about what it was going to take to win in her PFI in the next ten years, and realized she could learn new skills related to her industry. After she signed up for a few courses and found a mentor at work to help her learn more, she sent me this e-mail:

> Amazingly, at some point in my career I got so good at what I was doing that I forgot how much I really loved to learn. I took my eyes off what I needed to learn in the future. But today I finished an online course, and I can't describe how accomplished that simple act made me feel. It was like graduating from high school all over again. That kind of optimism for the future came back into my life because learning opens the mind and begs it to play. I can't believe changing how I feel was as easy as choosing to learn again.

You can follow Kate's lead. Try this:

1. Think about your PFI (primary field of interest) and write down three skills that make people successful in that field.

2. Under each skill, write down what you will do to develop it. Will you read, practice, get a coach, go to a training? When? Set up a plan to develop those skills, put it in your calendar, and stay consistent.

3. Now think about your PFI and write down three skills that you will need in order to succeed in that field five to ten years from now. In other words, try to imagine the future. What new skill sets will you likely need then? Keep those skills on your radar, and start developing them sooner rather than later.

Service

It had been too long since Kate felt the difference she was making. She had lost the spirit of service to others, and that's what had caused her to start merely going through the motions at work. Though nothing there had changed, she began perceiving her days as a series of empty tasks. Specifically, while she was a phenomenal leader at work and she truly felt the spirit of service in leading her teams, she had lost her connection to those ultimately affected by their work: her customers.

It turned out that Kate hadn't actually *spoken* with any of her customers in years. She had become an internal executive in a big company, far removed from the front lines—and the real people that her organization served. So she started a monthly practice of visiting her customers and really listening to them and asking what they wanted from her company in the future. Soon, her enthusiasm for work came roaring back.

The last of the Four Futures, after *self*, *social*, and *skills*, concerns how high performers look to tomorrow and consider their *service* to the world. Specifically, high performers care deeply about the difference they are going to make for others and in the future in general, so they cater today's activities to delivering those contributions with heart and elegance. This may sound like a broad description, but it's how high performers talk. They often speak of how all the extra efforts they make to wow people today are vitally important to leaving a lasting legacy tomorrow. That's why, for many high performers, the details of how they treat others or approach their work truly matter. The high performing waiter obsesses over whether the table is set with symmetry and precision, not just because it's his job but because he cares about the overall customer experience and how the restaurant will be perceived now and in the future. The extraordinary product designer obsesses about style, fit, and function, not just to create strong sales through this season but also to create devoted fans and to serve a larger brand vision. What ties all these things together is the future focus conveyed in this question: "How can I serve people with excellence and make an extraordinary contribution to the world?"

The opposite is easy to spot.

When someone becomes disconnected from the future and their contribution to it, they underperform.

They have nothing to get excited about tomorrow, so they stop caring about the details today. That is why it's so vital that leaders continually engage their people in conversations about tomorrow.

What will provide the *most value* to those you serve? This is a question high performers obsess about. And I don't use the word *obsess* lightly. In our interviews, we found that high performers give an extraordinary amount of thought to questions of service: how to add value, inspire those around them, and make a difference. Their attention in this area could best be described as a search for relevance, differentiation, and excellence.

Relevance has to do with eliminating things that don't matter anymore. High performers don't live in the past, and they don't keep pet projects at the forefront. They ask, "What matters now, and how can I deliver it?" *Differentiation* allows high performers to look at their industry, their career, and even their relationships for what makes them unique. They want to stand out for who they are, and to add more value than others do. *Excellence* comes from an internal standard that asks, "How can I deliver beyond what's expected?" For high performers, the question "How can I serve with excellence?" gets more attention than perhaps any other.

In stark contrast again, underperformers are too focused on *self* over *service*. They give more mindshare to "What do I want now?" than to "What do those I serve want now?" They ask, "How can I get by with the least amount of effort?" instead of "How can I serve with excellence?" Underperformers ask, "Why don't people recognize my unique strengths?" while high performers are asking, "How can I serve in unique ways?"

At the end of this chapter, you'll get a worksheet tying together all the ideas of the Future Four. For now, let me introduce you to a section that will conclude each of the practices in this book, called "Performance Prompts." These prompts are sentence-completion activities that will help you reflect further on the important concepts you're learning. I highly recommend you write out and complete each of these statements in a separate journal. If you would like a companion workbook with all the prompts included and more space for reflection, visit HighPerformanceHabits.com/tools.

Whether you use the worksheet or just grab a journal of your own and freeform your thoughts, I suggest you sit and write out what you want of life. No goals, no growth. No clarity, no change.

Performance Prompts

1. When I think about the Future Four—self, social, skill, and service—the area that I haven't had as much intention in as I should is . . .

2. The areas in which I have not been considering those I serve and lead are . . .

3. To leave a lasting legacy, the contributions I can start making now are . . .

PRACTICE TWO

DETERMINE THE FEELING YOU'RE AFTER

"Don't ask what the world needs.
Ask what makes you come alive, and go do it.
Because what the world needs is
people who have come alive."

—Howard Thurman

The second practice that will help you heighten and sustain clarity in your life is to ask yourself frequently, "What is the primary feeling I want to *bring* to this situation, and what is the primary feeling I want to *get* from this situation?"

Most people are terrible at this. Underperformers, especially, are neglectful of the kinds of feelings they are experiencing or want to experience in life. They bumble into situations and allow those situations to define how they feel. This explains why they have low self-awareness and weak self-control.

High performers demonstrate a tremendous degree of emotional intelligence and what I call "willful feeling." In performance situations, they can accurately describe their emotions, but more importantly, they can also calibrate the meaning they draw from those emotions and determine the feelings they want to endure.

Let me give you an example. I worked with an Olympic sprinter who was at the top of his game that year. But in prior years his performance was often erratic. Sometimes he won a competition; other times he didn't even make the qualifying cut. When I got the call to work with him, he had a yearlong winning streak. In our first session together, I asked, "If you had to describe why you're winning now, in just three words, what would they be?" He said, "Feeling, feeling, feeling."

When I asked him to explain, he said, "I got very clear about the feelings I needed in my mind and my body before I walked out onto the field, while I readied myself at the starting blocks, what I sensed in the middle of the sprint, and what I wanted to feel after I crossed the line and even all the way back into the tunnel."

I asked if that meant he got control of his emotions and didn't experience performance anxiety anymore. He laughed. "No. When I'm at the starting blocks, my body still senses the energy and emotion of it all—my body is naturally aware of what's at stake, and there's an emotion of [some fear] that's there no matter what. But I don't *feel* anxious. *I define the feeling.* I tell myself that what I'm sensing is a feeling of readiness, excitement."[10]

I've heard so many high performers describe this practice in some form or another. They can sense their emotional state in any given moment, but they often choose to override it by defining what they want to feel.

Let's pause to differentiate between emotions and feelings. While researchers differ in their definitions of what an emotion is, many agree that emotions are different from feelings.[11] Emotions are generally instinctive. A triggering event—which can be an external situation or simply our brain anticipating something—generates an emotional response like fear, amusement, sadness, anger, relief, or love. Often, the emotional response happens without much of our conscious will; we just suddenly feel the emotion because our brain interpreted something happening and attached a meaning and emotion to it, guided mostly from how we sensed the situation from the past. This doesn't mean that we are conscious of all our emotions, or that we can't also generate an emotion consciously. For example, seeing your baby smile at you may stir joy in your heart, but you could also illicit the emotion of joy simply by purposefully thinking about the same incident later on without the actual stimulus. Still, the vast majority of the emotions we feel in life are automatic and physical.

The word *feeling* here is used to refer to a *mental portrayal* of an emotion. This is not a precise statement, but it's helpful for our purposes here: Think of an emotion as mostly a reaction, and feeling is an interpretation.[12] Like the sprinter, the emotion of fear can come up but you don't have to choose to feel frightened and run away. You can experience the sudden emotion of fear, but in the very next moment choose to feel centered. Whenever you "calm yourself down," you are choosing a different feeling than the emotion that may have come up for you. Before entering any performance situation, high performers contemplate how they want to feel *regardless of what emotions might come up*, and they envision how they want to feel leaving the situation *regardless of what emotions might come up*. Then they exert self-control to achieve those intentions.

Here's another example that shows this dynamic at play. If I'm in a meeting and people suddenly start arguing with a negative tone, I'll probably experience immediate emotions like fear, anger, or sadness. The response is pretty predictable: My heart will start pounding; my hands will get sweaty; my breathing will get shallow. Those emotions can soon evoke feelings of dread or anxiety. Knowing this, I can choose to feel differently in the meeting *even if* those emotions come up instinctively. I can tell myself that the emotions are just telling me to pay attention or to speak up for myself or to feel empathetic toward others. Instead of allowing the emotion to evoke the feeling of dread, I can just let it be, take a few deep breaths, and choose to feel alert yet calm. I can keep breathing deeply, speak in an even tone, sit comfortably in my chair, think positively about the people in the room, choose to be a calm force amid the storm—all these choices generate a new feeling that's different from what "came up" earlier.

My automatic emotions don't have to be in charge.
My feelings are my own.

Over time, if I choose to create the feelings I want from my emotions, my brain will likely habituate to the new feelings. Fear suddenly doesn't feel so bad anymore because my brain has learned that I'll deal with it well. My old references for how I feel after the emotion has changed, and that can change the actual automatic emotion's power.[13] The emotion of fear still might get triggered, but now the feeling I sense from it is what I've created in the past.

Emotions come and go. They're mostly immediate, instinctive, and physical. But feelings last, and they're often a result of rumination, which you have control over. Anger can be the emotion that comes up, but bitterness—a lasting feeling—doesn't have to be your lifelong sentence.

This might sound as if I'm just parsing words, and again I acknowledge that my descriptions are imprecise.[14] (No description of any function of mind or body can be precise, because there is always variance and no thought or emotion is an island—our senses and intentions interact and overlap across a vast neural network.) **But I share this here because it's so thoroughly obvious that high performers are generating the *feelings* they want more often than taking the *emotions* that land on them.** When high performing athletes say they are trying to get in the zone, what they mean is that they are trying to use their conscious attention to narrow their focus and *feel* in the zone. Being in the zone is not an emotion that just happens—athletes will themselves there by minimizing distractions and immersing themselves in what they are doing. For high level athletes and high performers from all walks of life, flow is a feeling they choose. It is summoned, not a lucky emotion that conveniently happens to show up just in time for kickoff.

It's when we stop being conscious of our feelings that we get in trouble. Then the negativity of the world can start stirring negative emotions, which, if we don't control the meaning of, can evoke long-term negative feelings, which in turn set the stage for a horrible life. But if we seek to experience life and all its emotions and yet choose to feel centered, happy, strong, and loving right through the ups and downs, then we've accomplished something powerful. We've wielded the power of willful feeling, and suddenly life *feels* the way we want it to.

That's what Kate had been forgetting. She was too often lost in a sea of unpredictable emotions. She wasn't choosing to feel any one way over another. She wasn't aware of how she was treating the emotions and experiences, and so she just became reactive. She wasn't just going through the motions. She was going through the *emotions*, so she wasn't really *feeling* life the way she wanted to anymore.

All I had to do was get her to choose how she wanted to feel in each situation she entered, and that intention and activity alone brought more vibrancy and color back into her life.

In your everyday life, start asking, "What do I want to feel today? How could I define the meaning of the day so that I feel what I want to?" Next time you go on a date with someone, think about the *feelings* you want to create. Before you sit down with your child to work on math, ask, "What do I want to feel when I'm helping my kid? What feelings do I want them to have about me, about homework, about their life?" This kind of clarity and intention will change how you experience life.

Performance Prompts

1. The emotions I've been experiencing a lot of lately are . . .

2. The areas of life where I'm not having the feelings I want to are . . .

3. The feelings I want to experience more of in life include . . .

4. The next time I feel a negative emotion come up, the thing I'm going to say to myself is . . .

PRACTICE THREE

DEFINE WHAT'S MEANINGFUL

"Unhappiness is not knowing what we want
and killing ourselves to get it."

—Don Herold

High performers can do almost anything they set their heart and mind to. But not every mountain is worth the climb. What differentiates high performers from others is their critical eye in figuring out what is going to be meaningful to their life experience. They spend more of their time doing things that they find meaningful, and this makes them happy.

It is not want of strength that locks us into unlived lives. Rather, it is lack of a decisive cause, something worth striving for, an ambitious purpose that sets our hearts ablaze and our feet marching forward. Our striving for a meaningful life is one of the main factors associated with psychological well-being.[15]

But what do we mean by *meaning*?

When most people talk about having "meaning at work," they typically discuss (a) enjoyment of the tasks of work, (b) alignment of personal values with the work, and (c) fulfillment from the outcomes of the work.

When researchers try to identify what is meaningful to people, they often focus on how important you say an activity is to you, how much time you spend at it, how committed you are, how attached to it you are, and whether you would do the work despite low compensation. They try to figure out whether you see the work as just a job, or an important career, or a calling.[16] They often associate a clear sense of purpose with an overall sense of meaning in life.[17]

Do high performers approach meaning the same way? We randomly selected 1,300 individuals who scored in the top 15 percent on the HPI and asked them questions such as:

- How do you know when you're doing something meaningful?

- What does it feel like?

- If you had to choose between two good projects, how would you go about choosing the one that would be most meaningful to you?

- How do you know when you're doing something that isn't bringing meaning into your life?

- At the end of your life, how would you know whether you had lived a meaningful life?

Since the questions were open-ended, we combed through the responses looking for patterns. What emerged was that high performers tended to equate four factors with meaning.

First, they linked *enthusiasm* with meaning. When forced to choose between two projects, for example, many mentioned they would do the one they could be most enthusiastic about. This finding dovetails with research findings that enthusiasm independently predicted life satisfaction, positive emotions, fewer negative emotions, environmental mastery, personal growth, positive relations, self-acceptance, purpose in life, engagement, positive relationships, meaning, and achievement.[18] Clearly, if you want a positive life, you would do well to summon as much enthusiasm as possible. It was these findings that inspired me to ask myself this question every morning in the shower: "What can I get excited or enthusiastic about today?" That simple question has changed the way I walk into each day. Try it.

The second link to meaning was *connection*. People who become socially isolated report that their life has lost meaning.[19] Social relationships, especially with those closest to us, are the most frequently reported sources of meaning in life.[20]

Like everyone else, high performers value the relationships they have in life and work. What's unique about high performers, though, is that connection often correlates with meaning, especially at work. Connection is less about *comfort* than about *challenge*. In other words, high performers feel that their work has more meaning when they are in a peer group that challenges them. In their everyday life, too, they value being around inspiring people who push them to grow more than, say, people who are just fun to be around or are generally kind.

Third, high performers relate *satisfaction* with meaning. If what they are doing creates a sense of personal satisfaction, they feel that their life is more meaningful. Teasing out what "satisfaction" means to people is as difficult as finding out how they define "meaningful." But for high performers, there is a clear equation for what leads to personal satisfaction. When your efforts correspond with one of your primary passions, lead to personal or professional growth, and make a clear and positive contribution to others, you tend to call those efforts satisfying.

Passion + Growth + Contribution = Personal Satisfaction

Other researchers have found that security, autonomy, and balance can also be important to satisfaction, especially on the job.[21]

The fourth way that high performers say their efforts have meaning is by making them feel that their life "makes sense." Psychologists call this *coherence*.[22] It means that the story of your life—or of recent events in your life—is comprehensible to you in some way.

This sense of coherence seems to be particularly important to high performers. They want to know that their efforts align with something important, that their work is significant, and that their lives are creating a legacy and feeding a larger purpose.

Often, the desire for things to make sense is more important to a high performer than are autonomy and balance. They will put their own desires for control or work-life balance aside if they sense that what they are doing makes sense and adds to a greater whole.

Certainly, more research needs to be done on how high performers view meaning. The research my team and I have conducted gives us a good start, though. You may find this simple equation helpful:

Enthusiasm + Connection + Satisfaction + Coherence = Meaning

Not all these factors need to be in play at once to give us a sense of meaning. Sometimes, just watching your child walk across a room can do it. Or finishing that important report. A lovely date night or hosting a mentoring lunch can make life meaningful.

The important thing is this: *You need to bring more conscious and consistent thought to what you will find meaningful in life.* You start by exploring your own definitions of meaning and how to enhance it in your life. When you learn the difference between busywork and your life's work, that's the first step on the path of purpose.

Performance Prompts

1. The activities that I currently do that bring me the most meaning are . . .

2. The activities or projects that I should stop doing, because they are not bringing me any sense of meaning, are . . .

3. If I was going to add new activities that bring me more meaning, the first ones I would add would be . . .

PUTTING IT ALL TOGETHER

"The meaning of life is whatever you ascribe to it."
—Joseph Campbell

You have to have a vision for yourself in the future. You have to discern how you want to feel and what will be meaningful to you. Without those practices, you have nothing to dream of and strive for, no pop and zest in your daily life propelling you forward.

We've covered a lot in this chapter. How do we put all these practices together so that our practices for clarity are strong and consistent?

I recommend the same thing I did for Kate, who felt that she was just going through the motions in her work, her relationships, and her life. You'll recall that she was so good she didn't really need to try anymore. She forgot to look to the future and have strong intentions, which led to her being busy but unfulfilled. It led to her feeling lost. To help her reorient herself, I had her begin a simple habit of contemplation that would hit all the practices you've learned in this chapter. I gave Kate a tool called the Clarity Chart™. It's a one-page journal sheet that I asked her to fill out every Sunday evening for twelve weeks. You can find the short version below, and you can download the full-page version at HighPerformanceHabits.com/tools.

Of course, you don't *need* to fill out the chart every week. (You don't have to do anything I'm suggesting.) But I promise that this activity will help you, even if your responses don't change much from week to week. High performance clarity happens because we put these concepts up onto the dashboard of our conscious mind. Perhaps you've given occasional thought to the concepts we've covered in this chapter. But our goal is to *focus on these things more consistently than you ever have before.* That's what moves the needle. With greater focus will come greater clarity, and with greater clarity will come more consistent action and, ultimately, high performance.

The Clarity Chart™

Download a printable weekly version at HighPerformanceHabits .com/tools.

Self	Social
Three words that describe my best self are . . .	Three words that could define how I want to treat other people are . . .
_____	_____
_____	_____
_____	_____
Some ideas for how I can embody these words more often this upcoming week are . . .	Some people in my life whom I could improve my interactions with this week include . . .
Skills	**Service**
The five skills I'm trying to develop most in my life right now are . . .	Three simple ways I can add value to those around me this week are . . .
_____	_____
_____	_____
_____	_____
_____	
The way I can learn or practice those skills this week includes . . .	Something I could do this week with real focus and excellence to help someone else is . . .

Focus on the Feeling

The main feelings I want to cultivate in my life, relationships, and work this week include . . .

The way I will generate these feelings is to . . .

Define What's Meaningful

Something I can do or create that would bring me more meaning in life is . . .

GENERATE ENERGY

"The world belongs to the energetic."
—Ralph Waldo Emerson

RELEASE TENSION, SET INTENTION

BRING THE JOY

OPTIMIZE HEALTH

"If I keep up this pace, I'll eventually burn out, or probably just die."

Arjun laughs and shifts uncomfortably in his chair. "Then all this was for nothing."

He looks as though he's barely slept in months. His face sags. His eyes are red, the sparkle inside gone. He doesn't have the vibrant charge like he did on the cover of that business magazine last year.

I feign a look of surprise. "Die, huh. When do you think 'eventually' might happen? Are we talking next week? This year? Next year?"

"I'm not sure. But don't tell anyone."

It's brave of him to be telling me this. No one likes to admit they've been working themselves into the ground. Especially here in Silicon Valley, it's a badge of honor to work nonstop. There are a lot of young, smart workaholics here on this peninsula, pumped up on excessive caffeine and become-a-billionaire-in-a-few-years dreams.

Six hours ago, a friend called and asked me if he could conference in Arjun to introduce us. We exchanged pleasantries, and two hours later Arjun's private jet arrived to pick me up. Now I'm sitting in a glass conference room in his office near San Francisco. It's 3:00 a.m., and we're the only ones in the building. Some achievers won't let their guard down until after midnight.

I'm not entirely sure why he's flown me here. On the phone, he just said it was urgent and he thought I could help. I had wanted to meet him someday anyway, so I agreed.

"So what's up?" I say. "I'm guessing you didn't fly me here to play Mom and tell you to get more sleep."

He laughs and pulls back in his chair. "No. That's not it. I know I need more rest."

"And yet, you don't rest?"

"I will."

I've heard this before. The someday-I'll-take-better-care-of-myself story. "Right now I just have to hustle," they all say. "To build. To take over the world."

"Well, that's not true, Arjun. And that's okay. The truth is, you won't flame out. You'll keep working hard at an insane pace, just as you've done for the past fifteen years. You won't burn out. You'll just become utterly, tragically miserable. You'll wake up one day, even richer and more accomplished than you are now, and life just won't feel the way you wanted it to. You won't burn out then, either. But you will make a bad and abrupt decision. You'll quit or you'll fail. You'll realize your mind and body didn't let you down; your choices did. But I'm guessing you already know that."

"Yeah," he says, then rolls back his left shirtsleeve. He points to a needle mark. "Don't freak out. It's not drugs. I'm doing that Myers cocktail thing. Bunch of B vitamins and stuff. It's probably not helping, you know?"

I don't show a reaction. I've seen them all by now: all the quick fixes and prescriptions and fads people use in a desperate grab to revitalize their lives. When people want the edge, often the first place they look is outside themselves.

"So what *would* help, Arjun? You're a smart guy; you probably already know the answers. So, with respect, I don't want to waste your time. It's three in the morning. Why am I here?"

"I want to feel good again. I don't want the emotional roller coaster anymore. I don't want to be tired. There has to be a way to crush it and still be happy. People say it's possible. But in forty years I haven't figured it out, that's for sure. But I know you can help."

"And how do you know that?"

Arjun rolls the sleeve up on his other arm. He holds up his wrist and shows me a leather bracelet, engraved with one of my quotes. He jabs at it with his finger. "I want *this* again, man."

"Where'd you get that?"

"My wife. It's embarrassing, but I'll tell you. We're having issues. She went to your event. She's a different person now. She said she bought this for me because I needed it. Because *we* needed it."

"Was she right?"

He sighs and joins me standing, looking out into his offices. "I can't take us . . . I can't take everyone here higher when I feel so low. My energy is dipping. The team can sense it. I'm not happy and I don't want to feel this way anymore."

The engraving on the leather bracelet reads BRING THE JOY.

ENERGY BASICS

"Energy is eternal delight."

—William Blake

As you might expect, it takes a lot of energy to succeed over the long haul. High performers have the magical trifecta of capital "E" Energy—that holistic kind that includes positive and enduring mental, physical, and emotional vibrancy. It's the key force that helps them perform better in many areas of their life. It's why high performers have so much more passion, stamina, and motivation. If you can tap into the capital "E" Energy stored within, the world is yours.

In our high performance research, we measure energy by asking people to rate themselves on a scale of 1 through 5 on statements such as:

- I have the mental stamina to be present and focused throughout the day.

- I have the physical energy I need to achieve my goals every day.

- In general, I feel cheerful and optimistic.

We also reverse score with statements like:

- My mind feels slow and foggy.

- I am physically exhausted too often.

- I feel a lot of negative energy and emotions.

You'll notice that energy isn't just *physical*, which is how most people conceive of it. Mental alertness matters, too. So does positive emotion. In fact, all three have been correlated with high performance. When I use the word *energy* in this book, then, keep in mind it means the full spectrum of mental, emotional, and physical vibrancy.

The headline from our research on this topic may seem obvious to you: Low energy correlates with lower overall high performance scores. But the details of the findings should get your attention:

The *lower* your ratings in energy . . .

- the lower your overall happiness,

- the lower your enthusiasm for taking on challenges,

- the lower your perception of your own success versus your peers' success,

- the lower your confidence in the face of adversity,

- the lower the degree of influence you'll have with others, and

- the lower the likelihood that you'll eat well or exercise.

So low energy not only hurts your ability to reach high performance overall, it pervades all aspects of your life. You feel less happy. You don't take on the big challenges. You feel as if everyone is passing you by. Your confidence tanks. You eat worse. You get fatter. You struggle to get people to believe in you, buy from you, follow you, support you.

But of course, the flip side also applies. Increase your energy, and you improve *all* those factors.

And there's more. Energy is also positively related to educational attainment, creativity, and assertiveness. This tends to mean that the more energy someone has, the more likely they are to pursue higher levels of education, to come up with creative ideas at work, and to speak up for themselves and take action toward their dreams. That's why organizations and academic institutions worldwide should get *very serious* about developing employee and student energy scores.

Regarding job roles, CEOs and senior executives have the highest energy—significantly higher than those in other roles we've measured, such as managers, entry-level workers, students/interns, and caregivers. This holds true even when we control for age. In a stunning finding, CEOs and senior executives have energy equivalent to that of professional athletes. It turns out that to make it to CEO, you have to care about your energy as much as an NFL quarterback does, because it takes about the same level of energy.

Bottom line: The more energy someone has, the more likely they are to be happy and climb to the top of their primary field of interest.

It turns out, too, that marriage is good for your energy, just as it's good for your longevity. In our surveys, married people have more energy than their never married counterparts.[1] So go ahead and tell any fearful friends that their belief that marriage makes you dull, tired, or moody just doesn't hold up.

Finally, energy is significantly related to productivity.[2] If you ever want to get more done, you don't need to buy some new app or organize your papers better. It's less about doing e-mail better and more about doing energy better.

My personal experience coaching extraordinary people validates the data and then some. Often, I see people forget to focus on their energy as they build their career, and then disaster strikes. I've seen low energy destroy marriages, turn kind people into stress monsters, and wipe out years of several companies' financial gains in just months after its CEO burns out.

Almost all modern health research confirms the importance of our well-being, which is the term often used to describe a more holistic sense of energy. Unfortunately, we don't do well at taking care of our well-being. More than one-third of Americans are obese, costing the United States over $147 billion per year in medical expenses.[3] Only about 20 percent of Americans get even the minimum aerobic and muscle-strengthening activity recommended by the Centers for Disease Control and Prevention (CDC).[4] Other studies reveal that 42 percent of American adults say they aren't doing enough to manage their stress, 20 percent say they never do any activities to relieve or manage their stress, and one in five say they have no one to rely on for emotional support.[5]

One in three working Americans is chronically stressed on the job, and fewer than half say their organizations support employee well-being.[6] This even though companies that promote their employees' well-being are more productive, bear lower health-care costs, retain their people longer, and see their people make better decisions.[7]

Stress is the ultimate energy and well-being killer. It slows the production of new brain cells, reduces serotonin and dopamine (which are critical to your mood), and fires up your amygdala while simultaneously decreasing your hippocampus function—making you a frazzled person with decreased memory.[8]

We could devote several books to the subject of well-being and hardly scratch the surface. But I want to zero in on energy measures as described at the beginning of this chapter, and see just how they correlate with individual high performance.

The good news is, you can dramatically increase your energy and overall performance with just a few simple practices. Your energy is not a fixed mental, physical, or emotional state. Again, you don't "have" energy any more than a power plant does. A power plant transforms and transmits energy. In the same regard, you don't "have" happiness. Rather, you transform your thoughts into feelings that are or are not happy. You don't have to "have" sadness; you can transform it to something else.

This means you don't have to "wait" for joy, motivation, love, excitement, or any other positive emotion in life. You can choose to generate it, on demand, any time you want, through the power of habit.

Like any other area of your life or any other set of skills, it can be improved. Here are the big three practices I've seen high performers leverage to maintain their edge and their energy.

PRACTICE ONE

RELEASE TENSION, SET INTENTION

"Human excellence is a state of mind."

—Socrates

In a decade of coaching high performers, I've found that the easiest, fastest, and most effective way to help them increase their energy is to teach them to *master transitions*.

Every day, people lose tremendous amounts of focus, will, and emotional energy by managing transitions poorly. They also lose the benefit of greater mental and physical stamina throughout the day.

What do I mean by transitions? Well, every morning when you wake up and start your day, you experience a transition from rest to activation. The start of your day is a transition.

The time you drop off the kids and start your commute—that's a transition from family time to drive time. When you finish your commute to work, open your car door, and walk into the office, that's a transition from solitary time to working with others.

At work, when you finish creating that presentation and now go to check e-mail, that's a transition. You're going from creative mode to e-mail mode. When a meeting ends and you walk back to your desk, sit down, and jump on a conference call, that's a transition. The workday ends, you hop back into the car and head to the gym. Two more transitions. Pull up to your house after a long day and walk into your home and become Mommy or Daddy. Transition.

You get the idea. Our days comprise a series of transitions.

These transitions are immensely valuable—a powerful space of freedom between activities. And it's in this space that you'll discover your greatest restorer and amplifier of energy.

Think about all the transitions you experience during the day. Take a moment and write a few of them down here:

_____

_____

_____

_____

_____

_____

_____

_____

_____

Now let me ask you a few questions about all these transitions:

- Do you ever carry over any negative energy from one activity to the next?

- Do you ever feel depleted but still plow into your next activity without a break, even though you know you should take a breather?

- Are you losing a sense of presence and appreciation for life and others the further you go in your day?

Most people answer yes to all three questions.

I'm convinced that if we can get you to change the way you shift from one activity to the next, we can revitalize your life. So, are you ready for an experiment?

From now on, as you move from one major activity to another, try this:

1. Close your eyes for the next minute or two.

2. Repeat the word *release* in your mind over and over. As you do, command your body to release all the tension in your shoulders, in your neck, in your face and jaw. Release the tension in your back and your legs. Release the tension in your mind and spirit. If this is hard, just focus on each part of your body, breathe deeply, and repeat the word *release* in your mind. This doesn't have to take long—just a minute or two repeating the word *release*.

3. When you feel you've released some tension—and it doesn't have to be *all* the tension in your life!—move to the next part: SET INTENTION. This means think about what you want to feel and achieve in the next activity you're about to take on when you open your eyes. Ask, "What energy do I want to bring into this next activity? How can I do this next activity with excellence? How can I enjoy the process?" These don't have to be the exact questions you ask, but these are the kinds of question that will prompt your mind to be more present in the next activity.

This simple activity, practiced deliberately throughout the day, can help you better manage stress and gain more presence. It's remarkably powerful.

Don't believe it? Try it. *Right now.* You know what to do. Set this book down for just sixty seconds. Breathe fully during that time. Release the tension in your body. Then ask yourself, "What energy do I want to feel when I start reading again? How can I retain the information better? How can I enjoy reading this even more?" Who knows? You might feel more present reading, underline more passages, and move to your favorite place to read or grab some coffee so you enjoy reading even more. See how it works?

Now that you know how this practice works, you can imagine dozens of transitions to apply it to. Imagine that you're about to finish replying to some e-mails. Your next activity is to start creating a presentation. In the transition between the two, push yourself back from your desk a bit, then close your eyes for a minute or two. Repeat the word *release* until you feel the tension lift and you find a moment of peace. Then set an intention for how you want to feel creating your presentation and for how you want it to turn out. Easy.

I do this RELEASE TENSION, SET INTENTION activity before and after workouts, before I pick up the phone to call someone, before I write an e-mail to my team, before I shoot a video, before I get out of the car and go to lunch with friends, before I walk out onto a stage in front of twenty thousand people. It has saved me many times from anxiety and a poor performance: before I walked into a room and got interviewed by Oprah, before I sat down to dinner with a US president, before I proposed to my wife. All I can say is, *thank God for this practice!*

You, too, can find and summon new energy and life in the moments in between. Remember, just take a beat, close your eyes, and RELEASE TENSION, SET INTENTION.

If you'd like to go to another level of mastery, try a twenty-minute practice called the Release Meditation Technique (RMT). I've trained over two million people on RMT, and all over the world I meet students who consider it one of the most life-changing habits they've ever adopted. Just close your eyes, sit up straight, and, breathing deeply, let the tension fall away from your body as you keep repeating the word *release* to yourself. As thoughts inevitably come up in your mind, don't try to chase them away or ponder them—just let them go and return to the "release" mantra. The goal of the meditation is to release both physical and mental tension. It helps to have a voice guide you through it with some background music, so just visit YouTube and type in my name and "Release Meditation Technique."

Regardless of how you choose to take a break, meditate, or otherwise deal with stress, the idea is to form a habit and stick to it. Most meditation practices can lead to significantly less stress and anxiety, causing a bump in attention, presence, creativity, and well-being.[9] Neuroscientists continue to find that people with more meditation experience show increased connectivity within the brain's attentional networks, as well as between attentional regions and medial frontal regions that are critical to such cognitive skills as maintaining attention and disengaging from distraction.[10] The positive effects of meditation don't happen just during meditation, but continue to be evident in daily life as well.[11] One study saw the positive effects (such as decreased anxiety) from just a few months of meditation last more than three years.[12]

Remember Arjun, the hotshot tech founder from the beginning of this chapter? He wanted to avoid burnout and experience more joy in his life. So that night, just before we finished our conversation at around 4:30 a.m. and his driver took me back to the airport, I taught him this practice. Just two days later, I received this e-mail:

> Hey, man,
>
> I want to thank you again for flying out. I appreciated our conversation and your time especially under short notice. I look forward to working together. I also want to share a quick win with you. Tonight, when I pulled up to my house, I tried that release technique you taught me. I just sat in the car for a few minutes before going into the house. I closed my eyes and just repeated the word "release" to myself. I'm guessing I did this for five minutes tops. Then I asked myself, "How do I go into my house free from the work and business? How would I greet my wife if I were the best husband in the world? How would I be with my daughter tonight if I realized how precious this time in her life is? How would I show up if I were as energized as my best

self?" I don't remember all my thoughts, but I set an intention to go into the house and love my wife and give her my full energy. I walked in like a new man, as if I'd won the lottery of life. You should have prepared me for what happened next, because [my wife] thought I was crazy for a moment. But then she realized it was just me again. My daughter noticed, too. We just had the most wonderful night. I'm at a loss how to describe it. But you gave me my family back. They're getting ready for bed now. I couldn't wait to zap you a note of thanks. For the first time in a long time, I want you to know that I felt like I was alive again. [My wife] said you talk about people coming around to the power of intention. Count me as one more example. Thank you.

Performance Prompts

1. The things that cause me the most amount of tension each day are . . .

2. A way I could remind myself to release that tension throughout the day is . . .

3. If I felt more energy each day, I would be more likely to . . .

4. When I reset my energy each day with this practice, I'd like to start the next activity feeling . . .

PRACTICE TWO

BRING THE JOY

*"Most folks are about as happy as
they make up their minds to be."*

—Abraham Lincoln

Our research has shown that joy plays a huge part in what makes high performers successful. You might recall that joy is one of the three defining positive emotions of the high performance experience. (Confidence and full engagement in the moment—often described as presence, flow, or mindfulness—are the other two.)

That's why I suggest that if you decide to set one intention that will raise your energy and change your life more than any other, make it to *bring more joy* into your daily life. Joy won't just make you a high performer, it will cue almost every other positive human emotion we desire in life. I don't know of any more important emotion than love, though I also believe that love without joy can feel hollow.

Positive emotion, in general, is one of the greatest predictors of the good life—high energy and high performance. People with more positive emotion have more satisfying marriages, make more money, and have better health.[13] When positive emotion is present, students do better on tests,[14] managers make better decisions and are more effective with their teams,[15] physicians make better diagnoses,[16] and people are kinder and more helpful to others.[17] Neuroscientists have even found that positive emotions prompt new cell growth (plasticity), whereas negative emotions cause decay.[18]

High Performance Indicator data shows that those who get better overall high performance scores and report being more successful over a longer period than their peers also report being more cheerful and optimistic than their peers. They also experience less negative energy and emotion.

In interviews, it's obvious that high performers are joyful as they talk about their craft, career, and relationships. They don't always enjoy all the hard work that goes into becoming great, but they are grateful and giddy about their craft and their opportunities overall. It turns out that joy, more than anything else, is what gives them capital "E" Energy. If you feel joy, your mind, body, and emotional reality all get a lift.

You've heard it said that showing up is 80 percent of success? Well, if you want to be a high performer, show up *and bring the joy.*

This all sounds wonderful, but what if you *lack* positive emotion? What happens when life *isn't* joyous? What if people are around you are negative?

Well, then, you'd better change that. Positive emotion is a prerequisite for high performance. *And only you are in charge of your enduring emotional experience.* Remember the lesson from the last chapter: You can choose your feelings (the interpretations you have about the emotions that you sense), and the more you do that the more you rewire how you experience emotions. You're in charge of how you feel. That's perhaps one of the greatest human gifts.

This doesn't mean that high performers are *always* happy and perfect and awesome. Just like everyone else, they experience negative emotions. It's just that they cope with them better and, perhaps even more important, they consciously direct their thoughts and behaviors to generating positive emotion. Again, high performers *will* themselves into positive states. Just as athletes do specific things to get themselves into "the zone," high performers consciously cultivate joy.

To understand how they do this, I asked a group of randomly selected people who had scored high on the HPI to describe how they generated positive emotions and feelings in general. What specifically brought joy into their lives (and what didn't)? And what habits, if any, did they deliberately make themselves practice in order to stay in joyful states for longer? What emerged from their responses is that high performers tend to follow similar habits every day. They tend to . . .

1. . . . prime the emotions they want to experience, in advance of key events (or of the day in general). They think about how they want to feel, and ask themselves questions, or practice visualizations, that generate those feelings. (This aligns well with "focus on the feeling" from the previous chapter.)

2. . . . anticipate positive outcomes from their actions. They're optimistic and clearly believe that their actions will be rewarded.

3. . . . imagine possible stressful situations and how their best self might gracefully handle them. As much as they anticipate positive outcomes, they're realistic about hitting snags, and they prepare themselves for difficulties.

4. . . . seek to insert appreciation, surprise, wonder, and challenge into their day.

5. . . . steer social interactions toward positive emotions and experiences. They are what one respondent called "conscious goodness spreaders."

6. . . . reflect regularly on all that they're grateful for.

If you were to do these six things consciously and consistently, you'd feel pretty joyful, too. I know, because that's what happened for me.

Getting My Life Back

In 2011, while on a vacation in the desert with friends, I wrecked an ATV while speeding along the beach at about forty miles per hour. I broke my wrist, threw out my hip, cracked some ribs, and was later diagnosed with postconcussive syndrome from the traumatic brain injury. I wrote about the experience in the opening of my book *The Charge*, so I won't go into much detail here. What I will share is that it was a terrible time in my life. The trauma hurt my concentration, emotional control, abstract reasoning abilities, memory, and physical balance. For weeks, I fell victim to just going with the flow and letting my emotions get the best of me. I wasn't managing everyday frustrations well because—I have to be honest—I don't think I was trying hard enough to do so. I was so focused on recovering from my physical injuries that I neglected the need to recondition my own mind, which was also compromised from my brain injury. It left me being easily frustrated with my team, being short with my wife, failing to think about the future, and generally feeling out of sorts.

Then one day, after reading some of our findings about high performers, I realized I wasn't practicing my morning habits. I also knew that if I didn't set up some new mental triggers to help activate more positive emotions and experiences in life, my brain trauma would take over and my default mode would be reaction and misery. With the research on the six things high performers did to bring joy to their lives, I began a new morning routine and triggers.

Every morning in the shower, I asked myself three questions to prime my mind for a positive day:

- What can I be excited about today?

- What or who might trip me up or cause stress, and how can I respond in a positive way, from my highest self?

- Who can I surprise today with a thank-you, a gift, or a moment of appreciation?

I chose the first question specifically because so many high performers shared that they enjoyed the anticipation as much as the joyous event itself. Neuroscientists have found the same: Anticipation can be just as powerful in releasing hormones such as dopamine, which makes you happy, as the actual positive event.[19]

Of course, sometimes I'd stand in the shower and couldn't think of anything to get excited about. So I would ask, "Well, what could you make up or do today that you *could* get excited about?"

I chose the second question so I could follow the high performers' practice of imagining possible stressful situations and how their best self might gracefully handle them. I tend to ask this question out loud, from a second-person standpoint, and then respond to it out loud. That means I stand there in the shower and say, "Brendon, what might stress you out today, buddy, and how would your best self handle it if it came up?" Or "Brendon, when X happens, think about Y, and then do Z." I might even imagine myself dealing with the issue and describe how I might be feeling: "There's Brendon in that meeting, feeling a little nervous. His heart is beating too fast because he's forgetting to breathe and he's focused only on himself. He needs to relax now, get present, and focus on asking people questions and being of service."

It might seem bizarre: me standing in the shower, thinking of stressful situations every morning and talking to myself. But thinking through obstacles and talking to yourself in the second person can be much more powerful than speaking in the first person.[20] It allows you some perspective. I call this practice *self-coaching*, because you're basically distancing yourself and coaching yourself as you would coach a friend on how to deal with a difficult circumstance. A lot of high performers do this.

This process is similar to what psychologists call "cognitive defusion," a practice of trying to externalize and "defuse" difficult emotions or situations. For example, a person dealing with anxiety might be taught to give a name to their anxiety—say, "Downer Dave"—so that rather than being the issue personally, the patient has an external bad guy. It allows the patient to divorce from the issue. Now they can see that external issue come knocking at their door, and they can choose to answer or not.

I included the third question because I wanted to ensure that every day I could anticipate positive outcomes from my actions. I knew that thinking of how I could surprise others with appreciation would actually give me a double shot of goodness: I'd get a jolt of gratitude just by thinking of someone to appreciate, and I'd get another jolt when I shared my gratitude with them. Asking this question also helps me seek to insert appreciation, surprise, wonder, or challenge into my day.

By being mindful of these three questions at the start of the morning, I entered the day enthusiastic, ready to meet the challenges as my best self, and excited to engage others with appreciation.

This simple morning practice can create anticipation, hopefulness, curiosity, and optimism—all positive emotions proven to lead to happiness and to positive health outcomes such as lower cortisol, less stress, and a longer life span.[21]

New Mental Triggers

Every high performer I've ever interviewed speaks about how they take control of their thoughts and bend them toward positive states of mind. They don't wait for joy to land on them; they *bring it*.

So as I was recovering from my brain injury, I decided to develop a series of triggers that would remind me to steer social interactions toward positive emotions and experiences.

1. The first trigger was what I call a "notification trigger." I put the phrase BRING THE JOY into my phone as an alarm label. I set the alarm for three different times throughout the day, and I set

the text for the label of the alarm to read BRING THE JOY! I could be in a meeting, on a call, or writing an e-mail, and all of a sudden my phone would vibrate as the alarm went off and display those words. (As you learned in the chapter on Clarity, I also put other words and phrases in my phone to remind myself of who I want to be and how I want to interact with others.) When your phone vibrates, you look at it, right? So there I was in the middle of my day, sometimes just going through the motions trying to recover from my accident, and *bam*, my phone goes off. It reminded me to *bring joy* to the moment. For years now, that reminder has conditioned my conscious and unconscious mind to bring positive feelings into my everyday life.

2. The second trigger I set was what I call a "door frame trigger." Every time I walk through a doorway, I say to myself, "I will find the good in this room. I'm entering this space a happy man ready to serve." This practice helps me get present, look for the good in others, and prepare my mind to help people. What positive phrase or sentence could you say to yourself every time you walk through a doorway?

3. The third trigger I set up was a "waiting trigger." Whenever I'm waiting in line to buy something, I ask myself, "What level of presence and vibration do I feel right now, on a scale of 1 through 10?" By asking myself this question, I'm checking in on my emotional state, scoring it, and choosing whether it's sufficient to how I want to feel and how I want to live my life. Often, when I feel at a level 5 or below, my mind snaps to attention and says, "Hey, man, you're lucky to be alive. Raise your energy and enjoy life!" Sometimes, the guilt of knowing you're not feeling as vibrant as you should can be a good motivating force to up your game.

4.   The fourth trigger I set up was a "touch trigger." Whenever I'm introduced to someone, they get a hug. Not because I'm a natural hugger—I'm not. I started this trigger because I read so much research about how touch is vital to well-being and happiness.[22]

5.   The fifth trigger I created was the "gift trigger." Whenever something positive happens around me, I say, "What a gift!" I did this because so many high performers talked about how they felt a sense of reverence or sacredness in everyday life. Sometimes, this comes from a spiritual place—they feel joy because they feel blessed by God. Sometimes, it comes from a place of awe and wonder about how beautiful the world can be. Other times, they speak about the gifts in their life as a "grateful guilt"—they feel they've been given too much, too many opportunities, and so they deeply feel a responsibility to *earn those blessings* by giving back. Either way, they see their lives and blessings as a gift. (Some scientists have even called our ability to invest a sense of sacredness into our daily activities and interactions another form of human intelligence— specifically, a spiritual intelligence.[23]) So if a deal goes through or someone gets good news about a loved one, or anything positive and unexpected happens, you'll hear me say, "What a gift!"

6.   The sixth trigger was a "stress trigger." My brain injury was causing me to always feel hurried, almost panicked. And then one day I decided that hurry and stress were no longer going to be part of my life. Stress is self-created, so I decided to stop manufacturing it. I always believed that we can choose an internal calm and joy even amid the chaos, so I decided to do just that. Whenever things felt like they were getting out of hand, I'd stand up, take ten deep breaths, and ask, "What's the positive thing I can focus on and the next right action of integrity I should take now?" Over time, this practice took the power away from the stressful and hurried feelings caused by my injury.

To complement the triggers, I began an evening journaling activity in which I wrote down three things that made me feel good during the day. Then I took just a few moments to close my eyes and actually *relive* them. I put myself right back into the situation I experienced. I see what I saw, hear what I heard, feel what I felt. Often, in reflection, I appreciate the moment with even more care and focus than when it happened. I laugh harder. I feel my heart beat faster. I cry more. I feel an ever greater sense of wonder, contentment, thankfulness, meaning, or appreciation for life.

I also began doing this same thing every Sunday evening. I look back at my previous week's gratitude entries and relive them again with just as much emotional connection. If I can close my eyes for five minutes and for that full duration, easily think of a growing list of things to be grateful for, then I know I was paying attention during the week.

Of course, gratitude is the granddaddy of all positive emotion. It's also been the focus of much of the positive psychology movement—because it *works*. There's perhaps no better way to increase ongoing happiness than to start a gratitude practice.[24]

Gratitude is the golden frame through which
we see the meaning of life.

Together, all these things helped me keep joy at the forefront of my mind and life as I was recovering from my brain injury.

I've met a lot of high performers who began similar routines and triggers to bring them back from poor health. When I shared this with Arjun, the tech titan from the beginning of this chapter, we discovered that he had never created *any* conscious triggers in his life that activated positive emotions. He was, in his words, "generally even-keeled and good at just reacting to life with a cool presence." But he found that just *reacting* well to life still amounted to a limited life. If you don't put intention and set up reminders to *generate* joy in your life, then you're not experiencing the full range of life's zest.

With just three or four new triggers in his life, Arjun completely changed. He had two favorite triggers. His first was that whenever he felt stress and he was alone, he'd stand up, take ten deep breathes and then ask, "How would my best self handle this situation?" His other favorite was a trigger he set so that whenever his wife called his name, he would say to himself, "You are on this planet for this woman. Bring joy to her life."

His intention to elevate his energy for those around him is something I hope you will model. If you are always in a state of hurry, anxiety, stress, and busyness, then what energy are you teaching others to adopt? If you won't bring more mindfulness and joy into your life for the sheer personal improvement, then do it for those around you who might otherwise be harmed by unchecked emotional contagion.

High performers cultivate joy by how they think, what they focus on, and how they engage in and reflect on their days. It's a choice. They bend their will and behaviors to generate joy. This enlivens them but also serves others. And so it is now time to awaken and reemerge into the world with a youthful spirit.

Performance Prompts

1. Three questions I could ask myself every morning to prompt positive emotions for the rest of the day could be . . .

2. Some new triggers I could set for myself include (see my examples of notification, doorway, and waiting-in-line triggers) . . .

3. A new routine I could begin for replaying the positive moments of my days is . . .

PRACTICE THREE

OPTIMIZE HEALTH

"You may not feel outstandingly robust, but if you are an average-sized adult you will contain within your modest frame no less than 7×10^{18} joules of potential energy—enough to explode with the force of thirty very large hydrogen bombs, assuming you knew how to liberate it and really wished to make a point."

—Bill Bryson

Before I began writing this chapter, I stood up from my computer, walked to the kitchen, drank a glass of water, went downstairs, rode my stationary bike for a challenging three-minute sprint, and stretched out for two minutes doing some Vinyasa flow yoga. Then I came back up to my office, sat down, closed my eyes, and did my practice of RELEASE TENSION, SET INTENTION. If you could see me backstage at my seminars, you'd see me performing a similar routine: energizing my body and preparing my mind to serve. I learned this discipline from high performers who, I noticed, were always improving their energy with physical movements and breathing patterns. I noticed they ate healthier and worked out more than the general public, so I began doing the same things.

It wasn't always that way. In my late twenties, I was in pretty lousy physical health. I was working twelve-to-sixteen-hour days as a consultant. Most of my work was sitting in front of a computer and creating presentations and curriculum. All that sitting triggered back pain from old injuries, and the pain prevented me from working out as much as I wanted to. Soon, I fell into the trap so many of us do: I stopped taking care of myself. I slept poorly, ate bad food, and rarely worked out. I noticed that my performance at work, and my life in general, were suffering because of it, but it was hard to break the cycle, because I was telling myself stupid stories about how hard it must be to get healthy.

When people are unhealthy, it's not because they don't know how to be healthy. We all know what to do to increase our physical energy, because by now it's common sense: *Exercise*—work out more. *Nutrition*—eat healthier food. *Sleep*—aim for seven to eight hours. Nothing to argue about there, right?

Unfortunately, plenty of people do argue. They say a lot of non-sensical things that justify poor behavior in these areas. Too often, achievers blame their low physical energy on "how I'm built" or on the time demands of their industry, company culture, or personal obligations.

I did the same. I said well-meaning but poorly thought-out things such as these:

"Everyone in my industry works this hard, so I have to cut out something somewhere."

And the thing I cut out? Care for my health. Of course, when I said, "my industry," I was confusing industry norms with the five crazy diehards I was working with who were also neglecting their health and families. Luckily, at that point in my life I worked for a global company, and I noticed that plenty of people at my level were healthy. Clearly, some people had figured out how to be physically healthy doing the same job I did. In fact, I noticed plenty of people at and above my level taking better care of themselves, enjoying life more, and getting even better results than I was.

"Well, I've become successful sleeping only five hours, so sleep isn't a factor for me."

I said this, oblivious to the logical next thought: Imagine how much *more* successful I would be with just two more hours of sleep. Lack of sleep wasn't the correlate to my success. That was not what was giving me the edge. But I was young and dumb. I started researching ways to hack my sleep in order to get less of it. Fortunately, I couldn't deny the fifty years of sleep research I kept coming across that said that proper duration of sleep (around seven to eight hours for almost all adults) leads to higher cognitive scores, less stress, higher life satisfaction, better health, more productivity, more profitability, and less conflict. The literature was clear that poor sleep is associated with psychiatric disorders, obesity, coronary heart disease, stroke—the list goes on.[25]

"I'll focus on my health and happiness again in ninety days. I'm just busy now."

The person saying this tends to be on a perpetual fatigue cycle—they say ninety days, but it's really been, and will continue to be, *years* before they rest and feel human again. That was me at one point, too. I learned that what we do in daily life—yes, even during those sprint days—tends to gather into habits that are difficult to break.

"I'm just built this way."

I used to make biological or genetic arguments for how I felt physically, because of a spinal birth defect I had and because of my previous accidents. But this rationale didn't hold up very well, either. There is no doubt that family history or specific genetic factors cause or can cause human disease—family histories of cancer, cardiovascular disease, diabetes, autoimmune disorders, and psychiatric illnesses are particularly influential. But you don't have to spend very long looking at before-and-after pictures on Instagram to get the reality that we can alter our health dramatically. We have an extraordinary degree of personal control over our general and long-term health. Our daily habits and environment can activate genetic predispositions or not.[26] And no matter the area of study, physical inactivity proves again and again to be one of the leading culprits of all negative health outcomes.

"I don't have time for X."

In this excuse, "X" generally refers to working out, healthy eating/ shopping, or meditation. But I learned that none of these things necessarily *cost* you time. In fact, they often buy back time by making you more energized and productive. If you're sharper, more on the ball, and better able to output things that matter, *because* you took the time to work out and eat healthier, then the workout or healthy diet wasn't a deficit.

I share these things because I know I'm not the only one who falls prey to bad thinking such as this. Have you ever said things like that to yourself? What other stories do you tell yourself to allow your poor health choices to continue? Tough question, I know, but it's worth considering. In fact, let's gauge your physical health now. How physically healthy would you rate yourself on a scale of 1 to 10? Think of 1 as you're practically dead, whereas 10 means you almost always feel physically energized and strong. What's your number?

If you don't feel that you're a 7 or above, then perhaps this is the most important section of this book. You can get immediate and extraordinary gains in mental and emotional energy just by taking better care of your physical body. And you need to. What you see in the world is dependent upon your state of mind and physical energy. Thus, things appear their worst when you are feeling your worst. And the best when you're at the best. We want you at your best.

Get Fit Now

If you're being honest, you know that the research is conclusive: *You need to exercise.* A lot. Especially if you care about your mental performance. Exercise increases production of brain-derived neurotropic factor (BDNF). BDNF causes new neurons to grow in your hippocampus and other areas in the brain, creating increased plasticity and the ability to learn faster, remember more, and improve overall brain function.[27] This is a huge point that too many people miss: Exercise improves learning. Exercise also decreases stress, which is a killer of mental performance.[28] Stress actually lowers BDNF and overall cognitive function, and exercise is your best bet for throwing off much of that stress.

Because it increases your energy, exercise also enables you to perform general tasks faster and more efficiently. It boosts your working memory, elevates your mood, increases your attention span, and makes you more alert, all of which increase your performance.[29]

So if the demands of your job or life require you to learn fast, deal with stress, be alert, pay attention, remember important things, and keep a positive mood, then you *must* take exercise more seriously.

If you care about your contributions to the world, you'll care for yourself. This doesn't mean you have to kill yourself on a treadmill— almost all these positive effects were found with just moderate exercise. This means working out just a few times per week. It means getting back on a good workout plan. Just *six weeks* of exercise has been proven to enhance dopamine production and receptivity in the brain, which elevates your mood and mental performance. It also increases production of norepinephrine, which helps you make fewer errors in mentally challenging tasks.[30] Remember, energy is physical, emotional, and mental—and exercise improves each category.

One stunning finding from our research on over twenty thousand high performers is that the top 5 percent of all high performers are 40 percent more likely to exercise at least three days per week than the 95 percent below them. Clearly, if you want to join the top ranks of success in life, it's time to take exercise seriously.

If you have kids, you should take this doubly seriously. It's essential that you inspire your children to be healthy. Fit kids can pay better attention than unfit kids, and exercise makes a tangible difference in their IQ and long-term academic achievement.[31]

And if *you* aren't a kid anymore—you're in an older demographic —then exercise is *everything*. It's been shown to be as effective for depression as medications (though it should not be perceived as a replacement). People who exercise more have less depression, likely because of its effects on increasing dopamine in the brain.[32] Exercise also helps boost serotonin production and improves sleep, which in turn produces more serotonin.[33] (If you didn't know it, most antidepressants are formulated to target the release and reuptake of serotonin, which is why so many researchers recommend that depressive patients exercise whether or not they're taking medication.)[34] Exercise also decreases pain (almost equaling the effect of THC/cannabis) and reduces anxiety—both major issues for aging adults.[35]

I'm sure we can all admit that there's a growing sense of stress these days. It's in the air. The best way to deal with that threat is to experience more positive emotions (by intentionally bringing more joy into our lives) and by releasing tension through exercise. I promise you that if you make exercise a vitally important part of your life, a lot of other things will magically fall into place.

Once you get your workout routines in order, start improving your diet. In the United States, 60 percent of adults are currently overweight or obese, and we can't blame it all on the decrease in physical activity. Much of it has to do with overconsumption of food.[36] People simply eat too much, and it leads to terrible health outcomes and performance. Researchers have found that overeating is a lot like an addiction and can be a result of how some people's brains operate. Still, researchers also conclude that overeating is just a result of poor decision making—consciously choosing short-term gratification over long-term health.[37]

If health practitioners consistently repeat any rule above all others, it's that you should be aware of when you're eating not for nourishment but just to satiate yourself when you're in a bad mood. Beware of using meals as a way to push down negative emotions. If you feel bad, *move*. Go for a walk and change your emotional state *before* eating. It's not always easy, I know. But it's worth the effort, because if you can change how you feel before you eat, then you'll likely choose healthier meals. And that is key. It turns out that what you eat can be just as predictive of good health and productivity as exercise. "Eat well, feel well, perform well" is a truism. And not just for us as individuals. Access to good nutrition has major positive effects on the macroeconomic performance of entire countries.[38] For children especially, cognitive achievement and success in school have been tied directly to proper nutrition.[39]

You probably already know you need to eat healthier, and so I say to you, *begin*. I also recommend that you see a nutritionist who can help you test for food allergies—a common energy drain—and formulate the best diet to suit your performance needs.

Where to Start

After personally coaching many people trying to improve their energy, I've learned that if you're going to start anywhere to improve your health, you should start with a regular workout schedule, especially if you're in generally good health. When people work out, they tend to start caring more about their diet and sleep.

On the flip side, I've found that for those who were in poor health, starting them with good eating habits helped get them into exercise. This is because losing weight is often easier to accomplish by changes in diet than by hitting the gym three times a week. Going to the gym is a new thing; eating is not. Changing *what* people eat is easier than getting them to adopt an entirely new habit of regular exercise.

As always, consult your doctor before making any changes to your physical fitness or other health routines. Just know that if you're dealing with a good doctor, they'll always recommend good sleep, nutrition, and exercise routines. If you're dealing with a health-care provider who doesn't ask detailed questions about health routines and fails to recommend specific diet, exercise, and sleep patterns related to your current and future health goals, then I suggest you seek other opinions.

I also recommend that you look outside yourself and set up a good environment around you, where people care about health. If you're working at a company that isn't promoting exercise and all forms of well-being—your safety, health, happiness, and sense of fulfillment—be wary. Companies that don't care about their employees' well-being don't perform as well as their competitors.[40] Still, less than half of working Americans say their organizations support employee well-being, and one in three people say they are chronically stressed on the job. Only 41 percent say their employer helps workers develop and maintain a healthy lifestyle.[41] Clearly, it's on each of us as individuals to take control of our own well-being and health because no one else is going to do it for us.

When I work with executives, I draw a hard line: If the organization you spend your week serving doesn't promote well-being, then either you start an internal initiative that gets well-being on the map or you start looking for a new place to work. That is, if you care about working with high performers and becoming one yourself.

At my seminars, I challenge people to use the next twelve months to get in the best shape of their lives. It's astounding how many people have never truly committed to doing that. If you're willing, here are a few things you can do to begin:

- Start doing what you *already know* you should be doing to optimize your health. You already know whether you should start exercising more, eating more plant-based foods, or getting more sleep. If you're honest, you probably know exactly what to do. Now it's just a matter of commitment and habit.

- You should know every possible health measure about your body available. Visit your primary care doctor and request a complete health diagnostic. Tell them you want to get in the best health of your life during the next twelve months and that you want every reasonable screening she or he has that will help you assess your health. They'll help you figure out your body mass index, cholesterol, triglycerides, and risk factors via various tests. Don't just get a routine physical—ask for the most comprehensive health diagnostic they provide. If you're going to splurge on anything this year, make it your health. I recommend you go beyond the usual physical checkup and also find a place that does full lab work, chest X-rays, vaccination reviews, cancer screenings, and brain scans.

- In addition to a full assessment by your primary care doctor, I suggest you seek out the best sports medicine doctor in your hometown. Find someone who works with the pro athletes. Sports med doctors often have an entirely different approach to optimizing health.

- If you don't know what to do for nutrition, find the best nutritionist in town to help you put together a customized meal plan. Make sure you test for food allergies and leave with a clear understanding of what you should eat, how much, and when. One visit to a great nutritionist can change your life forever.

- Start training yourself to sleep eight hours a night. I say "training" because most people can't sleep a full night—not because of biology but from lack of conditioning for sleep. Try this: Don't look at any screens an hour before bed; drop the temperature in your home to sixty-eight degrees at night; black out the room from all light and sound. If you wake up in the middle of the night, don't get up and don't check your phone. Condition your body just to lie there. Start teaching your body that it has to lie in bed for eight hours no matter what. For other sleep tricks, read *The Sleep Revolution* by my good friend Arianna Huffington.

- Get a personal trainer. If you've made optimal fitness a primary goal in your life, under no circumstances should you try to optimize your physical health without a trainer. Yes, you can watch workout videos at home, but accountability to a trainer will make you better. If you simply can't afford a trainer, then find a friend who is in phenomenal shape and ask them if you can start working out with them. Don't let your ego get in the way—just because you can't keep up doesn't mean you can't *show* up. Get on a regular workout routine and make it social.

- If you want a simple starter plan, and your doctor approves, I recommend you start doing two-by-two's. That's two twenty-minute weight-lifting-based workouts per week, and two twenty-minute cardio-based workout routines per week. In all the sessions, give about 75 percent of your full effort—meaning, be more intense than casual during your workouts. That's just four sessions of intense exercise per week. On the other three days, you can walk briskly outside for twenty to forty-five minutes. Again, consult your doctor to see if this is a routine that is optimal for you.

And work up to it. Don't jump in at 75 percent effort if you're coming off the couch. Otherwise, you may hurt yourself or get so sore you decide that exercise just isn't for you. And that would be a terrible outcome.

- Finally, *stretch* way, way more. Just five to ten minutes of light stretching or yoga every morning and night will help you gain greater flexibility and mobility. It will loosen up your body so you're not carrying so much tension.

Performance Prompts

1. I want to get as physically healthy as I can at this stage of my life because . . .

2. If I was going to get in the best shape of my life, the first three things I would stop doing would be . . .

3. The things I would start doing include . . .

4. A weekly schedule that I could use to get healthier and actually stick to would be . . .

MAKE THE COMMITMENT

"Great effort is required to arrest decay and restore vigor."

—Horace

Energy is critical to high performance. You can have all the other habits up and running in your life, but without mastering this one, you won't *feel* good. No one wants to feel mentally foggy, drowned in negative emotions, or physically exhausted. Happily, though, these states are usually the results of bad decisions, not bad genetics. You can optimize your overall energy quotient in life if you choose to. And perhaps that is our ultimate duty since our vibrancy ultimately dictates how we work, love, move, worship, relate, and lead.

Make improving your energy a commitment. Start taking more moments during the day to release the tension in your body and mind. Choose to bring joy to your everyday life experience. And decide right now that over the next twelve months, you're going to get in the best shape of your life. I know, that's a high bar to set. But if that were the only decision you ever made from a book like this, the effort alone would change your life. If I got an e-mail from you a year from now that said, "Brendon, I did nothing you recommended except get in better health," well, that would bring me tremendous joy.

RAISE NECESSITY

"Only one who devotes himself to a cause with
his whole strength and soul
can be a true master. For this reason mastery
demands all of a person."

—Albert Einstein

KNOW WHO NEEDS YOUR A GAME

AFFIRM THE WHY

LEVEL UP YOUR SQUAD

"What else could I do?"

The three Marines sitting around Isaac nod as a waitress refills their coffees.

I ask, "You didn't have a choice?"

He laughs. "Well, there's always choice. Right about then I had three choices: Sh*t my pants. Run away. Or be a Marine."

I laugh harder than anyone at the table. The other guys are used to this kind of thing.

I ask him, "What did you say to yourself as you ran toward the explosion?"

Isaac was on foot patrol when one of his platoon's vehicles hit an improvised explosive device. The explosion knocked him down and out. When he came to, he saw the vehicle smoldering, engulfed in a spiral of smoke, and taking enemy fire. That's when he started running toward it.

"You just think you don't want any of your guys to die. That's all you really think: about the guys."

Isaac stares out the café window, and no one speaks. For a moment, everyone seems lost in his own stories.

"Sometimes," Isaac continues, "everything you are comes into play in a moment. It was just a few minutes. I can remember it like it was a two-hour movie. It's like your whole life and all that you stand for meets the needs of a moment."

He looks down to his wheelchair. "It just didn't end like I thought it would. I'm useless now. It's over."

Isaac may never walk again. He's a hero for providing the cover and action that helped evacuate one of the survivors of the blast. He was shot just as they got the injured survivor, one of his close friends, to safety.

One of the other Marines at the table scoffs. "It's not over, man. You'll recover. You're going to be just fine."

Isaac huffs back. "Do you even see me? I can't help myself. I can't serve my country. What's the point?"

His friends look to me.

"You're right," I say. "There is no point—unless you choose to make one. Either the point of your pain is to say to the world, 'This is how I've chosen to deal with this: by giving up.' Or the point is to show yourself, your fellow Marines, and the world that nothing will stop you or the spirit of service in you."

My words land flat. Isaac just crosses his arms. "I still don't see the point."

One of his friends leans in. "And you never will. If you don't have a reason to be, man, you're done. But the deal is, you choose the reason. You don't have to get better. Or you choose that you must get better. It's up to you. One choice sucks and makes your life miserable forever. The other gets you out of bed."

Isaac murmurs, "Why try?" then remains quiet. It's that silence no one wants to be a part of, watching someone on the edge, unsure whether to give up or live.

After a while, it becomes clear he doesn't feel he needs to make a choice at this moment. I can tell it's frustrating his friends. Indecision is not something Marines do well. Finally, one puts his face just inches from Isaac's and looks at him with an intensity only a military man can get away with.

"Because, damn it, Isaac, you don't have any other choice. Because you're going to obsess about your recovery the same way you trained infantry: like a Marine. Because your family is counting on you! Because we're here for you but we won't accept excuses. Because a warrior's destiny is greater than his wounds."

#

I share this story to illustrate a rather uninspiring truth: You don't have to do anything. You don't have to show up for life, for work, for your family. You don't have to climb out of bed on a tough day. You don't have to care about being the best you can be. You don't have to strive to live an extraordinary life. And yet, some people do feel they have to. Why?

The answer is a phrase that explains one of the most powerful drivers of human motivation and excellence: *performance necessity.*

Will Isaac get better physically? In many ways, it's up to him alone. The doctors have said he may walk again—if he works hard for it. There are no promises, they tell him, but there is a possibility. Will he get better emotionally? Again, it's up to him. He has plenty of support around him. But lots of people who need it are offered support and don't take it. The only difference lies in whether someone decides it is *necessary* to get better. No necessity, no consistent action.

Necessity is the emotional drive that makes great performance a *must* instead of a preference. Unlike weaker desires that make you *want* to do something, necessity *demands* that you take action. When you feel necessity, you don't sit around wishing or hoping. You get things done. Because you have to. There's not much choice; your heart and soul and the needs of the moment are telling you to act. It just feels right to do something. And if you didn't do it, you'd feel bad about yourself. You'd feel as though you weren't living up to your standards, meeting your obligations, or fulfilling your duties or your destiny. Necessity inspires a higher sense of motivation than usual because personal identity is engaged, creating a sense of urgency to act.

This "heart and soul" and "destiny" stuff might sound woo-woo, but it's often how high performers describe the motivation behind many of their actions. For example, in my interviews I often ask high performers *why* they work so hard and how they stay so focused, so committed. Their responses often sound something like this:

- It's just who I am.

- I can't imagine doing anything else.

- This is what I was made to do.

There's also a sense of obligation and urgency:

- People need me now; they're counting on me.

- I can't miss this opportunity.

- If I don't do this now, I'll regret it forever.

They say things like what Isaac said: "It's like your whole life and all that you stand for meets the needs of a moment."

When you have high necessity, you strongly agree with this statement:

"I feel a deep emotional drive and commitment to succeeding, and it consistently forces me to work hard, stay disciplined, and push myself."

People who report strong agreement with statements like this score higher on the HPI in almost every category. They also report greater confidence, happiness, and success over longer periods than their peers. When this emotional drive of necessity doesn't exist, no tactic, tool, or strategy can help them.

If I've learned anything from my research and a decade of interventions developing high performers, it's that you cannot become extraordinary without a sense that it's absolutely necessary to excel. You must get more emotionally committed to what you are doing, and reach that point where success (or whatever outcome you're after) is not just an occasional preference but a soul-deep necessity. This chapter is about *how*.

NECESSITY BASICS

"Necessity is the mistress and guide of nature.
Necessity is the theme and inventress of nature,
her curb and her eternal law."

—Leonardo Da Vinci

These are the factors in performance necessity (which I call the Four Forces of Necessity): identity, obsession, duty, and urgency. The first two are mostly internal. The second two are mostly external. Each is a driving force of motivation, but together they make you predictably perform at higher levels.

The nuances of necessity are not always obvious, so we will spend a few moments on description before we move to prescription. Bear with me, because I'm betting you will identify some significant areas of your life where greater necessity can change the game.

Performance Necessity

INTERNAL FORCES

"Whatever I have tried to do in life,
I have tried with all my heart to do it well;
whatever I have devoted myself to,
I have devoted myself to completely."

—Charles Dickens

Have you ever noticed that you feel guilty when you're not living your values or being the best version of yourself? Perhaps you believe you're an honest person but feel you lie too often. You set goals but don't follow through. Conversely, have you noticed how good you feel when you're being a good person and following through on what you say and desire? Those feelings of being frustrated or happy with your performance are what I mean by *internal forces*.

We humans have a lot of internal forces shaping our behavior: your values; expectations; dreams; goals; and need for safety, belonging, congruence, and growth, to name but a few. Think of these internal forces as an internal guidance system that urges you to stay "who you are" and grow into your best self. They are forces that continuously shape and reshape your identity and behaviors throughout your life.

We've found that two specific internal forces—personal standards of excellence and obsession with a topic—are particularly powerful in determining your ability to succeed over the long term.

High Personal Standards and Commitment to Excellence

"The quality of a person's life is in direct proportion
to their commitment to excellence, regardless
of their chosen field of endeavor."

—Vince Lombardi

It goes without saying that high performers hold themselves to a high standard. Specifically, they care deeply whether they perform well at any task or activity they see as important to their identity. This is true whether or not they choose the task. It's also true whether or not they enjoy the task. It's their identity—not always the choice or enjoyment of the task—that drives them to do well.[1] For example, an athlete may not particularly enjoy a workout their coach has given them, but they do it because they see themselves as an elite athlete willing to try anything to get better. Organizational researchers have also found that people don't perform well just because they're doing tasks they're satisfied with, but rather because they're setting challenging goals that mean something to them personally.[2] Satisfaction is not the cause of great performance;

it's the result. When we do what aligns with our future identity, we are more driven and likely to do a great job.

Naturally, we all want to do a good job on things that are important to us.

But high performers care even more about excellence and thus put more effort into their activities than others do.

How can we know that they care more? Because they report self-monitoring their behavior and performance goals more often. High performers don't just know that they have high standards and want to excel; they check in several times throughout their day to see whether they are living up to those standards. It's this self-monitoring that helps them get ahead. In conducting hundreds of performance reviews, I've found that underperformers, on the other hand, are often less self-aware and sometimes oblivious to their behavior and their results.

These findings align with what researchers have found about goals and self-awareness. For example, people who set goals and regularly self-monitor are almost *two and a half times* more likely to attain their goals.[3] They also develop more accurate plans and feel more motivated to follow through on them.[4] In one review of 138 studies spanning more than 19,000 participants, researchers found that monitoring progress is just as important to goal attainment as setting a clear goal in the first place.[5] If you're not going to monitor your progress, you may as well not set a goal or expect to live up to your own standards. This applies to almost all aspects of our lives, even the mundane ones. Imagine you envision yourself as a healthy person and you want to lose a few pounds. If you don't set a goal and track your progress, you're almost sure to fail. One meta-analysis found that self-monitoring was among the most effective means for improving weight loss results.[6]

So how does this relate to high performance? You need some sort of practice for checking in on whether you are living up to your own personal standards. This can be as easy as journaling every night and considering this line of questioning: "Did I perform with excellence today? Did I live up to my values and expectations for giving my best and doing a good job?"

Asking yourself these kinds of questions daily can bring up tough truths. No one is perfect, and inevitably you'll have days when you aren't proud of your performance. But that's part of the deal. If you don't self-monitor, you'll be less consistent and will advance more slowly. And if you do self-monitor, you may still feel frustrated from time to time. That's just how it goes.

High performers can certainly be hard on themselves if they don't perceive growth or excellence in what they're doing. But this does *not* mean they're unhappy or are turning into neurotic stress cases who always feel that they're failing. Remember the data: High performers are happier than their peers, perceive that they have *less stress* than their peers, and feel that they're making a greater difference and are being well rewarded for those efforts. They feel this way because they feel that they're on the right path. *And they feel that they're on the right path because they frequently check in with themselves.*

In every discussion I've had with high performers, I've found them more than willing to face their faults and address their weaknesses. They don't avoid the conversation. They don't pretend to be perfect. Indeed, they *want* to talk about how to improve, because at their core, their identity and enjoyment in life are tied to growth.

So how can high performers look themselves in the mirror so often and not get discouraged? Perhaps it's simply because self-evaluation is something they're used to. They're comfortable with it. They don't fear observing themselves, flaws and all, because they do it so often. The more you do something, the less it stings.

Still, high performers can be tough on themselves when they fail, because excellence is so important to their *identity*. When your identity says, "I'm someone who gets things done and does them with excellence," or "I'm a successful person who cares about the details and how things turn out," then you care when things go sideways. To high performers, those statements aren't just affirmations but an integral part of who they are. This means there is real internal pressure to do well, and that pressure can be hard to tame or turn off.

And, of course, if high performers aren't careful, these high standards can backfire. We can become *too* critical of ourselves, and soon self-evaluation begins to equate with pain. When that happens, either we stop asking whether we're doing things with excellence (because the answer is too painful) or we keep asking and psyche ourselves out. Over-concern with making mistakes increases anxiety and decreases performance.[7] When a star golfer suddenly chokes on the eighteenth hole, it's not because they lack the necessity to do well. It's that they allowed necessity to generate a debilitating level of expectation and pressure.

Still, choking is surprisingly rare for high performers because, again, they're so used to dealing with high necessity.[8]

It's important to consider our findings on low performers. They report self-monitoring only a third to half as many times per week as their high performing peers. And they rarely agree strongly with statements such as "I have an identity that thrives on seeking excellence, and my daily behaviors show it." Perhaps an identity of excellence is just too risky. If you regularly feel bad about yourself because you are underperforming, then naturally you might prefer to avoid self-evaluation. But this becomes the ultimate irony for underperformers: If they don't self-monitor more, their performance won't improve. And yet, if they do self-monitor more, they'll have to deal with the inevitable disappointments and self-judgments.

> The goal for all underperformers must be to
> set new standards, self-monitor more frequently,
> and learn to become comfortable with taking a hard,
> unflinching look at their own performance.

I don't pretend that it's an easy task. Avoiding potentially negative emotions is a deeply ingrained human impulse. I'm not blind to the fact that feeling intense necessity isn't always rainbows and roses. Striving to play at your best in any area of life can make you truly vulnerable. It's scary to demand a lot of yourself and push to the boundaries of your capabilities. You might not do a good job. You might fail. If you don't rise to the occasion, you can feel frustration, guilt, embarrassment, sadness, shame. Feeling that you *have to* do something isn't always comfortable.

But I suppose that's the ultimate tradeoff high performers make. They sense they *must* do something with excellence, and if they fail and have to endure negative emotions, so be it. They too highly value the performance edge that comes from necessity to let themselves off the hook. The payoff is worth the potential discomfort.

Don't fear this concept of necessity. Lots of people are leery of the idea when I introduce it to them. They fear they're not enough or can't handle the hardship of real demands. But necessity doesn't just mean something "bad" happened and now you "have to" react. It doesn't mean the demand is a negative load to bear.

This is why I often tell low performers:

> Sometimes the fastest way to get back in the game
> is to expect something from yourself again.

Go ahead and tie your identity to doing a good job. And remember to set challenging goals. Decades of research involving over forty thousand participants has shown that people who set difficult and specific goals outperform people who set vague and non-challenging goals.[9]

See yourself as a person who loves challenge and go for the big dreams. You are stronger than you think, and the future holds good things for you. Sure, you might fail. Sure, it might be uncomfortable. But what's the alternative? Holding back? Landing at the tail end of life and feeling that you didn't give it your all? Trudging through life safely inside your little bubble bored or complacent? Don't let that be your fate.

High performers have to succeed over the long term because they have the guts to expect something great from themselves. They repeatedly tell themselves they *must* do something and do it well because that action or achievement would be congruent with their ideal identity.

High performers' dreams of living extraordinary lives aren't mere wishes and hopes. They make their dream a *necessity*. Their future identity is tied to it, and they expect themselves to make it happen. And so they do.

Obsession with Understanding and Mastering a Topic

"To have long-term success as a coach or in any position
of leadership, you have to be obsessed in some way."

—Pat Riley

If an internal standard for excellence makes solid performance necessary, then the internal force of *curiosity* makes it enjoyable.

As you would expect, high performers are deeply curious people. In fact, their curiosity for understanding and mastering their primary field of interest is one of the hallmarks of their success. It's truly a universal observation across all high performers. They feel a high internal drive to focus on their field of interest over the long term and build deep competence. Psychologists would say they have high intrinsic motivation—they do things because those things are interesting, enjoyable, and personally satisfying.[10] High performers don't need a reward or prod from others to do something, because they find it inherently rewarding.

This deep and long-term passion for a particular topic or discipline has been noted in almost all modern success research. When people speak of "grit," they're talking about combined *passion and perseverance*. If you've heard of "deliberate practice"—often misinterpreted as the ten-thousand-hour rule—you know that it matters how long you focus on and train for something. The findings are straightforward. People who become world-class at anything focus longer and harder on their craft.[11]

But I've found that high performers must have something more than just passion. Passion is something everyone can understand. It's acceptable. We're told to be passionate, live with passion, love with passion. Passion is the expectation, the first door to success. But if you can stay highly emotionally engaged and laser focused over the long term, even when motivation and passion inevitably rise and ebb in waves of interest, even when others are criticizing you (and you know they might be right), even when you *fail* again and again, even when you are forced to stretch well beyond your comfort zone so that you can keep climbing, even when the rewards and recognition come too far apart, even when everyone else would have given up or moved on, even when all signs say you should quit—that's a leap beyond grit into the territory of what many might call an irresponsible obsession. It borders on recklessness. I took up this point in *The Motivation Manifesto*:

> Our challenge is that we have been conditioned to believe the opposite of these things—that bold action or swift progress is somehow dangerous or reckless. But a certain degree of insanity and recklessness is *necessary* to advance or innovate anything, to make any new or

remarkable or meaningful contributions. What great thing was ever accomplished without a little recklessness? So-called recklessness was required for the extraordinary to happen: crossing the oceans, ending slavery, rocketing man into space, building skyscrapers, decoding the genome, starting new businesses, and innovating entire industries. It *is* reckless to try something that has never been done, to move against convention, to begin before all conditions are good and preparations are perfected. But the bold know that to win, one must first *begin*. They also deeply understand that a degree of risk is inevitable and *necessary* should there be any real reward. Yes, any plunge into the unknown is reckless—but that's where the treasure lies.

Am I mincing words here? No—this is what high performers worldwide spoke with me about.

> **When you are passionate about what you do,**
> **people understand. When you are obsessed,**
> **they think you're mad. That's the difference.**

It is this almost reckless obsession for mastering something that makes us feel the imperative to perform at higher levels.

In any field of endeavor, those lacking obsession are often easy to spot: the half-interested browsers, the half-hearted lovers, the half-engaged leaders. They may lack intense interest, passion, or desire in general. But not necessarily. Sometimes, they have *lots* of interests, passions, and desires. But what they lack is that *one thing*, that abiding and unquenchable obsession. You know within minutes of meeting someone whether they have an obsession. If they have it, they're curious, engaged, excited to learn and talk about something specific and deeply important to them. They say things like "I love doing what I do so much, I'm sort of obsessed." Or "I live, eat, and breathe this; I can't imagine doing something else—this is who I am." They speak enthusiastically and articulately about a quest for excellence or mastery in their field, and they log the hours of study, practice, and preparation to achieve those ends. Their obsessions land on their calendars in real work efforts.

The moment you know that something has transcended being a passion and has become an obsession is when that something gets tied to your *identity*.

It changes from a desire to *feel* a particular state of emotion— passion—to a quest to *be* a particular kind of person. It becomes part of you, something you value more deeply than other things. It becomes *necessary* for you.

Just as some people fear setting high standards for themselves, many fear becoming obsessed. They prefer casual interests and passing flames. It's easier to live with passions that have no stake in who you are.

It's worth the reminder: High performers can handle this sort of internal pressure. They don't mind diving into the deep end of their passions. Obsession is not something to fear. Quite the contrary. It's almost like a badge of honor. When people are obsessed with something, they enjoy doing it so much that they don't feel the need to apologize to others for it. They lose hours working at a task or improving a skill. And they love it.

Are there "unhealthy" obsessions? I suppose that depends on how you define things. If you get so enthralled by something that you become addicted or think about it compulsively, then yes. That's not exactly healthy. If you define an obsession as a "persistent disturbing preoccupation," as Merriam-Webster does for one sense of the word, then yes, taking it to the degree of "disturbing" is probably unhealthy. But the dictionary also defines *obsession* in these ways:

- a state in which someone thinks about someone or something constantly or frequently, especially in a way that is not normal

- someone or something that a person thinks about constantly or frequently

- an activity that someone is very interested in or spends a lot of time doing

- a persistent abnormally strong interest in or concern about someone or something

I don't find any of those senses of the word particularly unhealthy. So again, it depends on the definition you choose. What I know about high performers is that they do indeed spend an enormous amount of time thinking about and doing their obsession(s). Is this "abnormal"? Absolutely.

But normal isn't always healthy, either.

Let's be honest: A normal amount of time spent on almost any-thing in today's distracted world is about two minutes. So, if an abnormal amount of focus is "unhealthy," then high performers are guilty as charged. But I don't observe high performers as being unhealthy—and I spend more time observing them than just about anyone does. If you're wondering whether you have an unhealthy obsession, it's pretty easy to figure out: When your obsession starts running you instead of you running it, if it starts tearing up your life and wrecking your relationships and causing unhappiness all around, then you've got a problem.

But that's just not a problem high performers have. Otherwise, by definition, they wouldn't be high performers. The data bears this out.[12] High performers are happy. They are confident. They eat healthy amounts of healthy foods, and they exercise. They handle stress better than their peers. They love challenge, and sense that they're making a difference. In other words, you could say they're in control.

That's why I encourage people to keep experimenting in life until they find something that sparks unusual interest. Then, if it aligns with your personal values and identity, jump in. Get curious. Let yourself geek out on something and *go deep*. Let that part of you that wants to obsess about and master something come alive again.

When high personal standards meet high obsessions, then high necessity emerges. So, too, does high performance. And that's just the *internal* game of necessity. The external forces are where things really get interesting.

Before we move on to the external forces, spend some time reflecting on the following statements:

- The values that are important for me to live include . . .

- A recent situation where I didn't live my values was . . .

- The reason I didn't feel it necessary in that moment to live my values is . . .

- A recent situation in which I was proud of living my values or being a particular kind of person was . . .

- The reason I felt it necessary to be that kind of person then was . . .

- The topics I find myself obsessed with include . . .

- A topic I haven't been obsessing about enough in a healthy way is . . .

EXTERNAL FORCES

"You never know how strong you are
until being strong is your only choice."

—Bob Marley

An external force of necessity is any outside factor that drives you to perform well. Some psychologists might simply describe this as "pressure."[13] I rarely use the term *pressure*, though, because it carries a lot of negative connotations. For the most part, high performers don't feel ongoing unwanted pressures causing their drive for excellence. Like all of us, they have obligations and deadlines, but the distinction is that they consciously *choose those duties* and thus don't see them as negative pressures to perform. They are not pushed to performance; they are pulled.

I used to get this wrong. In one of our pilot studies for the High Performance Indicator, we asked people to score whether they agreed strongly with this statement: "I feel an external demand—from my peers, family, boss, mentor, or culture—to succeed at high levels." To my initial surprise, this statement didn't correlate with high performance.[14] In asking high performers about this result, I learned that the reason is because the demands they sense to succeed do not come from other people. If they *do* feel pressure from others in a way that makes them perform better, it likely just reinforces choices or behaviors they may already have committed to. Another way of saying this is that high performers don't necessarily view external forces as *negative things* or as *causal reasons* for their performance.

This means that high performers are not functioning from what psychologists often call reactance, which are acts motivated by the will to fight back or act out against a perceived insult or threat. High performers' necessity for action in life does not stem from wanting to fight "the system" or whoever is putting them down. High performers aren't driven because they are rebelling or feeling threatened.

That type of "negative" motivation certainly exists, but alone it rarely lasts long or accomplishes much.

More often, high performers view "positive" external forces as causal reasons for increased performance. They want to do well to serve a purpose they find meaningful—fulfilling a high purpose serves as a positive sort of pressure. Even obligations and difficult-to-meet deadlines—which many people dislike—are viewed as positive performance enhancers.

With this in mind, there are two primary positive external forces that exert the kind of motivation or pressure that improves performance.

Social Duty, Obligation, and Purpose

> "Duty makes us do things well,
> but love makes us do them beautifully."
> —Phillips Brooks

High performers often feel the necessity to perform well out of a sense of duty to someone or something beyond themselves. Someone is counting on them, or they're trying to fulfill a promise or responsibility.

I define *duty* broadly because high performers do, too. Sometimes, when they speak of duty, they mean that they owe something to others or are accountable for their performance (whether or not anyone has asked for the thing they feel obligated to do). Sometimes, high performers view duty as an obligation to meet another's expectations or needs. Sometimes, they see duty as complying with the norms or values of a group, or following a moral sense of right and wrong.[15]

The duties that drive performance can be explained best by the truth that we will often do more for others than for ourselves. We'll get up in the middle of the night to calm an upset child even though we know we need sleep. It's just *more necessary* in our mind to do this thing for someone else. This type of necessity is often the strongest pull. So if you ever feel that you are not performing well, start asking, "Who needs me more right now?"

If you add to that accountability—when people know that you are responsible for helping them—necessity becomes stronger yet. A tremendous amount of research shows that people tend to maintain motivation, give more effort, and achieve higher performance when they are held accountable for their outcomes, are evaluated more often, and have the opportunity to demonstrate their expertise or gain respect from those they serve.[16] In other words, if you owe it to someone to do well, and you feel that doing well will exhibit your expertise, then you'll feel greater necessity to perform at higher levels. For example, when we are evaluated more and held accountable to team performance, we work harder and better.[17]

This all sounds nice, but we all know that often a sense of duty to others can *feel* like a negative thing in the short term. Few parents are eager to wake up in the middle of the night and change a diaper. Doing so is more an obligation than an expression of warmhearted love. Will parents complain about that obligation? Sure. But over the long term, adherence to meeting that "positive" obligation helps make them feel like good parents, which is at least part of what motivates them to do it. In other words, the external demands we feel to meet our obligations in life can feel bad in the short term but lead to strong performance outcomes later.

It's hard for underperformers to see that obligations are not always a negative thing, which is why we found that underperformers complain more about their responsibilities at work than their high performing peers. Some obligations can naturally feel like something to complain about. A sense of obligation to family, for instance, might lead you to live near your parents or to send them money. This kind of familial duty might feel like a ball and chain to many, but meeting such duties also happens to correlate with positive well-being.[18]

At work, a sense of "doing the right thing" drives positive emotions and performance as well. Organizational researchers have found that employees who are the most committed, especially in times of change, feel that it would be "wrong" to leave a company if their absence would hurt the company's future.[19] They often double down on their efforts to help their managers even though it requires longer work hours. Duty to the mission replaces their short-term comforts.

Because high performers understand the need to meet their obligations, they rarely complain about the tasks and duties they must perform to succeed. They recognize that fulfilling their role and serving the needs of others is part of the process. It's a positive thing tomorrow even if it's a pain now. It's these findings that have inspired me to view my obligations in life differently. I've learned to adjust my attitude to things I have to do, to complain less and realize that most of what I "have" to do is in truth a blessing.

I learned that when you have the opportunity to serve, you don't complain about the effort involved.

When you feel the drive to serve others, you sustain solid performance longer. This is one reason, for example, why members of the military are often so extraordinary. They have a sense of duty to something beyond themselves—their country and their comrades in arms.

It's also why most high performers mention "purpose" as motivating their best performance. Their sense of duty or obligation to a higher vision, mission, or calling propels them through the hardships of achievement.

In fact, when I talk with high performers, they regularly say they "don't have a choice" but to be good at what they do. They don't mean this as a lack of freedom, as if some autocratic leader were forcing them to do something. What they mean is, they feel that it's necessary to do something because they've been *called* to do it. They feel they have been given a unique gift or opportunity. Often, they sense that their performance now will affect their future and, perhaps, the futures of a lot of people, in profound ways.

This sense of duty to a higher calling is almost ubiquitous when you talk to the top 15 percent of high performers. It is not rare to hear them talk about legacy, destiny, divine timing, God, or a moral responsibility to future generations as primary motivators for their performance. They need to perform well, they say, because they know they are needed.

Real Deadlines

"Without a sense of urgency, desire loses its value."

—Jim Rohn

Why do athletes work out harder in the weeks immediately before walking into the ring or onto the field? Why do salespeople perform better at quarter's end? Why do stay-at-home parents report being better organized right before school starts? Because nothing motivates action like a hard deadline.

Real deadlines are an underappreciated tool in performance management. We'd rather talk about goals and timelines, setting "nice to have" dates to achieve those goals. But high performance happens only when there are real deadlines.

What is a "real" deadline? It's a date that matters because, if it isn't met, real negative consequences happen, and if it is real, benefits come to fruition.

We all have deadlines in life. The distinction that matters here is that high performers seem to be regularly marching toward real deadlines that they feel are important to meet. They know the dates when things are due, and the real consequences and payoffs associated with those dates. But just as important, high performers are *not* seeking to meet *false* deadlines.

A *false deadline* is usually a poorly conceived activity with a due date that is someone's *preference*, not a true need with real consequences if it's not met. It's what one of my clients, a Green Beret, calls a "circle jerk fire drill."

Here is how this distinction between real and fake deadlines plays out in my life. Whenever someone e-mails me a request, with or without a due date, I reply in this way:

> Thanks for your request. Can you give me the "real deadline" date for this? That means the date when the world will explode, your career will be destroyed, or a domino effect leading to both your and my ultimate demise will truly begin. Any date before that is your preference, and with respect, by the time you've sent me this request I have 100 preference requests in front of you. So, to serve you best, I have to put you in ranking order with the real deadlines. Can you please let me know that drop-dead date and why, specifically, it occurs then? From there, I'll decide the priority and coordinate appropriately with you and, as always, serve with excellence. Thanks!
>
> —Brendon

I send this e-mail because I know how quickly I can fall out of high performance by meeting other people's demands that aren't real demands. I'm a people pleaser. I'm a sucker for distraction. Habits such as clarifying real deadlines are what make me, and every high performer I know, so effective.

A recent survey of 1,100 high performers revealed that their underperforming counterparts get pulled into fake urgencies or deadlines *three and a half times* more often than they do.[20] High performers are more focused on doing what really matters *when* it matters.

But that's not simply because high performers are superhuman and always focused on their own deadlines. In fact, for the most part, the real deadlines that high performers are marching to have been placed on them *by others*, by outside forces. Olympians don't choose when the games will be held, and CEOs don't set the quarterly demands thrust on them by the marketplace.

Left to my own devices, I probably would never have finished this book. But I knew that at some point, if I didn't turn it in, my family would mutiny, my friends would abduct me, and my publisher would dump me. Sure, I missed a few false deadlines, which I had set. But once there was a real deadline, when my publisher promised the book to retailers, and my wife expected a vacation, *bam*, the words per hour increased exponentially.

This isn't to say that high performers are driven to meet a deadline only by the negative consequences of missing it. In fact, most want to meet their deadlines because they're excited to see their work out there in the world, as well as to move on to the next project or opportunity they have chosen for themselves. I was eager to finish this book not just because I feared the negative repercussions of being late; I was also excited to finish so I could get the book in your hands and turn more of my attention to my family and to reaching more students with this message.

This example illustrates another aspect of real deadlines: that they are inherently *social* deadlines. High performers are driven to get things done because they recognize that their timeliness affects other people.

> **The reality is that when you choose to care for others**
> **and make a big difference in the world,**
> **the number of deadlines coming at you will increase.**

Some might assume that time pressure makes people miserable. But that's just not what I've observed or what other research is finding. A recent study found that by having a deadline, not only did people focus more to complete the activity but they found it easier to "let that activity go" and devote greater attention to the *next* activity.[21] That is, deadlines help us get closure between activities, so we can give our full focus to what we need to be working on *now*.

KEEPING THE FIRE

Identity. Obsession. Duty. Deadlines. As you can imagine, any *one* of these forces can make us bring up our game. But when internal and external demands mix, you get more necessity, and an even stronger wind at your back.

I'll repeat the part about this being a sensitive topic. Lots of people really dislike necessity—they hate feeling any sort of pressure. They don't want internal pressure because it can cause anxiety. And they don't want external pressure because it can cause anxiety *and* real failure. Still, the data is clear: High performers *like* necessity. In fact, they need it. When it's gone, their fire is gone.

For an example of how this might play out, imagine you're working with someone who is in the top 2 percent of high performers. They say to you, "I feel like I'm not as consistent or as disciplined as I used to be." What would be your next move with them? Would you make them take a personality test or a strengths assessment or go to a retreat in the woods?

I sure wouldn't. I'd have a real conversation with them about necessity. I'd find out about a time when they did feel consistent, and I'd explore the Four Forces of Necessity with them to see what led them to such impressive performance in the past. Then I'd cycle through the Four Forces again, seeking to get the high performer more deeply connected to their hunger for achievement because of their identity, obsessions, and sense of duty and urgency. If they didn't have something they felt obsessed with, obligated to, or at risk of losing or missing out on, I'd have them *find* something to care deeply about. I wouldn't let them off the hook until we were clear about the Four Forces.

This is exactly what I did with Isaac, the soldier struggling with the feeling that he wasn't useful anymore. I got him to imagine his future in a new way, reconnect with some of the obsessions he had before his injuries, and commit to improving his health and mindset for his family and so he could get back to work. It wasn't easy, but eventually Isaac reconnected with himself and again found his enthusiasm for life.

Bottom line: We change and improve over time only when we *must*. When the internal and external forces on us are strong enough, we make it happen. We climb. And when it gets most difficult, we remember our cause. When we are afraid and battling hardship and darkness, we remember we came in the cause of light and we sustain positive performance over the long term. Here are three practices that can fire up a greater sense of necessity.

PRACTICE ONE

KNOW WHO NEEDS YOUR A GAME

> "Not only must we be good,
> but we must also be good for something."
> —Henry David Thoreau

To help you tap into both the internal and the external demands of necessity, try this simple practice. Set a "desk trigger" for yourself. From now on, whenever you sit down at your desk—that's the trigger action—ask:

"Who needs me on my A game the most right now?"

Butt hits chair; then you ask and answer the question. That's the practice. I love this practice for several reasons:

- It's simple and something anyone can do.

- The trigger is based on something you do frequently: sit down at your office chair. Whether your office chair is at the kitchen table or in a high-rise corner office, I bet you're there a lot.

- It forces you to do a quick gut check. The mere mention of your A game forces an internal review: What *is* my A game? Have I been bringing it today? What would my A game look like in the next hour or so?

- The question also forces you to think of someone else. Whether by duty, obligation, or purpose, they ended up on your radar, and now you can have an external person or group to work for. When you have someone external to take action for, you tend to perform better.

- Finally, I like the phrase "the most right now." It is immediacy focused, and yet "the most" makes you examine your priorities and—yep, you guessed it—your real deadlines.

I started teaching this practice to my clients because I've never met a high performer who didn't *consistently* ponder whether they were giving their best—and not just for themselves but for others. They have come to assess their performance at regular intervals. By giving you a desk trigger, I'm helping you bring that skill to your conscious habits. I'm also helping you step into a spirit of service because that's what high performers do. They're grateful for life, so they're generous with others.

People often ask me to clarify what it means to be on your A game, and *how* to get there. Being on your A game means that you are giving your best effort with full focus on the singular task at hand. To get it, you need to stoke the internal and external demands of necessity. Specifically, you assume the identity of a high performer and you set up situations that require full immersion. In other words, you get to your A game through the gates of identity and immersion.

In the game of life, you get to choose your identity—who you will aspire to be and how you'll show up. That choice of identity will dramatically affect how well you perform. Consider the difference between these identities:

Dabblers have a passing interest in the game of life. They look at many things and try many things. But they never really jump into anything with full engagement or commitment.

Novices have interest, too, but at least they are intent on developing some expertise in an area. They jump in deeper than dabblers, but their issue is, they don't deal well with discouragement. Novices stop at obstacles because they don't have much of their identity in the fight.

Amateurs have more than interest. They have passion. They've jumped in deep, and they truly engage a subject and want to get better. They get through more obstacles than novices do, but they tend to remain at an unskilled level unless they get fast and positive feedback or recognition. In other words, they need a lot of external validation to continue.

Players have passion but also greater commitment and skill. With great focus, they teach themselves to master one area of the game. They excel and find themselves happy as long as they get their turn and get compensation. If the game changes or the rules change, though, they're quickly embittered. Players desperately need the rules and routines. They don't like disruption or negative feedback. They need a high degree of fairness if they are going to participate—if someone on the team gets paid more than they do, they freak out and quit. They're committed to becoming a success in their position but rarely achieve a holistic level of success in other areas of the game (or life). To them, it's a game to be won and there's not much beyond that.

High Performers are like players but with greater all-around necessity, skill, and team spirit. They are all-in on the game. They play at a high level no matter what the recognition or rewards, because the game is intrinsically rewarding and also part of how they view their service to the world. Their identity is tied to the game but also to the team and those they serve. They don't want to master just one area of the game; they want to be known for the game itself. And yet, unlike players, they don't mind sharing the spotlight. They have such a high degree of personal excellence and duty to the team, they become the go-to person in every game. They stand out because they not only deliver exceptional individual performance but also make every person better through their influence.

These are more casual descriptions than I've made elsewhere in the book, but I often share them to help people realize they have a choice. If you want to be on your A game, you can't be a dabbler, novice, amateur, or player. You must consciously choose and try to will yourself into being a high performer. If you're going to bring your A game regularly, you have to describe that identity for yourself and step into it—every single day.

In addition to choosing a high performance identity, you'll have to immerse yourself fully in activities that force you to stretch. You can't just prance around thinking you're good. You have to put yourself in situations that *make* you good. Fortunately, research has clearly outlined exactly what will help you find those challenging and immersive experiences. This popular concept in positive psychology is known as *flow*. According to Mihay Csikszentmihalyi, flow happens when several of these elements are in play:

1. You have goals that are clear and challenging yet attainable.

2. Strong concentration and focused attention are required.

3. The thing you're doing is intrinsically rewarding.

4. You lose self-consciousness a bit and feel serene.

5. Time stops—you feel so focused on the present that you lose track of time.

6. You're getting immediate feedback on your performance.

7. There's a balance between your skill level and the challenge presented. You know that what you're doing is doable even if difficult.

8. You have a sense of personal control over the situation and the outcome.

9. You stop thinking about your physical needs.

10. You have the ability to focus completely on the activity at hand.[22]

You can use this list of conditions to increase the odds you'll bring your A game to those you hope to serve. Perhaps this last part, about serving others, is what makes flow even more powerful. That's why I ask that you frame this practice as an opportunity to bring your A game *for someone else*. Look beyond your individual performance or feelings and connect with a reason to be your best for others. Find somebody or something worth fighting for. If you can stoke the necessity to be your best in order to help others, you'll hit high performance faster and stay there longer.

Performance Prompts

1. The people who need me on my A game at this point in my life are . . .

2. The reasons each of those people need me include . . .

3. The reasons I want to become a high performer for each of these people are . . .

4. I know that I'm on my A game when I think, feel, or behave . . .

5. The things that throw me off my A game are . . .

6. I can deal more effectively with those things by . . .

7. A few reminders I could set up for myself to be my best for the people in my life could include . . .

PRACTICE TWO

AFFIRM THE WHY

"The moment one definitely commits oneself,
then providence moves, too."

—Goethe

High performers don't keep their goals, or the why behind those goals, *secret* or *silent*. They confidently affirm their goals to themselves and others. If there is one necessity practice that seems to divide high performers and underperformers the most, it's this one. Underperformers are often unclear about their why, and they don't use affirmations or speak about the whys they do have.

To affirm is to declare or strongly assert something as valid or confirmed. It is saying *with confidence* that something is true or will happen. This is the way high performers speak about their goals and their whys. They don't sound doubtful. They have confidence in the reasons they are working so hard, and they are proud to tell you about their purpose. In fact, I found that high performers love talking about why they do almost anything. High performing athletes, for example, take great joy in describing their workout and especially *why* they chose a specific exercise that day. They'll spend as much time telling you why they're doing the routine—"I'm doing three sets of squats at 75 percent today because I've felt off balance"—as on what the routine is or how to do it.

When I first started working with high performers, I often wondered whether they were just extroverts who liked to talk a big game. Or did they have some sort of charisma that made their reasons for action sound more appealing than other people's reasons? I was wrong on both assumptions. Personality isn't correlated with high performance. An introvert is just as likely as an extrovert to be a high performer.[23]

I also learned that while high performers are exuberant in sharing their whys with others, they rarely declare that their *approach* is always right. Yes, they are confident in their purpose, but in interviews it is clear that *most* high performers question whether their approach is the best one available. It's often by being open to better processes that they identify new ways of getting ahead. That is, high performers are confident about their why but open about *how*.

It's in affirming their whys with other people that high performers not only feel more confident but create social consequence and obligation. If I tell you I'm going for a goal and why it's so important to me, and if I speak as though it's going to happen, declaring that *I will make it happen*, then my ego is now on the line. There are social stakes. I promised that something was going to happen, and if it doesn't, then I didn't meet my promise. I didn't keep my word. I risk looking like a fool or like someone lacking integrity, neither of which I want.

All this leads me to suggest that you affirm your whys, to yourself and to others, more consistently.

When I say affirm your why to yourself, I mean literally talk to yourself using affirmations. Here's a personal example. About eleven years ago, I decided I wanted to reach more people with my work in motivation and personal and professional development. At the time, YouTube, online video marketing, and online education were all in their infancy but gaining steam. So I decided I should start shooting videos and creating online courses. The thing was, I was terrible on camera. I couldn't remember three sentences if you paid me, and I didn't know how to be myself, or what to do with my hands, when the lights went on. I was a mess.

But I did have one advantage. I knew about this practice of affirming the why to myself and others. So right before I started filming, I would say something like this to myself: "Brendon, you're doing this because it's important. Remember your students. You can inspire them and help them reach their goals. That's your purpose. Do good for them. You're going to love this, and you're going to help a lot of people."

When I said this, I wasn't trying to be confident in my ability to be awesome on camera. That's not the point at all. I was speaking confidently about *why* I wanted to do well on camera that day. And it was this reminder of the why that created the performance necessity.

Also, note that I spoke to myself in the second person and that the affirmation was based more on intrinsic rewards (helping people, loving the process) than on extrinsic rewards (finishing the video, making money selling the course, winning awards, or getting positive feedback). This is something you might want to model because not all affirmations are created equal—intrinsic affirmations are stronger.[24]

If any of this sounds hokey, then you really need to spend more time with high performers, because they actually say and do these kinds of things. They talk to themselves—out loud—and remind themselves what's really important. Go stand in the tunnel before Olympians walk out onto the field, and you see them talking to themselves. They're affirming their whys, even if that's not what they call it. Listen to a world-class speaker backstage. They're not just rehearsing their lines—they're connecting with *why* they are there. Researchers have found this in therapeutic settings, too. When those with anxiety disorders find the courage to overcome their symptoms, the strategy they list most commonly for how they did it is to remind themselves about the value of the goals they are after.[25]

To get better on video, I also affirmed my why to a lot of people who knew me. I started telling friends and family I was going to shoot an online course and why it was important to me. I declared I would send them access to my course the following week, and asked them to send me feedback that same week. Many, of course, laughed or played along. But I didn't need them to affirm me; I needed to affirm myself publicly so I could create a situation where I needed to honor my word. As soon as I promised it, my human need for congruence motivated me even further to perform well and on time. I created the external expectation that I was going to do something, and I did. Had I not done this, the million-plus students who have now completed my video series and courses would never have benefited from them. Affirming the why has always been my secret to being prolific.

When we verbalize something, it becomes more real and important to us. It becomes more necessary for us to live in alignment with that truth. So the next time you want to increase your performance necessity, declare—to yourself and to others—what you want and why you want it.

Performance Prompts

1. Three things I would like to become extraordinary at doing are . . .

2. My whys for becoming excellent in each of these areas are . . .

3. The people I will tell about these goals and the whys behind them include . . .

4. The things I can say out loud to myself to affirm these whys—my affirmations—are . . .

5. Some ways I can remind myself about these important goals and whys are . . .

PRACTICE THREE

LEVEL UP YOUR SQUAD

"Find a group of people who challenge and inspire you,
spend a lot of time with them, and it will change your life."

—Amy Poehler

When I'm hired to coach someone to high performance, one of the easiest quick wins is to have them spend more time with the most positive and successful people in their support network. Your support network comprises the people who are consistently closest to you at home, at work, and in your community. It's the people you talk with or see the most. I tell my clients that their job is to start spending more time with the best in their peer group, and less with the more negative members. That's an easy win. But it's not the full picture.

If you truly want to increase your performance in any area of your life, get around some *new* people who expect and value high performance. Expand your peer group to include more people who have greater expertise or success than you, and spend more time with them. So it's not just about increasing time with your current squad of positive or successful peers, but about adding new people to the squad as well.

You probably already know that you should do this because you've heard there is power in your peer group. But you may not appreciate just how powerfully your social environment affects you.

Over the past decade, researchers have made fascinating discoveries about a phenomenon called "clustering." They found that behaviors, attitudes, and health outcomes tend to form in social clusters. The people around you even affect how much you sleep, the food that you eat, and how much money you spend or save.[26] This dynamic, which has been dubbed "social contagion," has been shown to have both detriments and benefits.

On the negative front, researchers have found that bad behaviors and outcomes such as smoking, obesity, loneliness, depression, divorce, and drug use tend to grow in social clusters.[27] If your friends smoke, you probably will, too. The more of your friends who are overweight or divorced, the higher the odds you'll get there, too.

Likewise, positive things such as happiness and prosocial behavior also seem to spread within social groups.[28] For example, if you have a friend who is happy in life, your chances of feeling happy go up by 25 percent. Researchers have even noted that expertise and world-class performance in music, soccer, art, baseball, tennis, and other fields happen in clusters.[29]

This "contagion" effect is usually relevant up to three degrees of separation. This means that it's not just your friends and family who can affect you. Research shows that your friends' friends exert an influence. So do your friends' friends' friends. With each degree of separation, the effect of your environment becomes less, with nonsignificant effects beyond three degrees of separation.[30] This is why it's so important to carefully curate who is in your social circle.

Of course, we can't always determine who is in our circle, especially when we're young, which is why so many people have poor behaviors today—they had bad influences. Those who grow up in homes with major household dysfunction (e.g., divorce, drug abuse, mental illness, neglect, or abuse) have an increased risk of negative future outcomes related to mental and physical health.[31] These children also suffer significant cognitive and emotional ramifications of the abuse they experience (e.g., smaller prefrontal cortexes [the decision-making area of the brain], smaller hippocampi [the memory center of the brain], and hyperactive stress responses).[32] Kids who grow up in poverty also face significantly higher levels of crime, violence, incarceration, lack of parental supervision, drug use, and sexual and physical abuse.[33]

All this evidence may seem overwhelming for people who aren't lucky enough to have hit the social lottery. It can make people ask, "Am I just doomed to live at the level of my peer group?"

The answer is an unequivocal and resounding *no*. It turns out that high performance is *not* tied to your culture or social environment. That's because high performance, as you'll remember, is about the long game. And over time, you can take back your life from negative influences and direct your mind habits and social environment toward high performance. This isn't just rah-rah stuff. Research has consistently shown that people can rise above their cultural programming and influence if they have the right beliefs and strategy. Simply adopting the belief that you can improve with effort, for example, has helped kids in disadvantaged neighborhoods go from terrible scores to the top of their class in study after study.[34]

A recent study of over 168,000 tenth-graders helps us prove the point. Researchers collected data related to students' academic achievement, socioeconomic status, and beliefs about their ability to improve with effort.[35] As you might predict, students from higher socioeconomic strata performed significantly better than students from low-income families. This relationship, however, was offset in children who believed they could improve with effort. In fact, children who came from the lowest 10 percent socioeconomically yet believed in their ability to improve performed as well as kids in the top 20 percent who believed that their abilities were unchangeable. This means that the economic gap—and all the negative factors that often accompany lower economic status, such as higher stress, worse schools, poorer nutrition—were largely erased in children who *believed they could improve with effort.*

Scientific research consistently shows that certain people maintain their strength even when the environment or culture around them is less than ideal.[36] The difference is how they *think*. This means that with or without social support, you can use your thoughts to improve your mind, mood, memory, reactions, happiness, and performance.[37]

None of us is shackled to our past or environment. We have tremendous personal control over the factors that improve our lives and performance. I share this because too many people think they can't win without the ideal peer group. So before I tell you to improve your peer group, don't for one second think you can't improve your life on your own. Social support just makes personal development and overall life success *easier*, faster, and more enjoyable.

For all these reasons, high performers spend more time with positive people than with negative people.

> They are more *strategic* and *consistent* in seeking
> to work with others *at or above* their level
> of competence, experience, or overall success.

They seek networking activities or group affiliations with more successful people. At work, they communicate more with people who are more experienced and often "above" them on the organizational chart. In their personal lives, they volunteer more, spend less time in negative or conflict-ridden relationships, and ask for help from their more successful peers more than others do.[38]

This doesn't mean that high performers have gotten rid of *all* the negative or challenging people in their lives. Somewhere, there's this myth that to be happy or succeed, you have to "get rid of" all negative people in your life. We hear things like: "If someone doesn't support your dream, dump them as friend." "Your spouse doesn't cheer you on and meet your every need? Get a divorce!" "The kids at school don't like your son? Change schools!"

This is half-baked advice. Learning to live with people who are different from you and who challenge you is just part of becoming a mature and resilient adult. "Cutting people out" of your life just because they're not a bright and shiny ray of light all day every day will only result in you, alone on an island, talking to coconuts.

Everyone has bad days. Everyone struggles in life. And not everyone needs to cheer you on every step of the way. We need to accept that and not bail on everyone who isn't in a cheery mood all the time.

Your family, friends, and coworkers are going to have a lot of bad days, and a lot of their attitude toward you has *nothing* to do with *you*.

They're in their own world and going through difficulties. Most people will have their lives affected by a mental illness. Most of your friends will come and go in your life. This idea of just swiping people out of our lives isn't mature or reasonable. Sometimes love equals compassion and patience.

BUILD WHAT YOU NEED

"Make a conscious effort to surround yourself with positive, nourishing, and uplifting people—people who believe in you, encourage you to go after your dreams, and applaud your victories."

—Jack Canfield

Still, you don't need to spend extraordinary amounts of time or give tremendous mindshare to negative people. People on a path of purpose don't have a lot of time for drama. So here's what I advise: Instead of "getting rid of" all the negative people in your life (especially if they are family, friends, loyal peers, or those who are just in need), spend more time (a) hanging with your positive and successful peers and (b) *building a new positive peer group.*

You can give your time to the drama and conflict of telling people they aren't what you want or need in life, or you can use that same time to *build a new circle.* Tear down relationships or build new ones? I'd focus on building.

I also want to address the excuse I hear all the time, especially from younger people, that "I have no access to successful people." That's almost always an unexplored personal belief, not a reality. In fact, in a globally connected world, it's a pretty thin argument to say you don't have access to somebody, somewhere, who you can learn from, collaborate with, work for, or follow to advance your life. The real question isn't whether they exist; it's whether you're willing to do the work to find them, contact them, hound them, or work hard enough to rise until you get in their orbit.

How do you do that? Here's my go-to list for helping someone get around a more successful peer group:

1. Add one more awesome friend.

To make a difference in your life, you don't need dozens of new friends. You need one more positive person who brings out the best in you. So find your most positive and successful friend and ask him to bring one or two of his friends to your next night out. Then start hanging with them a little more often, just a half hour more per week. One more positive person leads you one more step toward the good life.

2. Volunteer.

This is always my first move in working with people who feel surrounded by negative people. Volunteers are spirited, positive people. They are givers. You want to be around that spirit of service for your own personal and spiritual development anyway. You also want to be around volunteers because they tend to be more educated and successful people. People with higher levels of education are more likely to volunteer than those with less education. In the United States, almost 40 percent of those over the age of twenty-five who have a bachelor's degree or higher volunteer. That compares with 26.5 percent for those with some college or an associate's degree; 15.6 percent of high school graduates; and only 8.1 percent of those with less than a high school diploma.[39] Often, the people who staff nonprofit organizations, especially at the board and committee levels, are the richest people in a community.

But volunteering isn't just about getting around richer or more educated people. It's about serving others and developing the kind of empathy and spirit of service required to deal with all your relationships in life. If you have a negative person who keeps getting under your skin, the perspective you gain about the world through volunteering might help you chill out.

To find great volunteer opportunities in your hometown, start by asking your friends. You'd be surprised how many already volunteer. Also, look up your town's name and "volunteer" and you'll see plenty of options. And do it this week. When you meet more people who strive to make a big difference in the world, it makes a big difference in yours.

3. Play sports.

Join that intramural league. Visit that racquetball club. Get that golf membership. Hit the park and join more pickup games. Being in competitive situations teaches you to pay more attention to your own performance, and as we've learned, self-evaluation of performance promotes increased performance. Competition can bring out the best in us when we view the process of competing as a striving for excellence, personal bests, and team contributions. It's only "bad" or maladaptive performance when all you care about is rank, outcome, or smashing the competition.[40]

4. Seek mentorship.

I tell high performers to have one or two lifelong mentors: older, wiser, highly respected, successful people. I want you to call them once per month. I also want you to have one new "domain mentor" every three years. This means someone who has precisely the expertise you need to succeed in your field. You should also call that person every month. These two mentors, one for life and another for specific domain expertise, will give you extraordinary perspective. To find mentors, start again with your friends and family. Ask, "Who do I know who has great wisdom and influence, who I might be able to learn from?" You might find a mentor at your workplace or by doing the actions above—say, volunteering or playing sports. You can also type my name and "how to find a mentor" into YouTube and watch my video for more ideas.

5. Earn it.

You want to get around more successful people? Then earn your way into that party by becoming exceptional at what you do. Work hard. Practice the high performance habits. Never give up, add a tremendous amount of value, and stay on the path to mastery. When you become supremely skilled and successful at what you do, doors will open and you'll meet more and more extraordinary people.

Imagine how much better your life would be if you got better people into your social network. And no, I don't mean your Facebook group. I mean real people with real pulses who you actually see, call, work with, hang out with, exercise with, have fun adventures with. Choose to surround yourself with people who bring joy and growth into your life and are secure enough in themselves to be real and solid whether you shine or struggle.

Bring your squad and their standards up. You'll become a more extraordinary person by having more extraordinary people around you.

Performance Prompts

1. The most positive people in my life who I should hang out with more include . . .

2. To add to the number of high performers in my network, I should . . .

3. Some new routines or get-togethers I could create to bring together the positive and supportive people in my life could include . . .

NO OTHER CHOICE

"First say to yourself what you would be;
and then do what you have to do."

—Epictetus

We all know someone who wasn't the smartest kid in the class, who seemed underprepared for life, who seemed to have more weaknesses than strengths, and who somehow went on to surprise everyone with their success. Asked how they rose above others who were more privileged or qualified than they, such people often say, "I was hungry. I *had* to succeed. There was no other choice." They had necessity. The flip side is how many people without this mentality never reach their full powers. No necessity, no drive, no fulfillment of their potential.

As with all high performance habits, you have to be deliberate about raising your level of necessity. You must consistently think it through: "Have I associated the important activities of my day with my identity and my sense of obligation? Why is chasing this dream so important to me? Why *must* I do this? When must I do it? How can I get around more amazing people who up my game and help me serve at the next level?" These questions, frequently revisited, can be the prompts for an entirely new level of commitment and drive.

You are only as strong and extraordinary as you give yourself reason to be. So determine your musts, my friend. Make them real. Feel them in your gut. Because the world needs you to show up now.

SECTION TWO

SOCIAL HABITS

HIGH PERFORMANCE HABITS

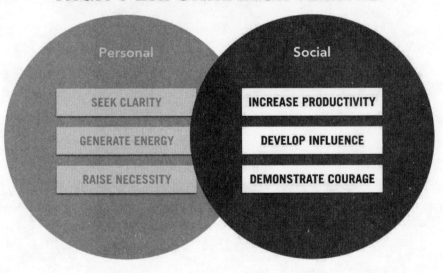

INCREASE PRODUCTIVITY

"Don't think about making art, just get it done.
Let everyone else decide if it's good or bad,
whether they love it or hate it.
While they are deciding, make even more art."

—Andy Warhol

INCREASE THE OUTPUTS THAT MATTER

CHART YOUR FIVE MOVES

GET INSANELY GOOD AT KEY SKILLS

"It's just not happening fast enough."

Athena, a school administrator, says this in a defeated tone.

We're in her office, discussing her goals and how productive she feels that her career has been. Thick binders are crammed into the shelves behind her. There's a tiny window next to her desk. No pictures adorn the white walls, which seem yellowed with time. I can't help but feel that this office—no, make it the entire admin building —was built in the 1970s and never painted again. Athena has worked in this room for fourteen years.

"I'm busier now than I've ever been in my whole career. There's a lot of urgency right now because they're about to close two of my schools. I barely leave this office, even for lunch." She points at two take-out boxes on the windowsill. "I have meetings all day with teachers, principals, parents, community leaders. In between, I try to cram in e-mail. I'm up late every night reviewing proposals. I've worked around the clock for what feels like four years. I don't feel like I'm making enough progress, even though I'm ticking off one thing after another."

I decide to ask a question that type A's dread when discussing their productivity: "Are you happy?"

Athena scowls. "I don't want to sound unhappy, Brendon. It's not like I'm saying life is awful or my career sucks. I'm just not as effective as I want to be, or everyone needs me to be. That's why we asked you here—to focus on being more effective."

I've found that when you're talking with really busy people, they usually leave the topic of happiness quickly.

"Okay. So, Athena, are you effectively happy?"

She laughs. "Happy enough, I guess. It's not like every day is a dream, but I do love what I'm doing. It's just, I think there *must* be a better way."

"A better way than what?"

"Than killing myself working this hard to get what feels like nowhere. I want to retire after twenty years. But that's six years from now. I don't even know if I can make it another two at this pace. And even if I do, I'm scared I'll retire and look back and think, *What was it all for? What did I really accomplish?*"

"What do you think it's all for?"

"Oh, the schools, for sure. I'm clear about that. That's why I started this career. I know if I can make the schools in my community healthy, I can make generations of kids have better lives."

"Okay. Sounds like a wonderful mission. You say you might wonder what you really accomplished. What do you hope that to be?"

"I hope to have accomplished some more big projects that these schools can benefit from for generations. But I can't imagine how I can get there—I'm already trying *so hard* just to maintain. I'm putting in the hours, but I haven't advanced as fast as I thought I would. I'm not making the difference I had hoped, because my projects move too slow. My work-life balance is a mess. It's just that I feel like I'm always pushing and pushing and juggling and juggling. I'm always having to reinvent the wheel with every project. I'm always fighting fires and scrambling to achieve anything that lasts . . ." She trails off and looks at the blank yellowed wall beside her. "It's like no matter what I do, I'm not getting these big projects accomplished, and I worry I'm not approaching them right. No matter what I do, it's just . . ."

I feel an intense energy coming from her. A lump has grown in my throat. I know where this is going. It hurts to see someone with vision caged here in this office. "It's just what?"

"Everything I do, it's just never . . ." She blinks back tears. ". . . *enough.*"

#

One of the worst feelings in the world is to be incredibly busy but feel that you're not making any progress. You're fighting the good fight, but your approach is wrecking your health or compromising your well-being. Projects seem to take forever. Progress comes too slow. Happiness is always a distant horizon never reached. Athena felt that. Most of us have at some point.

It was hard watching Athena experience these feelings because from the outside she seemed like a one-woman SWAT team. She finished each day with a lot of to-dos crossed off her list. What she had yet to learn was that not only was balance possible but so was increased progress. She also had to discover that sometimes all that busywork isn't your life's work. Sometimes, being effective isn't enough because achievement can be hollow if it gets out of sync with who you are, what you really want to be doing, what you're actually *capable of.* She had to learn the difference between just getting things done and reaching high performance productivity.

High performers have a very deliberate approach in planning their days, projects, and tasks compared to underperformers. Like most productive people, high performers score well on statements such as "I'm good at setting priorities and working on what's important," and "I stay focused and avoid distractions and temptations." (The stronger the agreement with such statements, the greater the overall high performance score.) The difference is that when they compare themselves to their peers, high performers are *more productive* and yet also happier, less stressed, and more rewarded over the long term.

The happiness finding is especially relevant since many people believe they can't possibly do more without compromising their well-being or sense of balance. But that's just not true. High performers have found a way to produce more but also eat healthier, work out more, and *still* feel a greater love for taking on new challenges than their peers do. And they don't just get more busywork done in the sense that they slop things together—high performers complete more activities and report being more excellence driven than their peers. My interviews with many high performers and their peers over the past decade confirm their statements.

None of this is because high performers are superhuman or over-caffeinated. Nor is it because of the feel-good ideals we're often sold today to become more productive. Believing that you give more than your peers or that you are making a difference can certainly increase your sense of motivation and satisfaction, but again, those things don't always lead to increased productivity.[1] Just because you're a giver doesn't mean you're good at setting priorities or avoiding distractions. Givers might feel a lot of heart, but they don't always finish what they start.

So how is it that high performers produce more but also maintain well-being and balance? It's because they have many of the deliberate habits you'll learn in this chapter.

To get the most out of this chapter, it's important that you set aside any preconceived notions about work-life balance or whether seeking tangible achievements in life is a worthy goal. Stay open-minded, because mastering this habit can have far-reaching consequences into every aspect of your life, especially in how you feel about yourself and the world in general. Our research found that if you feel you are more productive, you are statistically more likely to feel happier, more successful, and more confident. You're also more likely to take better care of yourself, get promoted more often, and earn more than people who feel less productive. These are not my opinions; they are important and measurable life outcomes that we've found in multiple surveys and studies.

In my coaching experience, it's clear that high performers are also the most valued and highly paid people in an organization. Organizations want high performance leaders because they are focused, manage tasks well, and succeed more often in taking projects through to completion. They get overwhelmed less, and they work on their goals longer, with a greater sense of joy and camaraderie than others experience.

Clearly, there is power in mastering this area of your life. Let's examine the basics, then move on to the advanced habits.

PRODUCTIVITY BASICS

"The day is always his who works with serenity and great aims."
—Ralph Waldo Emerson

The fundamentals of becoming more productive are setting goals and maintaining energy and focus. No goals, no focus, no energy— and you're dead in the water.

Productivity starts with goals. When you have clear and challenging goals, you tend to be more focused and engaged, which leads to a greater sense of flow and enjoyment in what you're doing.[2] Greater enjoyment gives you that intrinsic motivation that has been correlated with greater productivity in both quantity and quality of output.[3] The same goes for teams. Groups that have clear and challenging goals almost always outperform those without explicit goals. Research consistently shows that group goals inspire people to work more quickly and for longer periods, pay more attention to the tasks that matter, become less distracted, and increase their overall effort.[4]

Energy is another huge factor in determining productivity. As we discussed in chapter three, almost everything you do to take good care of yourself matters in increasing your high performance. Good sleep, nutrition, and exercise are huge enhancers of productivity.[5] And not just *your* productivity—the productive output of entire economies can be tied, for example, to their citizens' nutrition habits.[6]

You'll recall that capital "E" Energy wasn't just about sleep, nutrition, and exercise, but also about positive emotions. It's an undisputed fact that happier people are more productive. In fact, one meta-analysis of over 275,000 people across more than 200 studies found that happy people aren't just more productive—they also receive higher evaluations for quality of work, dependability, and creativity.[7] Another study found that students who were more cheerful in college were more financially successful than their peers over a decade after graduation.[8] Even that old advice of "smile and you'll get more done" plays true. One study found that just watching a comedy clip to bring some joy into your life before doing serious work can increase productivity.[9]

Finally, if you're going to be productive, you've got to maintain focus. This isn't easy in the modern era. Information overwhelm, distractions, and interruptions cause dire consequences in both our health and our productivity. Information overload causes demoralization and lower work quality.[10] Dealing with an endless stream of inputs, or having to spend a large chunk of our day poring over data or searching for it makes us miserable. That's why we have the term *analysis paralysis*—we're paralyzed by too much data and too much time spent gathering and analyzing that data. This is just one reason why you should never check your e-mail first thing in the morning. That big flood of e-mails causes overwhelm and reactivity—not the emotion or mindset you want to frame your day with. Instead, try some of the activities we discussed in the energy chapter.

Distraction is another downer. One study found that distraction lowers productivity by 20 percent.[11] It's even worse if we're working on challenging mental tasks—distractions then can slow our thinking by almost half.[12] Several studies have shown that multitasking itself is a distraction. It is incompatible with the peak-concentration states that are associated with high performance and quality work.[13] When people multitask, they cannot focus fully on the task at hand because their brain is still processing their last unfinished task.[14]

The final big culprit is interruptions. Most people in larger organizations are interrupted several times during any given task, activity, or meeting. When they are, they have trouble focusing again and catching back up to what they were doing. They don't "bounce back" to their original effort but instead turn to, on average, two other tasks or projects before reorienting themselves to the original effort.[15] With my Fortune 50 clients, even the highest achieving, I've noticed that one significant interruption in the workday can throw off important and scheduled tasks by two to three hours.

These facts should get you seriously disciplined about setting challenging goals and keeping your energy and focus on track. But that's hard work, and often those efforts are derailed by our assumptions that it's just not possible. Too many people say they can't set larger goals or maintain energy because their work-life balance would be upended. In fact, the conversation around work-life balance has become so absurd, I'd like to address it specifically before moving on to our habits.

THE WORK-LIFE BALANCE DEBATE

"One of the most common ways for the modern person to maintain self-deception is to keep busy all the time."

—Daniel Putnam

These days, many people have thrown in the towel on the concept of work-life balance. But not so fast. People can find balance in their lives, and to believe otherwise is a terribly disempowering and inaccurate assumption. Having trained literally millions of people on the topic of productivity, I have come to realize that those who don't think work-life balance is possible believe this because either (a) they've never made a fully conscious, consistent effort to define, seek, and measure that balance, or (b) they simply define "work-life balance" using an impossible-to-achieve standard.

First, let's address the often-voiced idea that work-life balance is impossible. Calling *any* human endeavor impossible typically proves to be a naive conceit, and this is no exception. When someone says to me that work-life balance is impossible, I remind them that human beings have crossed oceans, summited the highest mountains, built skyscrapers, landed on the moon, and guided vehicles beyond the solar system. What we are capable of is remarkable, and what we will attempt is constrained only by our beliefs. And so I say to you that if you believe a better work-life balance is impossible, you have already lost the fight.

I also remind many of my clients who have given up on this issue that they simply never tried as hard to find balance as they have tried in other efforts. They'll spend ten months planning the achievement of a work project, but not a single day planning more balance in their upcoming week. If you won't focus as attentively on balancing your life as on achieving any other project, then you've settled the matter. In that case, don't point an accusing finger at the entire work-life balance conversation; point the finger at the person looking at you from the mirror, who simply refused to try.

If we can keep an open mind in this discussion, we might realize that a major problem is the way we approach work-life balance in the first place.

The great mistake most people make is to think of balance in terms of evenly distributed *hours*.

They think they're supposed to spend equal time on work and "life." Their expectation is a quantity expectation versus a quality expectation, and anytime we confuse the two, we get into trouble. Still, despite how many people feel they don't have balance in this regard, most, in fact, *do*. The vast majority of us spend 30 percent of our lives working (assuming a standard forty-hour workweek), 30 percent sleeping, and 30 percent doing other stuff, such as hanging with the family, pursuing hobbies or health, handling life's basic needs. Indeed, most people have a lot more time off and more time with their families than they think. It's just that they're not intentional about that time and, hence, don't enjoy that time "enough." It's ironic that the average American who watches four-to-five hours of television per day says they have no time and no balance.[16]

To be fair, a lot of people do work a lot more than forty hours per week. And in the always-connected culture we live in today, where a response is expected at all hours of the day and night, it can *feel* as though balance is gone.

That's why I think there's a better approach to thinking about work-life balance. Instead of trying to balance *hours*, try to balance *happiness* or progress in your major life arenas.

Let me elaborate. When most people feel that they're "out" of balance, it's because *one area* of their life became more intense, important, and time-consuming than other areas. They got so obsessed about work that they let their health or their marriage slide. Or they got so focused on a family issue that their work suffered.

The solution is to keep perspective in life by keeping an eye on the quality or progress of the major life arenas. A simple weekly review of what we're after in the major areas of our life helps us rebalance or at least plan for more balance.

I've found that it is useful to organize life into ten distinct categories: health, family, friends, intimate relationship (partner or marriage), mission/work, finances, adventure, hobby, spirituality, and emotion. When I'm working with clients, I often make them rate their happiness on a scale of 1 through 10 and also write their goals *in each* of these ten arenas *every Sunday night*. Most of them have never done that before. But doesn't it stand to reason that only from measuring something in the first place can we determine whether it's in "balance"?

If you aren't consistently measuring the major arenas of your life, then you couldn't possibly know what the balance you seek is or is not.

This activity is really just a simple check-in, I know, but you'd be surprised how powerful it is. I once gave an executive team of sixteen people this weekly activity, and in just six weeks they reported dramatic increases in their sense of well-being and work-life balance. Admittedly, this was a small and informal study, but nonetheless, we saw double-digit increases when nothing changed in their work or personal lives except taking time each week to assess their ten life arenas.[17] Sometimes, just having a look at the larger picture can help us feel more in control, adjust course as needed, and, yes, find more balance.

That was what Athena, the school administrator at the beginning of this chapter, so desperately needed. That day in her office, I asked her to rate herself in the ten arenas. To her surprise, she hadn't even *thought about* many aspects of life outside work *for years*. Who's to blame in that situation? Is it her bosses' fault? The society we live in? No. If we're honest, our lack of attention to the important areas of our life is no one's fault but our own. What Athena discovered was that she needed a weekly ritual to assess where she was and what "balance" could even mean to her.

The other distinction generally missed about work-life balance is that it's not so much about evenly distributed hours as about *feelings*. It's not about the hours you spend but about the harmony you feel. Often, people simply feel unhappy with, or disconnected from, their work. If you don't like your work and you have to spend a lot of time doing it, then of course you feel as though life is out of balance. You would recognize that your busywork isn't your *life's work*, and that dissonance would cause you mental distress. That's why it's important to live in harmony with what you truly desire and to do the activities in the chapter on clarity.

You'll always feel out of balance if you're doing work that you don't find engaging and meaningful.

Other times, people *are* engaged and enjoying their work, but they're *fried* from too much stress and too many hours on the job. There's a fine line between busy and burned out, and when you cross it, no matter how great your life is outside work, you will feel out of balance. Burnout in one area of life easily scorches others. So what can we do? In the chapter on energy, we covered a lot of the basics: transition better, release tension, get more sleep, exercise more, eat better.

The good news is that if burnout is often just a feeling of fatigue, there's also a simpler fix. If we can just give you a short mental and physical refresh/reset every hour, then you can dramatically improve how you feel, and you'll sense a significant improvement in your work-life balance. This means that for most people, they didn't need to quit their job because of work-life balance problems; they just needed to change *what they did on the job* so that they felt more energetically balanced. Happily, that's easier than you may think.

TAKE A—GASP!—BREAK

"There is virtue in work and there is virtue in rest.
Use both and overlook neither."

—Alan Cohen

Your brain also needs more downtime than you probably think—to process information, recover, and deal with life so that you can be more productive.[18] That's why, for optimal productivity, you should not only take longer breaks—claim your vacation time!—but also give yourself intermittent breaks throughout the day.[19]

Researchers have long known that taking breaks at work leads to positive emotions and greater productivity.[20] For example, simple acts such as taking a lunch break away from your desk each day can significantly increase your performance at work.[21] Taking a short break to get outside to a nearby park for just a few minutes can give you cognitive benefits so that you return to work restored and with greater focus.[22] If you're unwilling to move away from the desk, simply standing up intermittently at your desk to work can increase productivity by 45 percent compared to sitting all day.[23]

Some researchers have argued that we need these breaks because we have limited cognitive resources and we "use up" our psychological bandwidth or self-control. While this theory has been questioned—perhaps we don't run out of self-control and focus at all but, rather, just lose motivation[24]—one thing is certain: Working straight through the day with no breaks makes people unhappy and less productive.

We've all sat at our desk and noticed our attention flagging even when we like our work. We've all felt tired even doing work we love. We've all run out of ideas even when our butt is on the line to solve a problem. In all these instances, that's your mind telling you that you need a break. We've all noticed, too, that simple things such as a chat at the cooler, a bathroom break, or letting our mind wander for a few minutes after lunch often refreshes us. It's self-evident that our minds need rest to restore neurochemicals and increase our future attention.[25]

The science is so conclusive on this that most organizational experts recommend brief breaks away from the desk at least every 90 to 120 minutes to increase employee satisfaction and performance.[26] But my research, as well as others', has shown that the number should be cut in half.[27]

> If you want to feel more energized, creative,
> and effective at work—and still leave work
> with enough oomph for the "life" part—the ideal
> breakpoint is to stop your work and give your mind
> and body a break *every forty-five to sixty minutes.*

This means you shouldn't work longer at any one thing without a mental and physical break for more than an hour tops. A break of just two to five minutes every hour can help you feel much more mentally alert and energized for your work and life overall.

For example, if you're going to work on e-mail or a presentation for two hours, I recommend you get up from your chair at fifty minutes in, then take a fast stroll around the office, grab some water, come back to your chair, and do a sixty-second transition meditation. As a reminder from the chapter on energy, a transition meditation means you simply close your eyes, focus on deep breathing, repeat to yourself a mantra such as "release," and then set an intention for the next activity. If you want extra credit, also ask the desk trigger question from the previous chapter (on necessity): "Who needs me on my A game right now the most?"

Notice what's *not* included during these breaks: checking e-mail, texts, or social media. Checking in is the exact opposite of our goal here: checking out so we can recharge.

Achievers often brush off this advice because they just want to sit and "power through" hours of activity at their computer or in meetings. But that's exactly why they are feeling so wiped out in their home life and thus report a terrible work-life balance. Remember, hours at home versus at work is not the issue. It's more about their feelings and overall sense of energy. Powering through is just bad advice. Studies of the world's top performers in dozens of fields found that they don't necessarily practice or work *longer* than others. It's that they are more effective in those practice sessions or simply have *more* sessions (not longer ones).[28] Putting in longer hours is almost always the wrong answer if you want to reach balance, happiness, or sustained high performance. It's counterintuitive, but it is true: *By slowing down or taking a break once in a while, you work faster, leaving more time for other areas of life.*

For my clients, this 45–60-minute break becomes a way of life. It's a strict protocol in the first months working together. I tell them, "If your butt lands in a chair, then set a fifty-minute timer on your phone or computer. At fifty minutes, no matter what you're working on, stand up, move, breathe, set an intention, and then return to your work." (If you want the fifty-minute timer I give them, just visit HighPerformanceHabits.com/tools.) The "stand up" part of my advice is important. You can't just close your eyes and meditate at your desk. You need to give your *body* a break from the posture you've been holding while sitting. So get up and move around a bit, and do some basic stretching. If all you did was stand up every hour, close your eyes, and bounce in place while taking ten deep, long breaths, you'd feel a total renewal of focus and productivity in your life.

No matter where I'm sitting—on a plane, in a café, at work, in a meeting, on the couch—I get up every fifty minutes. I do a short two-minute physical routine of calisthenics, Qigong, and yoga paired with deep breathing. This fifty-minute rule is something I never break, even when I'm in a meeting with other people. I often make them stand and do an energizer with me, or I excuse myself and go find a place to refresh for two to three minutes. Those short few-minute breaks buy me hours of added focus and effectiveness each day.

If you follow the steps outlined in this chapter, you can find greater work-life balance, so do not fear becoming more productive or seeking higher achievement. Just be sure to gauge your work-life balance every week by rating yourself in the ten arenas of your life and having goals in each. Then take a two-to-three-minute break every forty-five to sixty minutes of your day. That's the basics. Now let's get to the advanced practices for productivity.

PRACTICE ONE

INCREASE THE OUTPUTS THAT MATTER

"Nothing is less productive than to make more efficient
what should not be done at all."

—Peter Drucker

If you want to become extraordinary, you need to figure out the productive outputs that matter in your field or industry. Eminent scientists produce more important papers than their less known or less effective counterparts.[29] Mozart and Beethoven became great not only by their genius but also through their productive output. The same goes for Bob Dylan, Louis Armstrong, the Beatles. In its highest performing years, Apple launched products that were hit after hit. Babe Ruth took more swings than his contemporaries, just as Michael Jordan took a lot more shots and Tom Brady threw a lot more passes. Seth Godin cranks out blogs; Malcolm Gladwell cranks out books and articles; Casey Neistat keeps uploading those

YouTube videos; Chanel keeps the fresh designs coming; and Beyoncé keeps dropping great albums.

High performers have mastered the art of *prolific quality output* (PQO). They produce more high-quality output than their peers over the long term, and *that* is how they become more effective, better known, more remembered. They aim their attention and consistent efforts toward PQO and minimize any distractions (including opportunities) that would steal them away from their craft.

This point seems almost universally lost in a world where people spend over 28 percent of their workweek managing e-mail, and another 20 percent just *looking* for information.[30] People spend eons of time on worthless activities—say, creating folders and organizing their e-mail—even though these have nothing to do with real productivity. (Yes, sorry, your elaborate e-mail folders aren't helping you. A 2011 study of 85,000 actions by 345 e-mail users found that people who create complex folders are less efficient in finding what they need than those who simply use search or threading.)[31]

I bring up e-mail because achievers almost universally blame it for their poor productivity. But e-mail, per se, is not the problem. The real culprit is our very orientation to work itself. Real work isn't replying to everyone's false emergencies, shuffling papers, deleting junk e-mails, posturing to look good, or attending meetings. Real work is producing quality output that matters.

Part of your job is to figure out what "relevant PQO" means to you. For the blogger, it might mean more frequent and better content. For the cupcake store owner, it might be discerning the two best-selling flavors and expanding distribution on just those two flavors. The parent may choose to increase the frequency of free time and great experiences with the kids. The sales rep might go after more meetings with qualified prospects. The graphic designer might pump out more great images. For the academic, it might be the quality of the curriculum and classes, or the number of published papers or books.

Figuring out what you are supposed to produce,
and learning the priorities in the creation, quality,
and frequency of that output, is one of the greatest
breakthroughs you can have in your career.

Look back to almost any business icon, and you see a turning point in their career and wealth, which came about when they discovered their PQO. For Steve Jobs, it was dumping a bunch of products from Apple's list so he could focus on massively scaling fewer products, which would change the world. For Walt Disney, it was ramping up production of movies. In the modern digital era, some of the greatest success stories are of those who simply enabled others to share more original and prolific content—Facebook, Instagram, Snapchat, for example. Wherever PQO is found, it seems that breakthroughs and wealth follow.

I left a corporate consulting job in 2006 because I couldn't find fulfillment in the outputs that were being rewarded. When I looked to the partners at my old employer, the PQO was basically how many big clients they signed per year. Though a lot of wonderful things came with that—the ability to do deals, change things—I just didn't connect with the idea of dedicating my life to a career built on deals. For a guy at my lowly level, the informal culture supported a PQO of "project hopping"—getting on as many projects as we could so that we gain perspective, expand our network, and get paid for extra travel. Again, there were other benefits to all this, but I just didn't connect. Very little of the endgame at that job resonated with me.

One of the great realizations of life can come from discovering that the outputs you are being compensated for are not exciting or fulfilling. When that realization comes, it's time to honor that truth and make a change.

I chose to quit and begin my career as a writer, speaker, and online trainer. I saw the outputs of those efforts—creating content for inspiring and empowering others—as something that would be meaningful to me. The issue was, I had no idea how to start or what, specifically, to do. Like a lot of people new to the expert industry, I thought I had to figure out the writing industry, the speaking industry, the online training industry. I made the mistake of going to dozens of conferences to try to figure out each of the industries, without realizing that they all were the same career of being a thought leader and had similar outputs that mattered most.[32]

For almost a year, casting about with no clarity on which outputs really mattered, I was a mess. I was trying to write articles for magazines and blogs, begging people to let me speak to their groups and hoping to get paid, spinning my wheels learning a hundred online marketing ideas. Then one day, sitting in a café, I realized I'd spent all day "working" but had nothing really to show for it. I thought, *Not one thing I've done today is going to advance my career or be remembered —by me or anyone else—ten years from now.* I still remember that conversation in my head: "If you're honest with yourself, you *want* to create things that matter. You want to know that a good day's work produces *something* worthwhile, *something* that will be part of your important contributions to others and the world, *something* that shows you care about your craft."

Of course, I realized that not every day would be a magical, perfect day where every task I did was earthshaking, monumental. We all have activities that have to get done that don't make us feel like legends. Taking out the trash isn't adding to your body of great works, but it has to get done.

What changed the trajectory of my career that day was deciding, on a single page, what my PQOs would be. If I was going to be a real writer, then my productive output needed to become books. This book you're holding? It's the *sixth* I've published since that day. (Two more unreleased manuscripts are waiting in my drawer.) This says nothing of the thousands of e-mails, blog articles, sales letters, and social media posts I've written. But my main effort is books. Wayne Dyer, a mentor and dearly missed friend, wrote and published more than thirty books. I'm just a beginner, but I know my PQO, and that gives me what Wayne would have called the power of intention.

I decided that if I was going to be a professional speaker, my PQO would be the number of paid speaking gigs at a certain booking fee. I stopped all wasteful conversations asking people to give me a chance to speak and started building marketing materials and videos like those of other speakers who were getting booked at the levels I wanted to reach.

I knew that if I was going to be an online course trainer—a relatively new career back in 2006—then my PQO would be curriculum, training videos, and full online courses. As I shared in the chapter on clarity, I stopped trying to learn every new marketing technique that came along, and put my full effort into creating and promoting online courses. The rest, as they say, is history. Nearly two million people have enrolled in my online courses or video series, and my free instructional videos about how to live a fully charged life have been viewed over 100,000,000 times. If I hadn't figured out my PQO, I would never have had the blessing of reaching all these students. I would never have had been named "one of the most successful online trainers in history" by Oprah.com or to make *SUCCESS* magazine's list of the top personal development influencers for so many years. Please know that I'm not sharing this to impress you. But I am sharing it to convey the tremendous power of deciding what your PQO is to be, and *going for it*. The results in my career are not because I'm particularly special or talented. They happen because I honed the focus for the PQOs that mattered in my career, and gave those outputs my obsessive attention and dedication *continuously, over the long term*.

I cannot overemphasize the importance of this strategy. Whenever I have to help a client increase high performance, quickly discovering what output they should be creating is one of my go-to strategies. No matter what topic or type of deliverables they decide to get productive toward, I have them reorient their entire work schedule toward that endeavor. As quickly as possible, I want them spending 60 percent or more of their workweek oriented to PQO. In my experience over this past decade, that 60 percent figure seems to be the sweet spot where real results start happening for a person's career. For most people, the other 40 percent ends up in such buckets as strategy, team management, and the everyday tasks of work or running a business.

I spend 60 percent of my workweek on writing, creating curriculum for online training, and filming videos. The other 40 percent goes to strategy, team management, industry relationships, and customer engagement, which includes social media and communicating with students. The 40 percent is really just the things that support or facilitate the 60 percent—the *prolific quality output*. Not everyone has my career, of course, and the golden proportion of 60/40 is not feasible for everyone. But the goal isn't to do what I do. It's to find *your* best allocation of time and stick to it the best you can. I'm tenaciously consistent about my 60/40, and whenever it drops below that, I know I'm not producing my best.

If these time allocations sound extreme, please note that this is very different from the advice of those who tell you to "go all in" and give one of your passions 100 percent of your time. Such guidance is patently absurd, anyway. We can't give 100 percent of our time to anything—certainly not if we're working with other people, caring for our families, or trying to make a big impact. There's always going to be a percentage of time we must give to working with or leading other people, managing and administering the details of our jobs, and, yes, e-mail. My point is, you can't shirk those things, but you can and must strategize and maximize your time working on outputs that make your career important and influential.

Why don't more people focus on producing prolific quality output, especially given that they still have the 40 percent allocation for dealing with the inevitable obligations of work? The most common excuses (Is *delusions* a better word?) are procrastination and perfectionism.

Despite how familiar we are with blaming procrastination, it's not a real "thing." Procrastination isn't a part of the human psyche—it's not even a personality trait. It's also not a result of poor time management skills that can easily be pointed at. Instead, researchers have found that procrastination is really a motivational problem.[33] It's an issue that arises because you're not working on things that intrinsically matter to you. In rare cases, it can be about anxiety or fear of failure, but far more often it stems from working on things that don't excite you, engage you, or matter to you. That's why finding a PQO you can get behind is so important. If you *love* what you're creating or contributing in the world, you'll experience less procrastination.

Whenever I tell people to create more output, inevitably I run into the perfectionists. They say things like "Well, Brendon, I can't just put more stuff out there. I'm a perfectionist. I have to know that it's absolutely right and will be loved." Perfectionism, though, is just a delay logic fancied up to look respectable. The reason people don't finish more things isn't perfectionism; it's that they rarely even begin or they get tangled up in doubt or distraction. If someone were a true perfectionist, they would at least have completed and released their work, since the very act of "perfecting" something comes only after it is completed, released, and then improved on.

We could all find reasons why it's hard to be more productive. But rather than spending any more mental power there, let's just get to work. Let's remember what's most important, let's focus, let's produce real things that we're proud of. Let's be prolific and change the world.

Performance Prompts

1. The outputs that matter most to my career are . . .

2. Some things I could stop doing so I can focus more on PQO are . . .

3. The percentage of my weekly time I will allocate to PQO is . . .
   and the ways I'll make that happen are . . .

PRACTICE TWO

CHART YOUR FIVE MOVES

"I believe half the unhappiness in life comes from people being afraid to go straight at things."

—William Locke

Humans are masterful jugglers. We can manage several projects at the same time, achieve many tasks concurrently, carry on multiple levels of conversation—implicit and explicit—with several people at the dinner table. This strength serves all of us—up to a point. Then it destroys us.

Most people reach their first levels of success through their ability to multitask with excellence. The entrepreneur starting the cupcake shop plays every role necessary to succeed and chases every opportunity available to her. She's the person who orders inventory, the baker who makes the cupcakes, the cashier who takes the orders, the marketer who mails the coupons, the networker who wins friends in the neighborhood. She hustles in dozens of roles and takes on hundreds of tasks. At some point, she earns a profit. Over time, she succeeds. She might even hit high performance.

But with success comes new opportunities. Soon, she's advising other start-ups. She's dabbling in other opportunities. She hasn't reached her primary goal of a world-class cupcake shop, but she's comfortable. She'd tell you that her cupcake business is still a priority, but dig into her calendar and you can see that "priority" no longer equates to work. Look closer and you'll see that most of her efforts are unaligned. She's busy, but she's not *progressing* with purpose.

What should she do now to get back on track? She should simplify, strip things down to the essential parts, and favor deep work. Most importantly, she should get a *plan*.

A lot of highly driven people think they don't need well-defined plans. They have talent, so they just want to get in the game, hustle, wing it, and see what happens. That might work when they're just starting out and everyone on the field around them is also uninformed. At that point, perhaps their innate, God-given talent can help them get ahead. But the advantage dies quickly. As soon as the other teams and players have actual experience and plans—they know the X's and O's, the routes and play calls—and you don't, you're toast.

This is terribly difficult for high performers to hear. I can't tell you how many high performers lose their perch at the top because of the inevitable distraction that comes from unfocused efforts. I'm not talking about the *lazy* kind of distraction. High performers are making things happen, all right.

But when they start making a lot of things happen with no unifying trajectory, they begin losing their power.

Then they lose their passion. Then they're achieving a lot of little things but no big, meaningful things.

The issue is that some people simply got away with not planning, for a long time. That's because you don't need much of a plan to figure out simple tasks. Simple tasks usually require obvious steps, few interaction points, and your own independent actions. But for complex tasks and goals, planning is vital because there are usually a variety of strategies that can help achieve a goal, and some are more effective or desirable than others.[34] The bigger the goal, the more to manage and the more interaction points with other people. *To become a high performer requires thinking more before acting.*

This doesn't necessarily mean you must have the entire path and every task figured out in advance. Often, long-term projects require you to set a plan as best you can, then figure things out on the fly. Still, research continues to show that when goals or projects are complex, planning always improves performance.[35]

Having a plan and working through it step-by-step is more important than you think. A plan focuses scattered thinking. And finishing each vital task on your list fires off dopamine in the brain, making you feel both rewarded and more motivated to continue. A plan not only increases your likelihood of completing an activity but also increases your joy during the project, and your available cognitive resources for the next goal.[36]

And so, after all that we've discussed about finding the area where you want to create prolific quality output, it is now time to plan. Think of the most ambitious dream you'd like to take on, identify what you really want, then ask yourself:

> **"If there were only five major moves**
> **to make that goal happen, what would they be?"**

Think of each major move as a big bucket of activities, a project. These big five projects that move you toward achieving your dream can then be broken down into deliverables, deadlines, and activities. Once you're clear on these things, put them into your calendar, scheduling the bulk of your time in protected blocks during which you do nothing but make progress toward the activity that the specific block is dedicated to. So, if I show up at your house and say, "Show me your calendar," I should readily see the major projects you are working toward. If I can't discern from your weekly and monthly calendar what major moves you are working toward, then you're not optimizing your time and you're at risk of getting sucked into a life of reaction and distraction. That, or you're just going to have to take years getting a result that others could do in months.

High performers plan almost everything more than underperformers do: from workouts to learning, from meetings to vacation time.[37] It's easy to get confused at this point, though, and become lost in tasks and overplanning. Lots of people will overcomplicate this. So let's pause here and remember that the main thing is to keep the main thing the main thing. *Know the big five moves that will take you to your goal, break those moves down into tasks and deadlines, then put them in a calendar.* If that's all you did, and you made sure these moves aligned with your PQO, you'd be ahead of the game.

Here's a rather public example that I'm amazed worked so well. Earlier, I shared with you my dream of becoming a writer. As you may recall, I was all over the place, writing things here and there but getting no real progress until I identified my PQO as writing books.

Once I knew I wanted to be prolific at writing books, I stopped other activities. Then I started exploring what the five major moves were to getting a book out.

Specifically, I wanted to become a *New York Times* best-selling author. I wasn't after the accolade itself, but what it represented: lots of people improving their lives. But there was a problem; I'd already written a book, and it didn't hit the bestseller list. I was demoralized and made the mistake of thinking the "system" was broken and didn't reward new authors. I wanted to blame a lot of people but I had to face a tough truth: I hadn't planned well enough the first time. The entire process of writing and promoting a book was as haphazard as could be for a newbie.

This time, I decided, I wouldn't allow such unsystematic activity to seal the fate of my new book. I didn't just start writing tidbits throughout the day, as I had for my previous book. I didn't follow my impulses to go to writers' conferences or read a lot of books about writing. I didn't try to do a hundred things in a hundred directions. I knew that would lead to exhaustion, frustration, and failure again.

Instead, I interviewed several number one best-selling authors and deconstructed their major activities. I simply asked, "What five major moves made the most difference in moving your writing forward and landing your book on the big bestseller lists?" You can do the same thing. Find the successful people you want to emulate in some way, and discover their five moves.

What I learned wasn't what I expected:

- Best-selling authors didn't talk about the romantic idealism of "being a writer." They talked about the hard work and discipline of cranking out pages even when they didn't feel like it.

- No one credited attending writers' conferences as a determining factor in their success.

- They didn't talk about focus groups or audience demographics.

- They didn't talk about conducting years of research before writing their books as a determining factor in their sales (though some had done that).

- Few mentioned major media coverage or traditional book tours.

- No one mentioned book clubs.

- No one mentioned famous people writing a foreword to their book as a determining factor.

At the time, all this came as a shock. In my dreamy mind, I thought all those things were important. In fact, I thought that was how you went about it all. While I was interviewing the authors, I had a big, long list of things I was supposed to do. Here are a few:

- Go to writers' workshops and get feedback on my writing to "find my voice."

- Interview a bunch of people in my audience demographic to see what they want from my writing.

- Brainstorm media "hooks" and "angles" so I can incorporate them into the book for later use in getting major media coverage.

- Get famous people to endorse the book.

I suppose you could make the argument that these are perfectly fine tasks. Perhaps some would even be helpful. The issue is, *none* of the best-selling authors cited these moves as *determinant* of their success. None of these things put an author on a bestseller list or guided more people to pick their book up off the shelf.

I discovered that to get the result of number one bestseller, all that really mattered were these five basic moves:

1. *Finish* writing a good book. Until that's done, nothing else matters.

2. If you want a major publishing deal, get an agent. Or just self-publish.

3. Start blogging and posting to social media, and use these to get an e-mail list of subscribers. E-mail is everything.

4. Create a book promotion web page and offer some awesome bonuses to get people to buy the book. Bonuses are crucial.

5. Get five to ten people who have big e-mail lists to promote your book. You'll owe them a reciprocal e-mail—meaning you agree to promote for them later, too—and a portion of any sales they might make for you on other products you may be offering during your book promotion.

That's it. I know it's less inspiring than a "find your truth and write each day with magnificent passion and love for the audience whose hearts and souls you will impact forever" kind of thing. But these were the five major moves that most of the authors told me about. These were the ones that mattered most. I was stunned. And scared. I had *no idea* how to do any of these things.

And yet I had confidence. Because now I had a *plan*. And as you'll read later, real confidence just means you believe in your ability to figure things out. I had a dream. I now had the secret five moves. You'd better believe I was going to figure out how to make them happen.

So all my effort went into those five moves. I stopped almost all other activity. I set up a calendar for accomplishing each activity. The first one, *finish book*, consumed almost 90 percent of my schedule for some time. After I got that done, most of my week was blocked so I could do deep work on the other activities. I sequentially completed those five moves. Everything else was classified as either a distraction or something to delegate.

I know this sounds simplistic, but stay with me. Consider the first move: *finish writing a good book*. Think of the hundreds of ways to mess that up. I could keep researching. Learning about writing. Waiting to find my voice one day. Interviewing people. Procrastinating. Trying to write stupid little articles.

But all the best-selling authors had so clearly communicated this move to me: *finish the book*. "Until that happens, kid," they all told me, "nothing else happens."

And that's the magic of knowing your Five Moves. By knowing the first major activity, then the second, then the third, then the fourth, then the fifth, you have a map, a plan, a clear path forward. You don't get distracted.

So I stopped everything else, and I wrote. Then I swiftly followed the next four moves. I chose to publish with a company that basically helped me self-publish it—they didn't have to "accept me"; rather, I gave them the manuscript and they formatted it for a book. I designed the cover in PowerPoint. I had already started building an e-mail list and had about ten friends with e-mail lists who agreed to promote some of my videos. Lining them all up took two weeks of begging and prodding. I spent three days shooting videos, and four days uploading them to a blog and creating an e-mail sequence. In sixty days *total*, I took *The Millionaire Messenger* from idea to number one *New York Times* bestseller, number one *USA Today* bestseller, number one Barnes and Noble bestseller, and number one *Wall Street Journal* bestseller. That includes thirty days of writing the book, then thirty days getting it ready for printing; creating the social media, web pages, bonuses, and videos; and getting people to agree to e-mail links to the videos to everyone on their lists. Five moves. Sixty days. Number one bestseller.

Some will argue that I was lucky I could do this because I already had some promotional partners and the ability to create web pages and videos. That's completely true—but that "unfair" advantage was only the result of previous years' hard work. It's not as if I came out of the womb, and right there in the delivery room were promotional partners and a video setup. In fact, never in my life did I have promotional partners, until I knew they were crucial to my Five Moves.

This brings up an important point:

> **It doesn't matter whether you know *how* to achieve your Five Moves at first. The important thing is that for every major goal you have, you figure out the Five Moves. If you don't know the moves, you lose.**

The point of my story isn't speed—it's not what I did or did not do in sixty days. It's that I knew the moves that mattered, and I *executed* them. If it had taken two years, so be it—the result would still have been what I was after, and focusing on the five moves was the only way to get to the result. I've followed this simple plan and achieved dozens of major goals in my life. "5-Move Planning" has helped me build a business I love, meet US presidents, efficiently create blockbuster online courses, book huge speaking gigs, and help raise millions of dollars for nonprofits and causes that we deeply care about.

It's a simple process that my clients have used over and over again to achieve equally impressive results:

- Decide what you want.

- Determine the Five Major Moves that will help you leap toward that goal.

- Do deep work on each of the major five moves—at least 60 percent of your workweek going to these efforts—until they are complete.

- Designate all else as distraction, tasks to delegate, or things to do in blocks of time you've allocated in the remaining 40 percent of your time.

I know, this seems almost too simplistic. But I can't tell you how many hopeful strivers I meet who can't quickly answer "What are the five major projects you are working on, in sequential order, to achieve what you want?" Unfocused people respond with off-the-cuff thoughts, long lists of unnecessary things, a top-of-mind purge of ideas. High performers *know*. They can tell you what they're working on and why that order, in exacting detail. They can open their calendar and *show you* the blocks of time they've allocated to their major goals and projects.

So test yourself. If I showed up at your house, could you open your calendar and show me the blocks of time on your calendar that you saved and structured specifically to complete a major activity leading to a specific big goal? If not, you know your next move.

I know that at this point many people will say, "But I know someone extremely successful who doesn't 'do' plans. They just bumble from one thing to another and everything they touch turns to gold. They don't have any long-term projects or planning." No doubt these outliers exist. But the question isn't whether or not they exist; it's how much they're leaving on the table. Just a little more planning could significantly improve their contributions. For the rest of us it's good to remember that without discipline, our dreams will forever remain delusions.

Don't spend years on what could be done in months with better planning and more focused execution. Know your five moves. Work them hard and always be thinking about the next steps that will help you produce something that's significant, something that you're proud of, something that makes you extraordinary.

Performance Prompts

1. The biggest goal or dream I have that I need to plan out right now is . . .

2. The five moves that would help me progress swiftly toward accomplishing that dream are . . .

3. The timeline for each of my five moves will be . . .

4. Five people who have achieved that dream who I could study, seek out, interview, or model are . . .

5. The less important activities or bad habits I'm going to cut out of my schedule so that I can focus more time on the five moves in the next three months include . . .

PRACTICE THREE

GET INSANELY GOOD AT KEY SKILLS

"I believe the true road to preeminent success in any line
is to make yourself master in that line."

—Andrew Carnegie

To become more productive, become more competent. You have to master the primary skills needed to win in your primary fields of interest.

Mastery of key skills has long been associated with better productivity and performance at both macro and individual levels. Increased skill is often the goal of educational and economic policy because it tends to promote increased economic growth. Skill is also considered the silver bullet for individual workers, since those with deeper skills typically earn higher incomes and experience greater work satisfaction. That's not always the case, though. Skilled workers are sometimes undermined by bad strategy, leadership, job design, or human resource practices.[38] We all know someone who had a lot of skills but wasn't given a chance at work.

One thing is certain: *Not* having the requisite skills to reach success in your field is a serious deficit. Without greater skill acquisition, there's no progress in your career, so it's essential that you identify the major skills you need to develop so you can win today and in the future.

When we say "skill," we often mean a broad range of knowledge and capabilities that allow you to perform adequately in any given area. General skills might include communication, problem solving, systems thinking, project management, teamwork, and conflict management. There are also specific skills for any given task or company, such as coding, video production, finance, and computational skills.

And, of course, there are personal skills such as self-control, resilience, and other forms of emotional intelligence.

My goal here is for you to determine the five major skills you need to develop over the next three years to grow into the person you hope to become.

One principle lies at the heart of this effort: *Everything* is trainable. No matter what skill you want to learn, with enough training and practice and intention, you can become more proficient at it. If you don't believe this, your journey to high performance stops here. Perhaps the three best findings of contemporary research tell us that you can get better at practically anything if you keep a growth mindset (the belief that you can improve with effort), focus on your goals with passion and perseverance, and practice with excellence.[39]

When people say, "I can't," it's usually code for "I am unwilling to do the long-term training and conditioning necessary to achieve that." Remember: *Everything is trainable.* Those three words changed my life forever. I know I've shared plenty of examples from my own career, at the risk of making this book overly personal. However, this example is perhaps the number one question I am always asked about, so let's talk about public speaking because so many people fear it.

Twenty years ago, I returned to college after my car accident. I talked with my close friends about the wreck. I shared how I wanted to be a more intentional man so that the next time I faced my life's last questions—Did I live? Did I love? Did I matter?—I would be happy with the answers. Not everyone cared to hear about my lessons and experience. But some of my friends encouraged me to tell my story to their friends. "It's inspiring," they said.

Though my friends might have called me extroverted at that time in my life, in reality I was a very private person. I could joke and kid around with the guys. I was fairly comfortable talking to new acquaintances because I wanted to know people and connect and have a good time. But sharing personal matters was another thing. I rarely shared my real thoughts, needs, or dreams with others.

About the same time, I began studying psychology, philosophy, and self-help. I was looking for answers. I wanted to know how to live a better life. As I read more on these topics, I discovered that many of the authors' journeys were much like mine: Something had happened to them that inspired them to improve their life, explore how to become a better person, and want to help others on that journey. Reading their stories, I felt more compelled to share my own.

I also noticed that many of these authors listed "lecturer" or "professional speaker" or "workshop facilitator" in their bios. These authors tended to be speakers, so I sought out their audiobooks or speeches online. I began to realize that the better they could speak, the better they could impart their message and inspire others to change.

And so I decided that mastering the skill of public speaking was a must in my life. Sometimes, the desire to serve and to develop the relevant skills to do so outweighs our fears. I got committed and began a process of learning that I call "progressive mastery," which quickly changed my life.

Whenever you want to master a skill, you have two choices: You can hope to develop that skill with some practice and repetition, or you can ensure that you become world-class in that skill through progressive mastery.

The concept of progressive mastery is very different from how most people approach skill development. Most people get interested in an idea, try it a few times, and gauge whether they are "good" at it. If they are not good, they chalk it up to a lack of natural ability or talent. At this point, most quit. And those who carry on think they have to use brute repetition to get better, hoping that simply by doing a thing enough times, they will become proficient and progress.

For example, let's imagine you want to get good at swimming. If you're like most people, you'll get some guidance from someone who already knows how to swim. Then you'll start swimming. You'll swim more and more, hoping to increase your stamina and speed. You'll just keep getting in the pool over and over and trying to improve. You imagine that time in the pool is the secret to becoming a better swimmer.

This, it turns out, is one of the least effective ways to master a skill. Repetition rarely leads to high performance. And that's why it's important to understand "progressive mastery."

These are the steps to progressive mastery:

1. Determine a skill that you want to master.

2. Set specific stretch goals on your path to developing that skill.

3. Attach high levels of emotion and meaning to your journey and your results.

4. Identify the factors critical to success, and develop your strengths in those areas (and fix your weaknesses with equal fervor).

5. Develop visualizations that clearly imagine what success and failure look like.

6. Schedule challenging practices developed by experts or through careful thought.

7. Measure your progress and get outside feedback.

8. Socialize your learning and efforts by practicing or competing with others.

9. Continue setting higher-level goals so that you keep improving.

10. Teach others what you are learning.

These ten principles of progressive mastery are a more nuanced version of what is often called *deliberate practice*, a term coined by

Anders Ericsson.[40] Like deliberate practice, progressive mastery involves getting a coach, challenging yourself beyond your comfort zones, developing mental representations of what success should be, tracking your progress, and fixing your weaknesses.

The difference is that progressive mastery places a high emphasis on *emotion, socialization,* and *teaching.* In other words, you are more strategic and disciplined in how you attach emotion to your journey, enhance your capabilities by training or competing with others, and leverage the extraordinary power of teaching to discover greater insights into your own craft. I find it a more humanistic, social, and enjoyable approach to mastering a skill.

Let's see how these principles will make you a better swimmer much more quickly than mere repetition ever could. Instead of just jumping into the pool once in a while and trying to get better, what if you tried this:

1. You determined that you specifically wanted to develop your skill as a freestyle swimmer. (You decided you weren't going to mess with the backstroke, breaststroke, or butterfly.)

2. You set goals for how fast and efficiently you entered the water, swam a lap, executed a turn, finished your last ten meters.

3. Before every practice, you reminded yourself why it was so important for you to get better at this, and you talked about your goals with someone who cared about your performance. Maybe your why is to get fitter, win a swim meet, or lap your best friend a few times.

4. You determined that a critical factor to success was your ability to work your hips efficiently in the water and that your major weakness was a lack of finishing stamina.

5. Every night, you visualized the perfect race, imagining in detail how you would move through the water, kick off the turn, power through fatigue, go for it in the last few strokes.

6. You worked with an expert swim coach who could give you regular feedback and who helped you design harder and harder practices to reach higher and higher goals.

7. You measured your progress in a journal every time you swam, and reviewed the journal, looking for insights on your performance.

8. You consistently swam with people you really enjoyed swimming with, and you entered competitions so that you could face better swimmers than you.

9. After every swim session, you set higher goals for the next session.

10. Once per week, you formally mentored another swimmer on your team or taught a swim class at the local community center.

Can you see how this approach would lead to much better results than just hopping into a pool and trying to get better? Even if you spent exactly the same number of hours in the pool, these principles would help you outperform mindless repetition.

This is the same approach I devised for myself when I decided I wanted to become a master-level public speaker. I thought, *Well, I can just start trying to give more speeches and hope I get better, or I can approach the process with real emotion and excellence.* Choosing to focus on progressive mastery is one of the greatest decisions of my life.

I simply followed the ten steps you see above. The most effective principles for me were 2, 3, and 10. I set a goal to use fewer and fewer notes every time I gave a speech. For example, when I gave my first speech in college, I had the entire thing written out and I basically read it. The next time I gave a speech, I pared the notes down to one page. Then half a page of bullets. Then just five bullets of sentences. Then just five words on a notecard. By the time I finished college, I was giving full presentations without any notes. That was setting "specific stretch goals on your path to developing the skill."

This doesn't mean I was a marvel. The first time I was ever paid to speak—at a sorority, on the topic of relationships—I threw up just before. But I suppose that's because I cared enough to worry about how well I would do. That means I allowed myself to attach "high levels of emotion and meaning" to my journey and results. When I messed up, I allowed myself to get energized and mad at myself, without becoming discouraged. I kept reminding myself how important it was to improve so that I could inspire people with my words. I watched such great orators as Martin Luther King, Jr., John F. Kennedy, and Winston Churchill, and read hundreds of transcripts from what many consider the greatest speeches in history.[41]

Principle 10, "teach others what you are learning," was also a huge factor in my development. In graduate school, I was fortunate to teach a public speaking course for two semesters. Looking back now, I had no idea what I was doing as a teacher. But every day, I faced the task with an earnest devotion to helping my students become better communicators. I shared with them what I learned. But the reality is, they taught me more than I ever taught them. In teaching others, I felt their pain and rejoiced in their breakthroughs. By watching them, I learned what I call *vicarious distinctions*, which helped me improve my own skills.

With the full ten-step progressive mastery habit in place, everything changed for me. In just a few years, I went from a kid terrified of public speaking to a confident orator addressing audiences without notes. I teach four- and five-day seminars with thousands of attendees where I'm often the only trainer on stage for eight to ten hours per day. I've been blessed to share the stage with many of my heroes and with leaders and luminaries from dozens of fields in arenas full of tens of thousands of people. Though I was once painfully awkward in front of the camera, I've faced that dark lens without hesitation over and over again since, filming more than a dozen online courses and untold numbers of videos. I'm still a long way from where I want to be. I have much to learn, and I love this process of challenging myself to new levels, even though it means taking a hard look at all the places I fall short. But because of progressive mastery, I am no longer scared or an amateur. Had I just "tried" to be a better speaker, without a disciplined approach, I would never have excelled and been so blessed to reach so many people.

I've used progressive mastery techniques to help Olympians improve their times, NBA stars hit more jump shots, CEOs set better strategy, and parents organize their schedules more efficiently. There's nothing in your life you can't improve through practicing progressive mastery.

You certainly don't have to take on every new skill with such a strategic and disciplined approach. Sometimes, it's difficult to find a coach or mentor who can give you the feedback you need. Perhaps you don't have a lot of opportunities to teach others what you're learning. It's hard sometimes to keep pushing yourself out of your comfort zones and working so hard to improve.

But what if? What if you brought a more thoughtful structure to your next efforts in developing skill? What if you could become world-class in your primary field of interest? What if you could create more prolific quality output because you honed your skills? What if you powered through your five moves faster because you were competent and capable? What if, today, right here, you decided to seek that next level of momentum and mastery in your life?

ONLY ONE RIDE

"Only put off until tomorrow what you are willing to die having left undone."

—Pablo Picasso

Life is short. We're only allotted so much time to make our mark. I say that's all the more reason to get focused. Stop producing outputs that don't make your soul sing. Avoid trying to be effective or efficient doing things that you're not proud of and make no impact. Determine what outputs really matter to you at this stage in your life, chart your five moves to accomplish your big dreams, and go make it happen while getting insanely good at what you do. From there, the world is yours.

INFLUENCE

"Power is of two kinds: One is obtained by the fear of punishment and the other by acts of love."

—Mahatma Gandhi

TEACH PEOPLE HOW TO THINK

CHALLENGE PEOPLE TO GROW

ROLE MODEL THE WAY

The CEO is in crisis.

Juan's global apparel company has just had its seventh straight quarter of weak performance. Sales continue to plummet, and after a decade of seeing strong performance, analysts are beginning to question both Juan's leadership and his brand's relevance.

This is nearly all the information I know as I board his corporate jet on a hot August afternoon. His CFO, Aaron, is an old friend of mine and has asked me to fly cross-country with them and perhaps give them some perspective. The two of them are on their way out to an all-hands meeting with their top forty senior leaders from around the world.

After a few pleasantries, I ask Juan what he thinks is the core problem at his company.

"*She* is," he says, pointing to a page in a fashion magazine. A woman's photo takes up the entire page. "Daniela. She's the real problem."

Daniela is the company's new chief designer. She was poached from another fashion house, where her youthful edge grabbed the immediate attention of the press. Within months of her arrival, Juan tells me, they were butting heads. He wants his line to continue with his core designs and staples. She wants to push the brand into the future—an edgier seasonal approach. Now the entire team has split down the middle, taking sides. Without the full company backing the new lines, infighting and blame have swept through the culture. Projects stalled. Marketing failed. Revenues tanked.

As Juan describes all this to me, his disdain for Daniela is palpable. It seethes into his tone with me. "She's your age," he says with a hint of condescension, "so I'm hoping you can help me figure out how to handle her."

"I doubt it's about age, Juan," I reply calmly. "It's about influence strategy. And it probably begins with something the legendary basketball coach John Wooden said: 'You handle things. You collaborate with people.'"

The quote falls on deaf ears, and Juan launches into his ideas to minimize Daniela's influence in the company. He wants to slash her budget and shuffle team members so he can keep better tabs on her. He wants to start a new business unit that focuses exclusively on what he wants. He wants to limit the number of buyers who see her line. It takes him twenty minutes to describe these strategies, and his passion hasn't subsided a bit by the time he asks me, "What else do you think I could do?"

This is not a position I enjoy being in, though I often find myself here. Leaders blaming their people for poor performance, seeking control through internal politics and individual demoralization. It's not a game I'm interested in, and if I weren't stuck in a plane forty thousand feet in the air, I would simply excuse myself.

Aaron senses my disconnection and says, "Brendon, I asked you here to give Juan some perspective. He knows you have no skin in the game, and despite his passionate feelings, I assure you he's open to your coaching. I say just give it to him straight." He looks at Juan for verification.

Juan says, "Don't be shy."

"Thanks, Aaron," I say. "Well, Juan, it seems you have a strong point of view on this one. It's hard to give feedback without knowing your endgame or what Daniela is thinking. Am I correct in surmising that you want Daniela to fight you until you're both bleeding and she quits in a massive media storm that will tarnish your brand forever?"

Aaron, surprised, sits back in his chair and laughs uncomfortably. Juan remains stoic and replies, "Not exactly what I'm after, no."

I laugh along. "So you're not trying to get her to quit?"

"No," he says, shaking his head. "I'd probably lose half the team with her."

"Okay. Then what do you want?"

"I want her to play nicer."

"You mean agree with you and execute your plan?"

Juan thinks for a moment, looks to Aaron, and shrugs. "Is that such a bad thing?" It feels a little smug.

I look to make sure he's serious, and he is. This guy is cast in the old command-and-control mold. I reply, "For Daniela, yes, I'm sure it's a bad thing. I don't know her, but no one wants to work with a boss who can't see beyond himself. If your only goal for her is to play along with *you*, then there's nothing in it for her. Don't you want something good for *her*? I mean, why did you hire her in the first place? She must have had some qualities or vision you admired. What did you promise her that persuaded her to take the job?"

Juan struggles with the questions as if searching for a long-forgotten memory. In the heat of battle, we often forget the promises we broke that drew the other side's guns.

He recounts that he hired Daniela because she was a fine artist and good with people—a rare combination, he says. "And I promised her a platform for growth with our brand. Of course I wanted her to do well and wanted to give her opportunities. But she took advantage of those things and started making this company about *her* vision instead of mine."

Aaron jumps in. "So now, you see, we're stuck."

"No one is ever stuck," I say. "They've just lost perspective."

Juan asks, "So what's the perspective we're missing? We all know what Daniela wants."

"And what's that?"

"To take over the company."

"And you're sure about that?"

"She hasn't said it, but, sure, I think that's what's happening."

"Well, I can't question you on that assumption because I don't have a full view into this. And I can't ask her because she's not here. So let's assume it's true. If we know your perspective and we know hers, then I suppose all we've lost is perspective on what makes influence actually happen."

"And what's that?" Aaron asks.

"Raising ambition. The only way to influence another person is to first relate with them and then help raise their ambition to think better, do better, or give more. The first part happens when you ask rather than accuse. The second happens when you work to shape their thoughts and challenge them to rise. The problem I see is, you know Daniela's ambition and, instead of trying to help her rise to it, you're blocking her."

Juan shakes his head in astonishment and leans into the table. "Are you *kidding* me? You're telling me to give her the company?"

"Not at all. I'm saying you can't influence a person in any useful way by diminishing them or putting out the fire in their belly. People only like to work with leaders who make them think bigger and grow more. If you want to influence Daniela, you'll have to reconnect with her and surprise her by helping her think even bigger. Then you'll surprise her even more by challenging her to rise and meet a higher ambition with you. That ambition might not be to have her take the company over, but I doubt that's what she wants as much as what you fear. Regardless, the two of you need a new ambition to work toward. No new ambition together, same old problems."

Juan shakes his head. "So what, then? We need a new company vision?"

"No. You need a new vision for how to influence Daniela. If you influence her well, she'll be on your team and you'll achieve great things. If you fail, then, as you said, she'll take your team."

"So how do I do that?"

I can tell that Juan is frustrated, so I challenge him further. "I just told you. Help her think bigger. Issue a challenge to do something great together."

He crosses his arms. "I don't get it."

I cross mine. "No, you probably do get it. You just don't *like* it. I'm suggesting something simple here. I'm doing the same thing to you that you should do to her: I'm asking you to think differently, and challenging you to engage her differently. Think about her as a collaborator again. Help her think bigger about her role, her team, the company. That gets you influence. Challenge her to be even better than she is, doing what she loves. That gets you influence. Raise her bar; don't block her. That gets you influence. And it sounds like that's something you don't have with her now."

"Okay. So what's the point of all this? What do you propose I do with all that influence?"

I decide to take a risk and follow my own advice. I know that one thing all leaders share is that they love a challenge. And deep down, they want to be role models.

So I lay it on the line: "Juan, you be a better leader to her and the team than you were the first time around."

He sits back in his chair and uncrosses his arms.

For the first time since we met, he smiles and agrees.

#

After this exchange with Juan, I pulled out my journal and drew a model for influence, which you will learn in this chapter. I'll tell you the end of the story once you know the model. Sometimes, all we need is a new set of practices for developing influence, and everything can change.

But how do we get to the core of what influence really is? To measure influence, we ask people to score themselves on statements such as:

- I'm good at earning people's trust and building camaraderie.

- I have the influence needed to achieve my goals.

- I'm good at persuading people to do things.

And we reverse score on questions like these:

- I often say inappropriate things that hurt my relationships.

- I struggle to get people to listen to me or do things I ask.

- I don't have a lot of empathy for other people.

As you might imagine, people who strongly agree with the first set of statements, and strongly disagree with the second set, have higher influence scores and better overall high performance scores.

So what affects your influence scores on the HPI the most? Let's start with what *doesn't*. A sense of giving doesn't appear to affect influence scores. Though we all think that more giving people would have higher influence scores, that's not the case. For example, people who rate themselves high on "I am more giving than my peers" are not any more likely to actually have or report having great amounts of influence.[1] This is frustrating but common sense, too; we all know someone who gives and gives and gives but can't rally others around them to help out. There is nuance to this. Influence is strongly correlated with feeling like you're making a difference.[2] So it's not about feeling like you are giving more than others; it's about feeling like your efforts are making an impact. In coaching sessions, it's clear that those who feel like they give all the time but don't make a difference or receive reciprocation can end up feeling unappreciated, unhappy, and, yes, lacking real influence in the world.

Creativity is also not strongly correlated with influence.[3] Though we live in a culture obsessed with creativity and individual displays of creative work and art, respondents who identified with being creative in our studies didn't necessarily feel any more influential than others. Creative talent doesn't always come with people skills.

What does matter, just as in other HPI categories, is your perception of *yourself*. If you believe that your peers view you as a successful, high performing person, naturally you believe yourself to be more influential. But it's not just about perception. It's common sense and our coaching clients tell us it again and again: More influence really does equal a better life. When you have more influence, your kids listen to you more. You resolve conflicts faster. You get the projects you ask or fight for. You can get more buy-in on your ideas. You make more sales. You lead better. You're more likely to become a CEO, senior executive, or successfully self-employed.[4] Your self-confidence goes up and so does your performance.

Here is where a lot of people ruin their chances at doing just that. They say things like "Well, I'm not an extrovert, so I can't be influential," or "I'm not a good people person," or "I don't like trying to persuade people." Somehow, these people believe that personality has a connection to influence. But that's just not true. A comprehensive meta-analysis on social skills found that personality does not correlate with "political skill," which is how researchers often refer to influence or your ability to understand others and get them to act toward objectives. This skill predicts how well you do on tasks, your belief in yourself to do a good job (self-efficacy), and how positively others view you. It also lowers stress and increases the odds that you'll be promoted and experience greater overall career success. More than anything else, having this skill leads to a positive personal reputation, and that further enhances your ability to influence others.[5]

Couple these career outcomes with a proven increase in your overall life happiness, and it's no wonder I often tell people one of the primary skills they must master in life is influence.

INFLUENCE BASICS

"We're not who we say we are, we're not who we want to be. We are the sum of the influence and impact that we have, in our lives, on others."

—Carl Sagan

Most of the other high performance habits are under your direct personal control. You choose to seek clarity. The level of energy you feel is largely under your command. How prolific you are with productive output is up to you. But what about influence?

To keep a broad perspective on this topic, at least for the next several pages, let's define "having influence" as the ability to shape other people's beliefs and behaviors as you desire. It means you can get people to believe in you or your ideas, buy from you, follow you, or take actions that you request of them.

Of course, influence is a two-way street. But more and more, researchers are coming to understand just how much control you have over others' perceptions of you and, ultimately, how much influence you have with them. It turns out that no matter your personality, you can develop more influence in the world than you probably imagine.

Ask (No, Really, Just Ask)

One reason people struggle to gain influence in their personal and professional lives is that they simply don't ask for what they want. This is, in part, because people drastically *underestimate* the willingness of others to engage and help. Several replicated studies show that people tend to say yes over *three times* as often as people thought they would.[6] This means that people are terrible at predicting whether someone will agree to any given request. Another reason people fail to ask is because they think the other person will judge them harshly. But it turns out that here, too, people are lousy fortune-tellers. Studies show that people *overestimate* how often or to what degree others will judge them.[7]

You can't possibly know whether you have influence with your coworkers unless you ask them to do something. The same goes for your spouse, neighbors, or boss. This is why the kitchen table wisdom of "you never know until you ask" is so valid. It's biblical, too: *Ask and you shall receive.* Part of gaining influence is simply learning to make a lot of requests and getting better at making those requests (which comes only with practice). Lots of people dream of having influence, but they never wield the most fundamental tool in creating it: asking.

Underperformers fail to ask all the time. They let fear of judgment or rejection prevent them from speaking up, asking for help, trying to lead. And the sad thing is, they're usually wrong.

Throughout my career, I've been blessed to advise a lot of people in the media. You'd be surprised how sensitive they get. All those years in the spotlight often blind them with fears about what others think. Then, when they leave a show or try to do a business deal on the side, they struggle to ask for what they really want. I often have to share some tough love with them: "I understand you worry what others think. But if no one has ever said it to you, here you go: Most people aren't thinking about you at all. And even when you put yourself in front of them to make a request and they say no, within minutes they're right back to not thinking about you. They're not sitting there judging you; they're too busy dealing with their own life. So you might as well get on with it and ask. Otherwise, you've set aside your dreams for judgments that probably don't even exist."

I also share this research fact with them: If someone does say yes to helping you, they tend to like you even *more* after they've done something for you.[8] People don't grudgingly help you. If they didn't want to, they'd probably say no. It's counterintuitive, but if getting people to like you *more* is the goal, then just ask them to do you a favor.

Finally, when you do ask for what you want in life, don't just ask *once* and quit. Research shows that influencers understand the power of repetition, so they try multiple times to get their ideas in front of those they hope to influence.[9] The more you ask and share your ideas, the more people become familiar and comfortable with your requests, and the more they start to like the idea.

Asking isn't just about making requests to get what *you want*. If you seek greater influence with other people, learn to ask them a tremendous number of questions that elicit what *they* think, feel, want, need, and aspire to. Great leaders ask a lot of questions. Remember, *people support what they create*. When people get to contribute ideas, they have mental skin in the game. They want to back the ideas they helped shape. They feel that they're part of the process, not a cog or some faceless minion. It's universally agreed that leaders who ask questions and get those around them to brainstorm the path ahead are more effective than "dictator" leaders who just push their demands and requests on others.[10]

This same principle works in your intimate relationship, your parenting style, your community involvement. Ask people what they want, how they'd like to work together, and what outcomes they care about. Suddenly, you'll start seeing more engagement, and you'll have more influence.

If you want more influence, remember: Ask and ask often.

Give and You Shall Receive

In all the asking, don't forget to *give*. In just about any area of endeavor, giving to others with no expectation of return increases your overall success.[11] And, of course, it increases the likelihood that you'll get what you want. Researchers have long known that often you can *double* your ability to influence others by giving before you ask for something.[12]

High performers have a giving mindset. They enter almost every situation looking for ways to help others. They carefully consider the problems people face, and offer suggestions, resources, and connections. They don't have to be prodded to do this. They're proactive in seeking to give *something* to others, whether in meetings at work or while visiting in someone's home.

In organizational settings, often the greatest thing you can give to others is trust, autonomy, and decision-making authority. Researchers call this giving someone "authorship," meaning they get to choose what to work on or how to get things done.[13]

New achievers often worry about the specter of "giving burnout" —giving so much that it becomes stressful or exhausting. But that's just not a problem. Burnout is more an issue of poor energy management and low clarity than of overgiving.

All this sounds great, but often people *don't* view situations with a helpfulness bias. It's not because they're bad people; it's likely because they fear they're already teetering on burnout. You give less when you're tired or stressed. That's why it's important to master the habits on energy and productivity. People who score high in those categories tend to have more influence. It makes sense, right? If you're more energized and on the path toward accomplishing your goals, you're probably more willing to help others.

Be a Champion of People

According to the American Psychological Association's 2016 Work and Well-Being Survey, only about *half* of employed adults in the United States feel valued by their employer and sufficiently rewarded and recognized for their efforts. While most employees (68 percent) are satisfied with their work, half don't feel sufficiently involved in decision making, problem solving, and goal setting, and only 46 percent participate regularly in those activities.[14]

Imagine walking into a company and discovering that fully half the employees don't feel rewarded, recognized, or involved. Think of all the consequences of that: less motivation, lower morale, poorer performance, higher churn, more complaining at the water cooler, and more resistance in meetings.

The good news is that it's easy to change this situation simply by demonstrating sincere appreciation for those you seek to influence. Since so many people feel ostracized, unappreciated, or undervalued, when you show up and give genuine praise, respect, and appreciation, you stand out. Be grateful for people. Just by offering gratitude, you can more than double the likelihood that those receiving your appreciation will help you again in the future.[15] Give thanks in meetings; write thank-you notes; spend more time noticing positive actions by your people. If you're the one who appreciates people the most, you're the most appreciated.

Appreciating people is one step. The next is to become their champion. Find out what your people are passionate about, and cheer on their good ideas. Be excited for people when they do a good job, and publicly praise them. The ultimate measure of whether you really support someone is to trust them, give them the autonomy to make important decisions, and praise them in public when they do well. That's how people know they are truly cheered on.

Perhaps all this sounds too basic, but every leader I've ever worked with has acknowledged they needed to do a better job of expressing appreciation and giving people more trust, autonomy, and praise. In fact, I've never met anyone, myself included, who couldn't do a better job in these areas. And that's why I know that anyone, including you, can gain greater influence.

These ideas are the low-hanging fruit of gaining influence. Now we'll focus on the more advanced strategies.

THE DIFFERENCE MAKERS

"Blessed is the influence of one true,
loving human soul on another."

—George Eliot

Can you name the two people who positively influenced you the *most* in your life? Take a moment now to think about those two people, and answer the following:

- What, specifically, made each person so influential to you?

- What was the greatest lesson each person taught you about life?

- What values or traits did they inspire you to embody in your own life?

I've asked these questions to audiences from around the globe. People may name family members, teachers, close friends, first employers, or mentors. You can never guess *who* someone will say was the most influential. But I've found that you can predict *why* those people were the most influential.

Typically, those who positively influence people the most have something in common. They exert an effect on us, deliberately or not, by executing one or more of three influence actions. First, they shape how we *think*. By their example, lessons they impart, or things they say to us, they open our eyes and make us think differently about ourselves, others, or the world. Second, they *challenge* us in some way. They call us out on our stuff, or they raise our ambitions to be better in our personal life, relationships, and contributions to the world. Third, they serve as *role models*. Their character, how they interact with us and others, or how they met the challenges of life inspires us.

Now think again of the three people who most positively influenced you. Can one or a combination of these influence actions explain their impact on you? If they taught you to be a better person, it probably happened because of a combination of all three, even if perhaps in subtle or unexpected ways.

I call these three influence actions the Ultimate Influence Model. I've taught CEOs to use the model as an outline for crafting their speeches to their employees at all-hands meetings. I've seen wives sit down with their husbands and talk about how to use it to influence their teenagers. Members of the military have used it to understand how their enemy was influencing local resistance forces. Entrepreneurs have used it to structure their sales presentations and marketing materials.

The rest of this chapter will show you how to use the model by giving you three new practices. I'll also share how others have shaped my life with these practices. My hope is that one day someone adds *your* name to their list of those who most positively affected them. In the end, *that* is the ultimate influence we all hope for.

Ultimate Influence Model

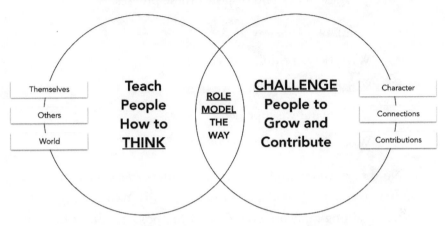

The Ultimate Influence Model© 2007, Brendon Burchard. Originally published in the online course titled the High Performance Master's Program. If you would like a downloadable thinking tool to help you journal, just visit HighPerformanceHabits.com/tools.

To gain influence with others, (1) teach them how to think about themselves, others, and the world; (2) challenge them to develop their character, connections, and contributions; and (3) role model the values you wish to see them embody.

PRACTICE ONE

TEACH PEOPLE HOW TO THINK

"He who influences the thought of his times
influences the times that follow."

—Elbert Hubbard

I want to give you some day-to-day examples of how you start gaining influence in people's lives, because I don't want you stuck in an abstract conceptual model. Framing how others should think is what we all do in real life, usually without realizing it. Consider how many times you've said or heard these phrases:

- "Think of it this way . . ."
- "What do you think about . . ."
- "What would happen if we tried . . ."
- "How should we approach . . ."
- "What should we be paying attention to . . ."

No doubt, you've said one of these things to someone recently. You were trying to elicit an idea or guide their thinking. In doing so, you were gaining influence even though you probably didn't know it.

My goal is simply to have you start doing this more deliberately. When it becomes a habit, you'll notice how good at it you've become and how much your influence with others has grown.

Imagine you have an eight-year-old child. She's doing homework at the kitchen table. She's getting frustrated and says, "I hate homework." How do you respond?

While there's no universal rule, no "right" or "wrong" approach, what if you thought of talking to her—not to get her to do her tasks, but to shape the way she *thinks* about homework? When people complain, be they children or our peers at work, we have an extraordinary opportunity to direct their thinking. What if you shared with your child how you used to think about homework, and how a simple change in the way you thought about it helped you do better in school and even enjoy the process? What if you asked her what she thought of *herself* while doing the work, and helped her reframe her identity? What if you brought in how to think of her teachers and peers? What do you think might happen if you spoke with her about how the world perceives people who follow through?

When I work with leaders, I'm consistently telling them they should *always* communicate how their people should be thinking about themselves as individual contributors, about their competitors, and about the overall marketplace. I mean that literally—in every e-mail to the full team, in every all-hands meeting, in every investor call, in every media appearance. In the all-hands meeting: "This is how we should be thinking about ourselves if we're going to win. If we're going to compete, this is how we should be thinking about our competitors. If we're going to change the world, this is how we should be thinking about the world and the future."

Take a few moments now and think of someone you want to influence. How can you shape their thinking? Begin by identifying how you want to influence them. What do you want them to do? Then know your responses to these questions before you meet with that person:

- How do you want them to think about themselves?

- How do you want them to think about other people?

- How do you want them to think about the world at large?

Remember, there are three things you want your people thinking about: themselves, other people, and the greater world (meaning, how the world works, what it needs, where it's headed, and how certain actions might affect it).

LEARNING HOW TO THINK

"The words that a father speaks to his children in the privacy of home are not heard by the world, but, as in whispering galleries, they are clearly heard at the end, and by posterity."

—Jean Paul Richter

In interviews, I'm often asked about the influences in my life. Who shaped my perceptions of myself, others, and the world at large? That answer begins with my parents.

I remember countless events in which my parents taught me how to think. When I was five or six, we were living in Butte, Montana. One winter, the heater broke. In some places, that's an inconvenience. In Butte, where winter temperatures regularly dip below minus twenty degrees, it's a dire situation. The challenge was that we couldn't afford to fix the heater. Though Dad and Mom worked hard to care for us four kids, we were living paycheck to paycheck. It would be at least a week until my dad got paid and we had enough money to fix the heater.

Looking back, the situation could have been terribly stressful for us kids, let alone for our parents. But they were resourceful people, and they both sought to bring joy into everyday life. So instead of panicking, my mom went into the garage, found our camping tent, and set it up in the living room. She threw in our sleeping bags and coats and electric blankets. We kids, oblivious of the dire situation, just thought we were camping. We'd walk to school and ask the other kids, "Where did you sleep last night?" When they said in their bedrooms, we'd brag that we were camping out in our living room. My parents made a difficult situation fun. Turning adversity into a good time is one of life's highest arts, and Mom and Dad were good at it.

Through all the challenges my parents faced raising us kids, they taught us to be self-reliant. That's how they wanted us to think of ourselves: that no matter the situation, we could handle it and make the best of it. Throughout life, Mom was always telling me that I was smart and I was loved, and that I should care for my brothers and sister because we were all we had. Dad was always telling me, "Be yourself." "Be honest." "Do your best." "Take care of your family." "Treat people with respect." "Be a good citizen." "Follow your dreams."

By guiding my childhood with directives such as these, my dad and mom taught me how to think of myself.

They taught us how to think of other people, too, by the way they treated others: with compassion. When I was in middle school, Dad ran the local Department of Motor Vehicles (DMV) office. His team's job was to give qualified people their driver's licenses. The operative word in that sentence is *qualified*. A lot of people couldn't pass the written test, or their vision was too poor, or they couldn't park a car or remember to stop at a red light. Others just forgot to bring their ID or Social Security card. What most had in common, though, was their reaction to being told they wouldn't get their driver's license that day. They were *irate*.

What often makes people's DMV experience worse is that the department is terribly underfunded. That's why you often have to wait in long lines, deal with old technology, or feel confused about what you're supposed to do. The DMV employees, who don't receive great pay and have to deal with unhappy people all day, are hampered by endless red tape and bureaucracy. They're doing the best they can. At least, my dad was.

I have a lot of memories of accompanying my father to work. He was a genuinely happy and thoughtful man. He had served twenty years in the United States Marine Corps. After retiring from the Marines, he worked three jobs, all the while going to night school to get his college degree. He and Mom had very little growing up, and very little as they worked hard to raise us four kids.

I had great respect for my dad, so you can imagine how it felt watching person after person literally scream at him because they forgot their paperwork or failed a test. I heard people insult his intelligence, his team, his office, his face, his very existence. I saw people fling their test papers at him. People spat at him.

As people belittled or blamed my father, I always wanted to tell them, "Don't you know how hard he works? Don't you know he's doing the best he can given the rules set by the state? Don't you know he served twenty years and got all shot up to protect your freedoms? Don't you know he's in a lot of pain? Don't you know he's my dad? My hero?"

I watched people treat my dad terribly. But I also watched his responses. He rarely let them throw him off. He would handle conflict situations at work with grace and aplomb. He would try to make people smile or laugh. He always had a good joke, and he always tried to be helpful. He would patiently guide people through their paperwork or exams even when they were negative. He would pat his team members on the back and whisper words of encouragement to them after someone at the counter was rude. Most nights, Dad came home calm and cool. Other times, you could sense all that confrontation bottled up within him. On rare occasions, it spilled out toward us. But for the most part, especially in his later years, it was as if Dad left the stress at work, and at home he would just chill on the couch and read his paper, go golfing, take me to play racquetball, or take care of the yard. He became more and more of a peaceful warrior.

As a kid, I didn't understand how hard it must have been to keep his composure at work. Looking back, I'm in awe that the old gunnery sergeant never reached across the counter and throttled someone.

As many times as I saw him treated poorly at work, many more were the times he came home and described how someone was kind enough to bring in some cookies to thank his team. He told me he didn't overreact because he understood that most people were good and caring; it was just that when they were in a hurry they could be oblivious, dismissive, or rude. He always gave people the benefit of the doubt. To Dad, everyone was like a neighbor, and he wanted to help them.

That's how Dad taught me to think of other people: as neighbors whom I should always give the benefit of the doubt and be helpful toward. And when hurry or disappointment soured their attitude, I should meet them with patience and humor.

My mother, too, is remarkable. She was born in Vietnam to a French father and a Vietnamese mother. Her dad was killed in the French-Vietnamese conflict long before my father, her future husband, ever served in the US-Vietnam war. After her dad died, Mom was sent to France under the Children of War program. She was separated from her brother and sent to live in abusive boarding schools. When she turned twenty-one, she immigrated to the United States. Eventually, she met my father in a Washington, DC, apartment building where they both lived. They fell in love and soon moved to Montana—where my dad had grown up—to raise us kids.

There's no doubt what drew my dad to my mom: She is the most joyous and energized person you could meet.

After they were married and had moved to Montana, Dad worked the DMV while Mom kept various part-time jobs—cutting hair, working at a nursing home—to support our growing family. By the time I was in middle school, Mom was working as a nurse's aide at a local hospital. Many of my teenage memories revolve around seeing my mother crying on the couch at nights while my dad tried to comfort her. The women at the hospital were mean to her. She had an accent. She wasn't "from here." With English as her third language, she struggled with the medical terms and pronunciations, and her coworkers belittled her and held her back because of it. Sometimes, in a small town, being from another place is hard.

Still, Mom kept a good attitude and expected us kids to treat everyone with compassion—even the mean people. Like Dad, she always gave them the benefit of the doubt. She would remind us that people were doing the best they could and often just needed our help. Many of my childhood memories of my mom involve her baking food for people or delivering them groceries or gifts. Other people, she said, needed our attention and generosity.

To this day, my mom is one of the most positive, giving, loving people you could ever meet. At my seminars, she is often helping out on my team, though attendees don't know she's my mom. She'll help check in and serve thousands of people. Often, on the last day of the event, I'll bring Mom onstage to thank her. When she walks out and people realize she's been one of the crew all weekend, I can tell that some are thinking, *How wonderful!* and others are thinking, *Uh-oh, I would have been nicer to her had I known.* Regardless, they always give her a standing ovation. Seeing my mom, who put up with so much in life, receive a standing ovation from thousands of people is a feeling I can't put into words.

Watching and listening to my parents, I learned how to think of other people. Mom and Dad didn't teach me that other people were mean or bad. Instead, they trusted in the goodness of others in general, and showed me that with patience, grace, and humor, people could open up, change, and be friendly.

More than anything, my parents gave me the gift of how to think of the world in positive terms. They were always grateful for what the world gave them, and excited about the possibilities for tomorrow. This doesn't mean they had big dreams or grandiose plans. They were simple, kind people who just believed that with hard work, the world will give you a fair shake. They showed me that life is what you make of it, and that it's here to be enjoyed. I can't imagine my life without these lessons.

We all have stories of people who influenced us to think better or bigger. Perhaps these stories will bring to mind stories of your own about who influenced you, and how you might teach your family or team to think.

Performance Prompts

1. Someone in my life I would like to influence more is . . .

2. The way I would like to influence them is . . .

3. If I could tell them how they should think of themselves, I would say . . .

4. If I could tell them how they should think of other people, I would say . . .

5. If I could tell them how they should think of the world in general, I would say . . .

PRACTICE TWO

CHALLENGE PEOPLE TO GROW

"The most important thing is to try and inspire people so that they can be great in whatever they want to do."

—Kobe Bryant

High performers challenge the people around them to rise to higher levels of performance themselves. If you could follow them around as they lead their lives, you would see that they consistently challenge others to raise the bar. They push people to get better, and they don't apologize for it.

This is perhaps the most difficult practice in this entire book to implement. People are afraid to challenge others. It sounds confrontational. It sounds as though it might make people push back, feel inadequate, or ask, "Who the hell do you think you are?"

But this isn't about confrontation. It's about issuing subtle or direct *positively framed challenges* to motivate others to excel.

As with any communication strategy, intent and tone really matter. If your intent is to diminish others, then your challenges will likely influence people in negative ways. Look for a similar result if you sound condescending. But if your intentions are clearly to help someone grow and become better, and you speak to them with respect and honor, then your challenges will inspire better action.

There is no doubt that regardless of how well you communicate, some people may not like it when you start pushing them to grow and contribute. That's a price you must be willing to pay to effect change and gain real influence in life. You have to be willing to challenge your kids to develop character, to treat others better, to contribute. The same goes for the rest of your family, your coworkers, and anyone else you serve and lead.

We are in a precarious time in history, when people are shying away from setting standards with others. "Setting standards" is really just another way to say "issuing positive challenges." People think that challenging others will lead to conflict. But that's rarely true, especially when dealing with high performers—they *like it*. They're driven by it. Not only can they handle it, but if you are in a position of influence with them, they also *expect* it of you. If you feel some hesitation in doing this, let me remind you of the data: High performers *love challenge*. It's one of the most universal observations we've made in our research. Consider the following statements:

- I respond quickly to life's challenges and emergencies rather than avoiding them or delaying.

- I love trying to master new challenges.

- I'm confident I can achieve my goals despite obstacles or resistance.

People who strongly agree with these statements are almost always high performers. This means that facing challenge is a huge part of what high performers do well and want to do well. Don't deny them that by being hesitant to issue the challenge.

CHARACTER

Influencers challenge others in three realms. First, they challenge their *character*. This means they give people feedback, direction, and high expectations for living up to universal values such as honesty, integrity, responsibility, self-control, patience, hard work, and persistence.

Challenging someone's character may sound confrontational, but in practice it's a supportive, helpful gift. I'll bet someone influential in your life once told you, "You could do better," or "You're a better person than that," or "I expected more from you." These were standard setting statements that challenged your character. You may not have liked hearing them, but I'll bet they got your attention and got you to rethink your actions.

Of course, challenging someone to develop more character can happen in subtler ways, through *indirect challenge*. Asking someone, "How would your best self approach this situation?" challenges that person to be more intentional in how they behave. Other indirect challenges might sound something like:

- "Looking back, do you feel you gave it your all?"

- "Are you bringing the best of you to this situation?"

- "What values were you trying to embody when you did that?"

For leaders, I suggest the direct approach of asking people to think of how they can challenge themselves in future scenarios. Ask, "What kind of person do you want to be remembered as? What would life look like if you gave your all? Where are you making excuses, and how might life turn out differently if you showed up stronger?"

CONNECTION

The second area where you can challenge others concerns their *connections* with others—their relationships. You set expectations, ask questions, give examples, or directly ask them to improve *how they treat and add value to other people.*

What you wouldn't condone is poor social behavior. High performing leaders call out anyone who is being inappropriate, rude, or dismissive of someone else on their team. High performing parents do the same thing with their children. They just don't let bad behavior slide.

What's important to note here is that high performers are explicit in their expectations for how people should treat each other. I'm always surprised at how direct they are in telling people, over and over, how to treat one another. Even when people around them are treating one another well, they still keep pushing for them to unite even more.

If you've observed a high performing leader in a team meeting, you've probably noticed how often they suggest how the team should be working together. They say things like:

- "Listen to one another more."

- "Show each other more respect."

- "Support each other more."

- "Spend more time with each other."

- "Give each other more feedback."

The word *more* seems omnipresent when they are challenging others.

As I've taught this point around the world, I've noticed that some misconstrue this as high performers being "hard" on their teams. But that's not necessarily the case. No doubt, high performers do have high expectations for those they influence. But their challenging you to connect with others better is clearly in an effort to help bring a sense of cohesion and solidarity to those you live or work with. High performers want to help you experience greater unity with others because they know that will increase your results.

CONTRIBUTION

The third area where you can challenge others is in their *contributions*. You push them to add more value or to be more generous.

This is perhaps one of the more difficult challenges that high performers issue. It's hard to tell someone, "Hey, your contributions here at work aren't enough. You can do better." But high performers don't shrink from saying this kind of thing.

When high performers issue challenges to contribute more, usually they are not giving feedback solely on the quality of what you're delivering *now*. Rather, they challenge you to contribute more *looking ahead*—to create or innovate so that you make the future better.

In almost every in-depth interview I've done, it's clear that high performers are future oriented when challenging someone to contribute something meaningful. They don't just challenge people to make better widgets today; they challenge them to reinvent the product suite, to brainstorm entirely new business models, to find adjacent markets to go after, to push into unknown territory, to add new value.

Though I initially thought that high performers were doing this on a large scale, telling their entire team to create a bigger future, I was wrong. Instead, high performers challenge individuals specifically. They go desk to desk and challenge each person on their team.

They adjust the level of challenge they issue to *each person* they are leading. There's no one-size-fits-all approach to pushing people to contribute. That's how you know you're working with a high performing leader: They'll meet you where you are, speak your language, ask you to help move the entire team toward a better future, in your own unique way.

MY CHALLENGE TO ENDURE AND LEAD

"A teacher affects eternity."

—Henry Adams

Aside from my parents, the other great influence in my early life was Linda Ballew. Linda came into my life at a critical moment—when I was about to drop out of high school.

Not that I didn't love school. The issue was that my family had the opportunity to go and see relatives in France. Because of my parents' work schedules, the only time we could go was during the school year. Unfortunately, the timing of the trip coincided with the district's strict new absence policy, under which any student missing more than ten days of school would be expelled from school for that semester. Our trip was going to be fourteen days. If I went on the trip, I wouldn't be allowed back into school that semester. The only way to graduate with my class, then, would be to take summer school—a time when I was usually working full-time to make and save money for college. My parents and I fought with the principal and the school board to make an exception to let me go and return to class. Our argument was that for my family, this was a once-in-a-lifetime opportunity, and that we had already worked with my teachers to make up for the lost time by coming back from the trip and giving reports to my classes about my experiences.

Unfortunately, we lost the fight. If I went on the trip, I wouldn't be allowed back into school. And since work prevented me from taking summer school, I probably wouldn't be able to graduate with my friends. I was devastated.

We went on the trip anyway because, as Mark Twain said, "Never let school get in the way of an education." I wrote an editorial to the local newspaper condemning the school board and then hopped a plane to Europe. On the trip, I took a lot of photos and significant notes about the culture and places we visited. It was the greatest learning experience of my life, and the trip brought my family closer together.

As expected, when I got home from the trip, I wasn't allowed back into school. My French teacher did allow me to come in and show some of my photos and tell my class about my experiences in France. I did the same for my art class. But when the principal found out I was in the school, he had me escorted out. I was so embittered by the whole ordeal, I considered just quitting. My grand plan was to drop out of high school and start my own grounds-keeping business.

Then I met Linda Ballew. Linda was an English teacher and the journalism adviser for the school's student newspaper, the *Iniwa*. She had read my editorial in the newspaper and heard about my photos of France from the art teacher, and sought me out.

When we talked, she praised my editorial and then, practically in the same breath, told me it could have been much better. She asked how I thought through the writing process, and gave me some tips. Then she asked to see my photos from France. She praised them, too, and also told me they could be better. She had this way of praising and challenging me that just worked. I suppose you could say our relationship began through her challenging my contributions.

"None of it matters anyway," I told her, "because I'm not coming back to school." I'll never forget how she handled the situation. What she didn't do was tell me it was a dumb idea. She didn't try to convince me that the school administration was just following its policy. She didn't try to explain the value of high school. Instead, she respectfully challenged my character:

"You aren't a quitter, Brendon, and you don't want to be one. You're too strong a person to let the administration make you quit."

Linda also told me I had potential and that I should join the student newspaper when I returned to school the next semester. She just assumed that my returning and joining would be the most obvious, natural thing in the world. I told her again that I was dropping out. And then she challenged my character, connections, and contributions all in one fell swoop, saying something along the lines of . . .

"That's too bad. You could have been good. A lot of students here need someone like you—someone willing to stand up for what they believe in. You could do a lot of good at the school, and you could learn to create good art and writing here. You have too much talent and potential not to use them in a creative endeavor. Just think about that. And if you ever think it's a good idea to come back, let me know and I'll be here for you. You don't seem the type to quit anything."

I can't remember my counterargument, but I do remember how she responded to it. She listened. She accepted and honored my point of view. She formed a real connection with me and said she hoped to see me again.

The next semester, I went back.

That year, Linda took a group of students, including me, and inspired us to think, work together, and contribute in ways we never had. She led us to hope that we could become the best high school newspaper in the country, even with our few resources and limited experience. She created an expectation of excellence, not so we could win awards but so we could look in the mirror and at each other and feel a sense of pride and camaraderie for giving our best effort. She wanted us to become leaders who led with integrity.

Linda's leadership style was the embodiment of "people support what they create." Every front page, headline, photo, byline, and layout, she let *us* choose, even though she was an expert in every aspect of journalism. She showed us how to analyze our competition and strive to improve on our last issue. She guided us to come together as a team, supporting one another and building on one another's strengths. With steadfastness and compassion, she helped us become more competent and confident. In more ways than one, Linda helped us become better human beings.

Every weekend and every late night spent working to make our deadline, Linda was there. She always role modeled what she wanted us to do as journalists: ask questions. I can still hear her voice behind me as I would place a final photo or article in the layout: "Is that where you want that? Is this our final-final? Is there anything else you'd like to add?" She was always asking us more questions: how best to handle a situation, what kind of people we wanted to be, what messages we wanted to communicate to the world, how to complete our work with excellence, how we wanted to represent ourselves and our school.

That year at the national Journalism Education Association convention, our paper won "Best of Show." We were *number one* in the country. A small school from Montana, beating big schools that often had ten to twenty times our budget and resources. Under Linda Ballew's leadership, I won national and regional first- and second-place awards for photography, layout and design, newswriting, and investigative reporting. I eventually became a managing editor. After I graduated, the paper went on to another decade of top awards.

Linda Ballew ran an underfunded high school journalism program in an underfunded school district in an underfunded state. And yet, she consistently took in new classes of inexperienced students and developed them into outstanding young journalists who won the highest national and international awards. Her students' newspapers won number one rankings across almost every category awarded in high school journalism, and Linda became perhaps the most decorated high school journalism teacher in our nation's history.

What made her so remarkable? It comes down to three things: She taught us how to think. She challenged us. And she role modeled the way to influence a team to perform with excellence.

In one conversation, on that precious, pivotal day when I was about to drop out of high school, Linda Ballew changed my life forever. If not for her, you would not be reading this book.

Performance Prompts

Think about a person in your life you are trying to influence positively, and complete the following sentences:

Character

1. The person I am trying to influence has the following character strengths . . .

2. She could become a stronger person if she . . .

3. She is probably too hard on herself in this area . . .

4. If I could tell her how to improve who she is, I would tell her . . .

5. If I could inspire her to want to be a better person, I'd probably say something like . . .

Connection

1. The way I want this person to interact differently with others is to . . .

2. Often, this person doesn't connect as well with others as I would like, because he . . .

3. What would inspire this person to treat other people better is to . . .

Contribution

1. The greatest contribution this person is making is . . .

2. The areas where this person isn't contributing well enough are . . .

3. What I really want this person to contribute more of is . . .

PRACTICE THREE

ROLE MODEL THE WAY

"Example is leadership."

—Albert Schweitzer

High performers give a lot of mindshare to thinking about being a role model. Seventy-one percent say they think about it *daily*. They say they want to be a good role model for their family, the team, and the greater community.

Of course, everyone would say they want to be a role model. Who doesn't, right? But what I've found with high performers is that they think about it much more often and *specifically in relation to how they are seeking to influence others*. Meaning they aren't just seeking to be a good person in general, as you would typically think of a role model—someone who is kind, honest, hardworking, giving, loving. They go a step further and think about how to act so that others might follow them or help them achieve *a specific outcome*. It's less "I'm trying to be Mother Teresa" and more "I'm going to demonstrate a specific behavior so that others will emulate that exact behavior, which will help us move toward a specific result."

To be clear, high performers *do* want to be perceived as good people and good role models. But that just makes them human. What makes them high performers is the laser-focused intention on how they can act in a way that gets someone to improve who they are, or achieve a specific result.

To illustrate this point, let's return to the story from the opening of this chapter. Remember Juan, the apparel company CEO? He was butting heads with Daniela, his new head of design. I had challenged him to be a better leader to her and his team, and then drew out the Ultimate Influence Model. We worked through the model together, exploring how he wanted Daniela to think about her role, her team, and the company. Then we discussed what challenges he might inspire her to take on regarding who she was, how she connected with others, and what she contributed. Importantly, we also flipped the scenarios and went through the model again. In other words, I asked him to imagine that she was going through the model and had to give *him* advice on how to think and what challenges he should take on. How, in his best estimation, did she want him to think about his role, team, and company? How would she like to challenge his character, connections, and contributions? Going through the model from her perspective was difficult for him, but it opened his eyes to the idea that perhaps he was perceiving her attempts at influence as threats rather than leadership. He began to realize that she was challenging him and the status quo at the company in significant ways that might actually be helpful.

Of course, we could only speculate on her perspective. What we knew for sure was that if he wanted to change the situation, *he* must change. We had to get him into the role model mindset, which is very different from the defensive mindset.

To open that way of thinking, I asked him to tell me about the most influential people in his life. As he did, I drew out components of the UIM to show him specifically why they were so influential—how they had challenged him and taught him to think. His most influential people were his father and his first business partner. After he described them to me, I asked how he could honor their legacies by bringing their values and spirits into his organization. I said, "How can you bring what made them so amazing into your company and your own leadership style? How can you be a role model to your people the way these two were to you?"

This conversation clearly shook him. Most people don't think about that kind of thing.

Then I said, "Now let's get back to the issue at hand. Why do you think so many people in your company see Daniela as a role model?" Although he hadn't a good word to say about her only minutes earlier, he found a few points of grudging admiration. He respected how outspoken she was—even though he didn't like it—because he was never so gutsy at her age. He was impressed by how quickly she got other people on board with her vision, stealing away some of his supporters. He admired her tenacity. He believed that people saw her as a role model because she was challenging them to look forward— *more than he was.*

For a moment, I didn't know whether these efforts were working. Was he becoming embittered, or perhaps seeing things from a new perspective? So I pushed further. "Juan, I'm just wondering if you could perhaps one day be just as good a role model to her as she is being to others and as your role models were to you. What would that look like?"

That last question was when everything clicked. I literally saw the light come on for him. I can't describe it exactly, but it seemed that months of frustration lifted off him.

> **There's just something magical that happens**
> **in our life when we let all the drama go and decide**
> **to ask how we can be role models again.**

Juan realized that to be a role model in this specific situation, he must demonstrate the very thing he wanted from her: He had to lead with questions instead of take solid stances; he had to be open to everyone's thoughts; he had to let her lead. If he hoped that one day she would be open to his thoughts, he had to open himself up to hers. If he was to be respected, he had to give that same respect. The most important thing he realized, though, was that he was not embodying the values his father and his business partner had instilled in him.

"I feel like I'm being petulant, and that's not how they'd want to see me lead."

By the time we landed for their all-hands meeting, Juan had worked through the UIM several times and brainstormed some ideas with Aaron and me. But when we arrived at the meeting, unbeknownst to either of us, he had also decided to throw out the entire agenda for the meeting. Instead, he would teach his team the UIM and, along the way, create a real dialogue with the whole group—including everyone who had been in Daniela's corner. He would go on to ask them how they, as a united group, should be thinking about themselves, their competition, and the market. He challenged them to come up with plans for how they could improve individually as leaders, how they could grow as a team, and how the company could make greater contributions to the marketplace. He was enthusiastic and open, collaborative and inspirational. It wasn't fake. I could see that the entire team was surprised by how differently he was addressing them, and they were liking it.

At the end of the training, he asked Daniela, the head designer, to the front of the room. He admitted his erroneous thinking about her, the team, and the brand. He shared what challenges he felt he faced in his own character, connections, and contributions. He asked her to share her own version of the UIM, and then he sat down. She was surprised at first, and treaded carefully. But he kept cheering her on and asking her to share more. Two hours went by. All the while, he sat, listened, asked for more insight, and took notes. As she finished, he led the group in a standing ovation for her. That night at their team dinner, she toasted him with one of the most heartfelt and emotional toasts I've seen in my career.

On the flight back, Juan said something I'll remember for a long time: "What if our real ability to be truly influential is our ability to be influenced?"

Performance Prompts

1. If I were going to approach my relationships and career as an even better role model, the first things I would start doing are . . .

2. Someone who really needs me to lead and be a strong role model right now is . . .

3. Some ideas on how I can be a role model for that person are . . .

4. If, ten years from now, the five closest people to me in my life were to describe me as a role model, I would hope they said things like . . .

A BEAUTIFUL LACK OF TRICKERY

"You will get all you want in life if you help enough other people get what they want."

—Zig Ziglar

Whenever I talk about influence with others or share the UIM model, inevitably someone asks about manipulation. I suppose that's because we've all been dealt our blows from past loves, friends, and businesspeople who manipulated us in some way. We know marketers and media heads who tell us how to think, and challenge us to buy things we really can't afford. Could these ideas be used to manipulate or negatively influence others? Of course they could.

My hope is that you gained some insights into a higher level of service from this chapter. High performers just don't do manipulation. That sweet spot in the middle of the UIM—that ideal of being a role model—is just too compelling a drive. No doubt, high performers are capable of manipulating others; they just don't. How do I know? Because I've interviewed and tracked and trained and coached so many high performers in the world, and in that process I've gotten to know their teams and families and loved ones. The people around high performers don't feel manipulated. They feel trusted and respected and inspired.

Is it possible to get ahead in life by manipulating others? You betcha—for the short term. But ultimately, manipulators burn all bridges and find themselves disconnected, unsupported, alone. They find no long-term success with relationships or their own well-being. If they achieve any success, it's built on deceit and discord and poisonous energy. Of course, you may find an extreme example of some deceitful person who is an external success. But that is merely one of the rare outliers. A handful of manipulators are not the mean. What I'm trying to impress on you is this: Of those who have achieved long-term success, far more are role models than manipulators.

I share this because we live in a chaotic world, and there is plenty of dark intent. But that also gives us an opportunity to be the light. The question we all face in these turbulent times is, how diligently will we work to be the role model? How much focus and effort will we bring to our days to help others think bigger? How many bold challenges will we share to help others rise? After all our years on this planet, how well will we inspire the next generation to be role models themselves?

"There are two ways of meeting difficulties:
You alter the difficulties or you alter
yourself to meet them."

—Phyllis Bottome

HONOR THE STRUGGLE

SHARE YOUR TRUTH AND AMBITIONS

FIND SOMEONE TO FIGHT FOR

The phone wakes me. I croak a barely audible hello and look to the clock. It's 2:47 a.m.

A woman's voice says, "I need you to look at something. I'm getting a ton of hate on social. I think I'm in danger."

"*What?*" I mumble as I sit up in bed. Sandra, the woman on the phone, is one of my celebrity clients. She can be overly dramatic. "What danger? Are you okay?"

"Yes, I'm safe for now. But can you click the link I just texted you?"

I click the link and see a video of Sandra on YouTube. The title of the video is "CONFESSION." It has over 300,000 views. "One sec," I say as I fumble to pull on a shirt, then slip out of the bedroom so I don't further disturb my wife.

As I head down to the kitchen, where I can talk, she continues in a desperate tone. "Can you watch it? Can you look at the comments? Then call me back, okay?" The phone goes dead.

The video is just Sandra sitting there, talking to the camera. She begins by telling the viewer that she hasn't been honest with the world. That she's been fake. She says she's always bright and happy but that the cameras and press don't cover what's real. That she feels bad for misleading people and she wants them to know she'll be more honest about her struggles.

I immediately dislike the video. It feels disingenuous. The title feels like clickbait. She shares her tale with convincing emotion but with no details whatsoever. The impression is one of "Oh, poor celebrity, you want us to know it's hard on you," but without specifics, it falls flat. By the look of the comments, most people agree with me. A lot of people are making fun of her. Those who aren't are asking for more details. There's not a lot of sympathy—not so much because people don't care, but because the video is so vague. There's nothing to connect to.

I text Sandra. *I've watched it and read the comments. What danger are you in? Seems like people don't love it, but I'm sure you'll be fine.*

She texts back. *NO. I DON'T KNOW. LUNCH TOMORROW?*

We agree to meet for lunch, and end the conversation. I shake my head and sit down to read more comments. I'm too annoyed to go back to bed.

I start imagining the conversation at lunch tomorrow: "I thought I was being courageous like you say to be, Brendon." Then she'll remind me that I've been telling her to share her real self more often. If the past is any indication, she'll blame me or scream at me. She's one of the rare volatile clients I've ever continued working with, because I know she has a good heart.

Still, I'll have to hold back. I already know what I'll want to say. I'll praise her for posting a video, but I'll also want to say, "Sorry, Sandy, posting a video doesn't qualify as courageous."

I will have to check myself because I'll want to go on a rant about how "courage" has been inflated to a comical degree these days. I tend to get snarky about this. When someone posts their first diary-like video on social media like this, we are expected to applaud and say, "Oh, what courage!" If someone shares an idea during a brainstorm meeting, "Oh, what courage!" If a kid finishes a race, even if he comes in dead last, "Oh, what courage!"

But please. Posting a video is an act of self-expression, sure. It's also just an effort to be noticed or share a message, and just sharing a message isn't courage when everyone is doing it, right? A billion people posted something today. Does that make them all courageous? Sharing ideas during a brainstorm meeting at work is your *job*, so if you don't get a hug for your courage, be satisfied with "great idea." Does the child who got fifty-ninth place really need double high-fives for being so brave and crossing the finish line when he didn't try, whined the whole time, and didn't want to be there?

I hear myself saying these things in my mind, and I know I'm getting snippy. Yet my mind continues. When Washington crossed the ice-clogged Delaware River to attack a superior force, *that* was courage. When astronauts piloted a capsule into the great darkness between Earth and the moon, *that* was courage. When Rosa Parks refused to give up her seat and sparked the Civil Rights movement, *that* was *courage*!

Maybe this is what I need to tell Sandra: "Look, you don't need to win a revolution or start a historic social movement to be some kind of hero or martyr. But the kinds of courageous acts that you will be proud of at the end of your life are not these tiny acts of self-interested sharing. No, the kinds of courageous acts that you are proud of at the end of your life are those where you faced uncertainty and real risk, where the stakes mattered, when you did something for a cause or person beyond yourself, without any assurance of safety, reward, or success.

Oh, yes, that's *the kind of courage we're going to talk about tomorrow,* I think as I go back to bed.

The next day, driving to the café to meet Sandra, I think more about her idea of courage. I've worked with Sandra long enough to know that she really needs to view courage in a new way. I'm convinced of it.

Sandra is sitting in the back corner booth of the café, wearing sunglasses, hidden from most of the customers' view.

I sit down and take a breath and try to release my expectations about this meeting. Good coaches, I remind myself, show up open. I know I'm not doing great on that one so far, but I try.

"Okay, Sandy, how are you?"

"The video has 1.3 million views now. Most people hated it," she says in a tone of defeat.

"What do you think of it?"

"I was proud of it. It was scary to post that. I had hoped for a better response, obviously."

I want to address the "scary" comment and launch into my rant about true courage, but a waitress comes by. I order some tea, and Sandra gets another coffee.

"Do you want some food?" she asks. "We might be here a long while. I really need your help."

I had planned on a shorter meeting. *It's just a dumb video,* I think. We sit in silence.

I can barely wait to get into it. "Okay, Sandy, what was so scary about this? I don't think there's much to do about the video. Just let it play out. Maybe release another one with more detail later this week. It'll blow over. These things do, you know."

I see a tear slip below Sandra's sunglasses. "Sandy? You okay?"

"It's not just about the video, Brendon. It was scary. I thought I was doing something brave. It was a cry for help, but it was just stupid." She starts crying, and I lean forward and take her hand.

"Hey," I say, "are you okay? What's this *really* about? What's going on?"

Sandra takes a sip of coffee, then casually removes her sunglasses. She has a black eye.

"Oh, my God, Sandy!" I gasp. "What happened?"

She sobs for few moments, then tells me. "It's my husband. I should have told you a long time ago. I've been . . . He's been abusive for a long time. I've been so scared for so long. Then yesterday I decided I had enough. I posted that video. I just felt like it was my first step to . . ." Her words melt into tears.

A wave of regret washes over me. I made stupid assumptions. I know better, and I immediately start kicking myself. Sometimes, a person's first step is courageous no matter what you think of it.

"He saw the video and went berserk. I should have thought it through. I just wanted to do *something*, you know?"

Sandra and I sit for three hours and plan her escape, where she'll stay, her future. She never returns home that day. Her friends go and collect her belongings. She leaves him and never looks back. She crossed her own Delaware. She revolutionized her life. She taught me about courage.

#

High performers are courageous people. The data show that courage is significantly correlated with high performance. In fact, higher courage scores are related to higher scores on *all* the other HP6. This means that individuals who have developed greater courage in life also tend to have more clarity, energy, necessity, productivity, and influence. Courage can revolutionize your life, just as it did for Sandra. In fact, our coaching interventions suggest that demonstrating courage is *the* cornerstone habit of high performance.

Demonstrating courage doesn't mean you have to save the world or do something grandiose. Sometimes, it means taking a first step toward real change in an unpredictable world. For Sandra, it was posting a video—just a small step, but it started the process of sharing that would give her the confidence to take bigger steps and, ultimately, reclaim her freedom. It was just a video. But it was the first light of courage.

To assess courage in our research, we ask participants to indicate how strongly they agree or disagree with statements such as these:

- I speak up for myself even when it's hard.

- I respond quickly to life's challenges and emergencies rather than avoid them.

- I often take action despite feeling fear.

We also have respondents score themselves on less upbeat statements:

- I don't feel that I have the courage to express who I really am.

- Even if I knew it was the right thing to do, I wouldn't help someone if it meant I would be judged, ridiculed, or threatened.

- I rarely act outside my comfort zone.

From assessing tens of thousands of people, what has become abundantly clear is that high performers report taking action despite fear much more than others do. This fact shows up in our interviews and coaching sessions as well—it seems all high performers have a real sense of what courage means to them, and can articulate times when they demonstrated it.

Of course, almost everyone, if prompted or helped to explore the topic, can remember performing one act of courage in their lives. But not everyone who has courage becomes a high performer unless they also have clarity, energy, necessity, productivity, and influence. As always, the HP6 work together to create long-term success.

Why do some people "have" more courage than others? Our research shows that the significant difference is not age or gender.[1] The people who are *more likely* to self-report high levels of courage are those who . . .

- love mastering challenges,

- perceive themselves as assertive,

- perceive themselves as confident,

- perceive themselves as high performers,

- perceive themselves as more successful than their peers, and

- are happy with their life overall.[2]

This makes sense. If you like to take on a challenge, the odds are, you won't shrink when it's time to rise and face a difficulty or obstacle. If you feel that you're confident and a take-action kind of person, you'll go into action when you're needed. But why are *happy* people more courageous? This was a head-scratcher for me, so I conducted structured interviews with twenty high performers to find out. They said such things as "When you're happy, you worry less about yourself and can focus on others," "Happiness makes you think you can do incredible things," and "To have gotten to a point of being happy in your life, you have to have developed some self-control, and once you have that, you feel more capable of taking control in uncertain situations." These were good descriptions, but there clearly was not a consensus on *how* happiness made people more courageous.

This reveals a general truth about courage: It's hard to explain no matter what angle you approach it from. In fact, most people struggle to define courage in the first place, let alone consider it a habit. Perhaps more than with any other individual characteristic we research, people think of courage as a human virtue that some have and others don't. But that's incorrect. Courage is more like a skill, since anyone can learn it.[3] And once you understand and demonstrate it more consistently, everything changes.

COURAGE BASICS

"Courage is resistance to fear, mastery of fear,
not absence of fear."

—Mark Twain

Psychologists agree with Twain's quote: Courage is not fearlessness; it is taking action and persisting despite that fear.[4] But courage can *lead* to fearlessness in many domains. For example, psychologists found that most parachuting trainees are fearful when jumping out of a plane the first time. Their first jump feels courageous. But the more they do it, the more confidence they gain and the more fearless they become.[5] Eventually, even jumping out of a plane can feel routine—exhilarating, certainly, but no longer fear inducing. Researchers found the same for bomb-disposal operators, soldiers, and astronauts: The more experience they had in facing their fear, the less fear and stress they felt.[6]

This happens to all of us. The more we do something successfully, the more comfortable we become with it. That's why it's so important for you to start living a more courageous life *now*. The more actions you take facing fear, expressing yourself, and helping others, the easier and less stressful these actions become.

But when you face down your fear, something else is also going on. Courage, it turns out, is *contagious*, just like panic or cowardice.[7] If your kids see you fearful of life, they'll feel it—and they'll model it. And it's the same for your team and whomever else you lead or serve. Demonstrating more courage is a gateway for our society to develop greater virtue.

Many Kinds of Courage

Defining and classifying *courage* is difficult, and there's little agreement even on what, exactly, the word means to researchers or the general public.[8] Ultimately, what we can agree on is that for someone to demonstrate courage, these things are likely present: risk, fear, and a good reason to act.

Still, it's useful to have a look at the different kinds of courage so we can think through them. There's *physical* courage, when you put yourself in harm's way to meet a noble goal—for example, jumping into an intersection to save someone from being hit by a car. It might also include fighting for your life when you're sick.

Moral courage is speaking up for others or enduring hardship for what you believe is right, to serve the greater good. Stopping someone from bullying a stranger, refusing to sit in the back of the bus despite an unfair law, posting a video about your beliefs on a controversial topic—these are all expressions of moral courage. Moral courage shows in selfless acts that protect values or advance principles to benefit the common good. It's about social responsibility, altruism, "doing what's right."

Psychological courage is the act of facing or overcoming your own anxieties, insecurities, and mental fears to (a) assert your authentic self instead of conforming—showing the world who you really are even if someone might not like it—or (b) experience personal growth even if it's only a private victory.

Everyday courage could mean keeping a positive attitude or taking action despite great uncertainty (such as moving to a new city), bad health, or hardship (such as sharing unpopular ideas or showing up every day for work even when things are tough at the office).

While none of these types of courage are definitive or mutually exclusive, the terms are useful in conceptualizing courage.

The important thing is that you define what being more courageous means to you, and start living that way.

I think of courage as taking determined action to serve an authentic, noble, or life-enhancing goal, in the face of risk, fear, adversity, or opposition.[9] The "noble" and "life-enhancing" part is important to me because surely not all fear-facing acts are courageous. Suicide bombers, for example, might seem to meet some criteria; they take determined action even though they must surely feel scared, and they have what they believe are noble goals. So, too, do burglars, running the risk of jail or worse. Are their acts courageous? Most would say no.[10] That's because even if they meet some criteria for courage, their actions are, at least according to most of society, harmful or destructive. *Do no harm* is an important concept in courage.

Taking action despite fear of rejection isn't always courageous, either. For example, a teenager taking a dangerous dare to jump off a high balcony to gain acceptance into a peer group *seems* courageous. The teenager is afraid, but jumps to be accepted. Courageous? To some. Others might simply call it conformity or stupidity.

Courage isn't always about taking a bold action either. Doing nothing when you're expected to can be courageous—that's a truth revealed in nonviolent demonstrations. Not accepting an invitation to fight and walking away to protect your body is courage. Refusing to jump into an argument even though you might look weak is a courageous act if it preserves your integrity.

While this may sound like mincing words, definitions are important. Courage is more than merely overcoming fear, though many people confuse the two. The outcome is what you're after, and the outcome that happens matters a great deal. If your well-intended actions hurt someone, that's not likely to be viewed as courageous. In fact, researchers have found that many people consider an action courageous *only if* it gets completed or ends in a good result.[11] For example, if you start to speak up for yourself but immediately stop at the first interruption, will you later feel that you were courageous? If someone jumps into a river to help another person but ends up only drowning them or requiring rescue themselves, are they courageous, or merely foolhardy? Probably the latter.

Still, at the heart of our courage research is the clear pattern that high performers have a *bias toward action* even when that action's outcome is scary, risky, or uncertain. After listening to so many high performers' stories over the past decade, I know this to be true:

You are capable of remarkable things that you could never foretell and will never discover without taking action.

Almost all the stories of courage I hear about are stories of surprise. A high performer faced doubt or fear or suddenly rose in service to help someone. They didn't "have" courage or find it through contemplation. Action woke their heart, and their path was revealed. They didn't hope for an opportunity to do something one day; they didn't hem and haw. They acted. They knew that hoping to achieve good things without taking action is like hoping for help without asking for it.

I also heard a lot of stories of people changing course in life. People talked about quitting a job, leaving an abusive relationship, or moving to a new town as an act of courage. Though we often think of courageous actions as stepping forward, I also heard a lot of people talk about going backward in a sense—back to an old dream that they had given up on. If you've quit on your dream, and your heart still longs for its achievement, only action will remedy the suffering. It's never too late to change course.

What high performers didn't talk about is how they delayed and complained for long stretches of time. Continual whining leads to diminishment. The human will shrinks when we don't quickly pair the complaint with real work toward progress. "Don't complain," dozens of high performers told me. "Act."

While many of my interviewees described acts of courage as spontaneous, the stories that inspired me the most—and, perhaps, best show the replicable nature of courage as a habit—were those where courage had been planned for. People knew what they were afraid of, and so they prepared themselves. They studied. They got mentors. Then they faced their fears. Only when our fears become our growth plan have we stepped onto the path of mastery.

I could share more personal observations here, but ultimately, you must decide what living courageously means to you. Courage is most often judged from the eye of the actor. So the important thing is that you determine whether you're living courageously *enough* at this stage in your life. To help people think through this, I like to ask this question:

If your future best self—a version of you ten years older, who is even stronger, more capable, and more successful than you imagined yourself to be—showed up on your doorstep *today* and looked at your current circumstances, what courageous action would that future self advise you to take right away to change your life? How would your future self tell you to *live*?

Read that question again and spend a few minutes pondering it.

I've asked a lot of people this, and while I don't know your response, my guess is that the future you wouldn't tell you to *play small*. Your best self would tell you to *go for it in life*. To do that, you'll have to go beyond the basics. You'll need a new way of looking at your fears and obstacles. You'll need these three high performance practices.

PRACTICE ONE

HONOR THE STRUGGLE

"Success is giving 100 percent of your effort, body, mind,
and soul to the struggle."

—John Wooden

Why is it that so many people are clearly *not* living courageous lives? They know they *should* speak up for themselves. But they don't. They *want* to face their fears and take some risks. But they don't. They tell you they're going to be bolder, strive for greater dreams, help people in significant and noble ways. But they don't. Why?

This was one of the most frustrating questions in my early coaching career. Many clients would talk about vision and big dreams, about wanting to live an exemplary life and make a difference. But they wouldn't *do anything* about it. They'd say they wanted a great life, but when we discussed new habits to get them there, they would often deflect, saying they were too busy or fearful. They would show me their vision boards from some seminar, and I would ask, "So what are the top three big leaps you're going to make, starting on Monday, now that you have these new vision boards?" They usually lacked any sort of response or plan, never understanding that one act of courage is better than a hundred vision boards!

I'm sure you've been frustrated with others, or even yourself, about the inability to take bolder action. So what was the real problem, and what was the solution? I've learned that the issue is really one of mindset. We're less courageous as a society today because we avoid struggle, and that decision leaves us with underdeveloped character and strength—two key ingredients for courage.

Here's what I mean. We're at a unique time in history, when more countries and communities have greater abundance than ever before. But in such blessings, there can be a curse—people can become resistant to struggle. Today, making any recommendations that would require real effort, trial, difficulty, or patient persistence is out of fashion. Ease and convenience reign. People often quit marriages and school and jobs and friendships at the first sign of difficulty. If you quit at the first sign of difficulty in your everyday life, what are the odds you'll persist in the face of real fear or threat?

If we're ever going to develop the strength that courage requires, we'll have to get better at dealing with life's basic challenges. We'll have to stop getting so annoyed and start seeing the struggle as part of growing our character. We must learn to honor the struggle.

Unfortunately, struggle is a hard sell. In my industry, for example, I'm constantly told to make my advice and curriculum less complex and rigorous, and more appealing. "Don't make them work," they say. "Don't give them too many steps that are hard, Brendon, because they won't implement them. Dumb it down. Make it easy. Make sure it's digestible for a sixth-grader. People don't want to try, so just give them easy things to do." (I was told each of these things while writing this book.)

The presupposition in these statements is that people are lazy, hate challenge, and will trade growth for comfort and certainty. Consider how often we're sold this assumption. In the general media world especially, every "tip" and "hack" is framed so that it's making life super easy, pulling us away from any pain or strain. Focus only on your strengths, because you'll feel better and serve better. No need to suffer through facing your shortcomings; that would be uncomfortable and not worth the effort. Outsource everything, because there's no value in learning real skills. Hack your diet with a magical pill so you don't have to change your horrible eating patterns.

We're surrounded by memes and media and influencers telling us we're not supposed to struggle, that life should just be an easy flow or we're on the wrong track. Imagine what that's doing to our abilities. *Imagine what that is doing to our odds of ever taking courageous action.*

If we keep telling people to do what's easy, why would they ever think to do what's hard?

The good news is, I think people worldwide are discovering that all these quick fixes, hacks, and silver bullets aren't enough. People are beginning to remember something they knew already: To achieve excellence requires hard work, discipline, routines that can become boring, the continual frustrations that accompany learning, adversities that test every measure of our heart and soul, and, above all, courage. I hope the research in this book has helped you discover a bigger picture: that high performance requires real intention and the mastering of complex habits. The practices here are doable, but they will still require focus, struggle, and faithful diligence over the long haul.

I'm sure older generations could tell us about a time when struggle wasn't something to be avoided. They knew that living a comfortable life free of all difficulty and all passion was never the goal. They didn't expect to have a smooth ride. They would tell us that toil and struggle are the fire in which we forge character. They championed the ideals of getting dirt under your fingernails, working harder than anyone else would expect, striving for a dream with a fierce tenacity even in the face of hardship because those efforts made you a better, more capable human. Meeting struggle with poise and dignity got you respect. It made you a leader.

Forgive me if this sounds nostalgic, but it's nonetheless true. No one who achieved greatness avoided struggle. They met it, engaged with it. They knew that it was necessary, because they knew that real challenge and hardship pushed them, extended their capabilities, made them rise. They learned to *honor the struggle*. They developed a mindset that *anticipated* the struggle, *welcomed* the struggle, *leveraged* the struggle into reasons to give more.

By meeting the conflicts and difficulties and outright messes of life straight on, willingly, we dismantle the walls of fear, brick by brick. This mindset, more than any other, is at the heart of my work. Read *The Motivation Manifesto*, *The Charge*, or *Life's Golden Ticket*, and you will see a deep respect, almost a reverence, for struggle.

When we learn to see struggle as a necessary, important, and *positive* part of our journey, then we can find true peace and personal power.

The alternative, of course, is crippling. Those who hate the struggle, or fear it, end up complaining, losing motivation, and quitting.

Our most recent research also backs up this idea of honoring the struggle. One of the strongest predictors we've found is that courageous people agree with the statements "I love trying to master new challenges" and "I'm confident I can achieve my goals despite challenges or resistance." High performers simply do not dread challenge, failure, or the inevitable difficulties that learning and growing entail. Instead, they *love* trying to master new things, and they feel confident they can achieve their goals despite potential hardships. Talk to them about difficult times in their past, when circumstances forced them out of their comfort zones to perform, grow, or win, and they'll speak of those times with reverence, not dread.

Our findings align with decades of psychological research on people with a growth mindset. People with such a mindset believe they can improve, love a challenge, and engage with difficulty rather than run from it. They don't fear failure as much as others do, because they know they can learn and, through hard work and training, become better. This makes them more motivated, more dogged in their pursuits, more resilient, and more successful over the long term in practically every area of their lives.[12]

Those with "fixed" mindsets believe and behave the opposite. They believe that their abilities, intelligence, and traits are set, fixed, limited. They don't think they can change and win, and that creates fear anytime they are faced with something that lies beyond their "natural" strengths and capabilities. They *dread* failure, because failure would be a commentary on *them*. They feel that a mistake or error makes them look incompetent. If something isn't easy, they give up. To illustrate how destructive this can be, research has shown that those with a fixed mindset are *five times* more likely to avoid challenges than those with a growth mindset.[13] This jibes with what we see in high performers versus low performers.

If you are unwilling to anticipate or endure the inevitable struggles, mistakes, messes, and difficulties of life, then it's a rough road. Without courage, you'll feel less confident, happy, and successful. The data confirms it.

THE TWO HUMAN STORIES

"You should never view your challenges as a disadvantage. Instead, it's important for you to understand that your experience facing and overcoming adversity is actually one of your biggest advantages."

—Michelle Obama

There are only two narratives in the human story: struggle and progress. And you can't have the latter without the former. All those ups and downs are what make us most human. There are supposed to be lows, and there are supposed to be highs, so that we may experience the full range of what it is to be human, knowing both joy and despair, loss and triumph.

We know that, but we often forget it when things get tough. It's easy to hate the struggle, but we mustn't, because over time hate only magnifies its object into a phantom far greater and more ominous than the actual thing. We must accept that struggle will either destroy us or develop us, and the hardest of human truths is that, ultimately, it's our choice. No matter how difficult it gets, the next step is still your choice. For that, let's be thankful.

We can go beyond gratitude to true reverence for life's challenges. In talking with high performers, it's clear that, to excel, you must teach yourself to view struggle as a stepping-stone to strength and higher performance. That's part of the high performing mind: Struggle must be seen as *part of the process*—and a vitally important part of any worthwhile endeavor. And the very decision to accept struggle draws courage from deep within us.

The struggle I'm now facing is necessary, and it's summoning me to show up, be strong, and use it to forge a better future for myself and my loved ones.

Honoring the journey doesn't mean you just take the adversity and roll with the punches, doing nothing to improve. This isn't about just being Zen and accepting life as it comes, without trying to exert your will when you're unhappy. It just means that you adopt the mindset that facing hardship and trying to learn *can bring the best from you*. Accepting that difficult times will come allows you to wake with a sense of realism and readiness, to anticipate problems and be prepared for them, to maintain calm when the winds of change might topple lesser leaders.

Having that affinity for engagement and action defines part of the high performance mindset. The difficulties in life that you can't avoid? *Engage them wholeheartedly.* Even when you feel overwhelmed, choose to go for a walk, focus on your breath, and consider the problem rather than avoid it. Look the problem in the eye and ask, "What is the next right action for me to take right now?" If you aren't yet ready to take that action, plan. Study. Prepare yourself for when the fog lifts and you are called to lead.

I'll end this section with two related sayings that my students find helpful. The first, I learned from working with members of the US Army Special Forces. They told me about a common maxim they use to help people realize they must deal with the hardships of service: *Embrace the suck.* Sometimes, doing your duty sucks. Training sucks. Patrol sucks. The weather sucks. Circumstances suck. But you can't just avoid them or be bitter. *You have to deal with it, face it, and will yourself to persevere and rise.* You have to embrace the suck. If there's one thing I respect most about the military, it's how little complaining there is. Complaining isn't respected or perpetuated. That inspires me. In any area of your life, if you have the opportunity and blessing to serve, you don't complain about the effort involved.

The second saying that might serve you in embracing and honoring the struggle: *You will make it through.* Just because they can't see your potential or don't share your vision, just because you're uncertain or afraid, that doesn't disqualify you. Just because the sky is cloudy doesn't mean there's no sun.

Trust that things turn out. People often say to "count your blessings" in times of hardship, but I'm reminding you to count *on* the blessings, too. The universe is abundant and giving, so you can trust that good things are coming your way. I suppose that's the ultimate message in times of difficulty: to have faith in yourself and the future. It's something I wrote on an index card and carried in my wallet when I was struggling through my brain injury: Remember, you are stronger than you think, and the future holds good things for you.

Performance Prompts

1. A struggle I've been facing in my life is . . .

2. The way I could change my view of this struggle is . . .

3. If something great could come from this struggle, it would be . . .

4. The way I choose to greet life's inevitable hardships from today forward is . . .

PRACTICE TWO

SHARE YOUR TRUTH AND AMBITIONS

"As far as I can judge, not much good can be done without disturbing something or somebody."

—Edward Blake

In *The Motivation Manifesto*, I argued that it is the main motivation of humankind to be free, to express our true selves and pursue our dreams without restriction—to experience what may be called *personal freedom.* Our spirits soar when we feel unencumbered by fear or the weight of conformity. When we live our truth—expressing who we really are, how we really feel, what we really desire and dream of—then we are authentic; we are *free.* This requires courage.

Surely, no one wants to live a constrained, conforming life. But since *Manifesto*'s release, I've received thousands of letters and comments about just how *hard* personal freedom is to achieve. Showing the world who you are, authentically and unapologetically, brings a great deal of risk. People often talk about that—how they *want* to be real, but doing so invites so much judgment or rejection. They're worried that if people could see who they really are, the show would be over. They wouldn't measure up to others' expectations.

But I say the only time you should try to measure up to someone else's idea of who you are or what you're capable of is when that person is a role model cheering you on. If someone believes in you and sees greatness in you, sure, try to live up to that.

But for anyone who doubts or diminishes you, forget about it. Don't bother trying to please them. Live a life that is yours. Don't seek the approval of the doubters. You'll find no lasting joy in seeking acknowledgment from others. If it comes, it'll never be enough. So the only path left is to express your own truth and pursue your own dreams.

When you do this, you'll meet with inevitable criticism. Anticipate that as just one more part of the struggle. Judgment will always be there, just as there will always be cloudy days. *Don't let their criticisms sway you from your convictions.* If you believe in your dream, stay on your path. You need no permission beyond that tingling hope in your soul.

After talking with so many high performers, I have to confess that I *hope* you meet with judgment and friction. It's a sign you're on your own path and aiming for great things. Indeed, if no one has looked at you sideways lately or, better yet, said, "Who do you think you are? What, are you *crazy*? Are you sure that's a good idea?" then maybe you're not living boldly enough.

I've shared this sort of coaching before. Once, I got a message from a fan who countered, "But, Brendon, I'm not proud of who I am. And so I don't want to put myself out there. I'm embarrassed at who I am. My truth isn't something I want to share." I could only reply, "My friend, if you're ashamed of the truth, then you've yet to find the truth."

MINIMIZING OURSELVES

"Only those who will risk going too far
can possibly find out how far one will go."

—T. S. Eliot

One thing I didn't expect from readers of *The Motivation Manifesto* was a different kind of fear in sharing their truth. Many people wrote in and said they weren't worried that others would judge them as insufficient; they were worried that by being their best, they would make *others* feel insufficient. *They were fearful of expressing their true ambitions, joy, and powers, because the people around them could feel bad about themselves.*

They felt they had to minimize their dreams, keep their big ideas bottled up, dumb themselves down, tone it down, look down—all so others could feel good about themselves.

When I receive concerns like this, I'll often send my readers a video I shot from my phone:

Do not dare play small, my friend. Do not feel guilt because you have high aims. Those dreams were seeded in your soul for a reason, and it is your duty to honor them. Do not hold back in life just to comfort or placate those around you. Holding back is not humility; it's lying. If the people in your life do not know your true thoughts, feelings, needs, and dreams, do not blame them. It is your lack of voice or vulnerability or power, not their lack of understanding or ambition, that is building the barricade to your potential. Share more, and you'll have real relationships that can support you, energize you, lift you. Even if they don't support you or believe in you, at least you lived your life. At least you put it all on the table. At least you honored the hopes of your heart and the calling of your soul. In your full expression lies your freedom. My friend, your next level of performance begins at your next level of truth.

I know, you're getting a lot of coaching in this chapter, but this is crucial. Readers still write me *years later* saying my message helped them. I want you to keep this message handy so you can read it again—out loud—the next time concern for someone else's feelings tempts you to hold back your own dreams.

So please stay with me. I have no doubt that accessing the next level of courage in your life requires a new degree of openness and honesty about who you are, what you want, and what you're really capable of and ready to do. All that stands in your way is that fearful part of you that feels like *minimizing yourself* so that you don't make others feel bad. But don't for one minute think that's humility. *That's lying about your real ambitions.* That's apologizing for the gifts that God, the universe, fortune, or hard work—take your pick—blessed you with. And it's insidious. Unless you choose to let it go, that fear will forever prevent you from feeling truly authentic and fulfilled and living out your real potential. It will drive you to lower your sights and miss out on excellence—and for what, exactly?

You may think, *People will be threatened by my drive and desire. They might not like my ambitions. They might make fun of me. So I'd best keep quiet. It's better to downgrade my ambition or work ethic, anyway.*

I've heard every version and permutation of that misbegotten idea. But I want to say it again and etch it on your mind: This kind of thinking is not humility, my friend. It's fear. It's lying. It's suppressing. It's adolescent concern. And it will destroy any real aliveness and authenticity in your relationships. I know, it may feel better in the short term to minimize yourself so someone else can feel good about themselves, but consider this:

No one wants to be in connection with a fake person.

How would you feel if you were in a relationship with someone for five years, and out of nowhere they said to you, "You don't know the real me. I haven't been honest with you. All this time, I've been holding back my real dreams from you. Because I was scared of you or I thought you were too small-minded to handle it."

Would that bring you close to them? Or would it upset you? How would you respond to that person?

You'd probably be astounded. And hurt. *So why would you do that to someone else by holding back?*

Look. If you're gulping back your real thoughts and dreams just to "fit in" or make others feel better, then you can't blame them or anyone else. Because it's *you* choking yourself. And while you're at it, you're squeezing the life out of your relationships.

I've seen a lot of people from all over the world martyr themselves under the guise of a poorly conceived "humility." But there's nothing humble in saying, "I'd better not shine, because the timid souls around me couldn't handle it." Please.

I've worked with enough people to know your likely gut reaction to this. You'll think, *Well, Brendon, you don't understand my husband . . . my community . . . my culture . . . my mom . . . my coach . . . my fans . . . my brand . . . my* [insert excuse here].

And right now it's my job to call you out on this.

> **No one can quiet you without your permission.**
> **No one can minimize your self-image but you.**
> **And no one can open you up**
> **and release your full power but you.**

You can always blame "them" for your failure to be real and vulnerable. Or you can choose this very day to start speaking up and living in full, even though some may not like it. Will some people make fun of you? Might a person you love doubt you or leave you? Could your teammates call you crazy and marginalize you? Can your neighbors or fans turn on you for wanting "more than you deserve"? To each of these questions, *yes*. But which is nobler: falling dutifully in line with what everyone wants, or speaking up for what's right for you? Ultimately, you must ask which your life is about: *fear or freedom?* One choice is the cage. The other—that's courage.

My passion on this topic is boundless because I've been in the trenches with enough people to know that at some point, someone—I or one of your mentors or a whisper from deep inside you—will get through and get you to share yourself with the world.

You don't have to listen to all this from some author you've probably never even met. But if I've somehow held your attention this far, then you may as well bear with me a little longer. You must beware; holding back will weigh on your mind and your life with stresses you may not see for a long time. It will cheat the people around you from ever discovering your true beauty and abilities. Worse, it will prevent the *right* people from coming into your life.

I see this all the time. A successful person fails to achieve the next level of success because they chose to strive in *silence*. They don't want to share or speak up. They're trying to be "appropriate," "realistic," "level-headed." They're trying to make others "happy" or "comfortable." And so they have these brilliant ideas, and not only do they not share them, they make the most lethal mistake of all: *They don't ask for help.* If you don't ask for help, the right people can't come into your life. So if the universe isn't giving you what you want, perhaps it's because amid all your distractions and silence, the universe just doesn't know what you're asking for.

Recently, I worked with an Olympic gold medalist. I asked, "When did the biggest gains come in your career?" She said, "When I finally started voicing my dreams to do this. Suddenly, people started pointing me in the right direction. They told me what to do, what skills I would need, who I should talk to, what equipment the pros used, who the best coaches were. I learned that if you open your mouth and shout from the rooftops what you want to do with your life, sure, some village idiots will show up and shout back all the reasons why you can't. But all the village leaders come over and want to help. Life's great that way."

The people who are in your life for the right reasons will listen to your truth. They'll applaud your ambition. They'll be happy to meet the person behind the face. They'll thank you for sharing, for being real, for trusting them. Trust others with your truth, and the golden values of real friendship and love reveal themselves like lost treasures.

To find even more courage, remind yourself that you owe it to those who have supported you in the past. Stay strong in recognition of the strength they have given you. As a gift to all those who have been good to you, don't complain; act. Don't criticize; cheerlead. Don't conform; live your truth. Don't be selfish; serve. Don't take the easy path; strive for growth and an extraordinary life.

And when things are falling apart, stay true to the best of who you are, for those are the moments when you're forging who you will become.

The Simple Conversations

The most important thing in connecting authentically with others is to share your true desires with them. They don't have to approve or help or even brainstorm with you. This isn't about them. This is about you having the courage to open to others just as the universe remains open to you. Try it. Each day, reveal to others a little bit more of what you're thinking, feeling, dreaming of. Even if you don't get the immediate support of the humans in front of you, who knows? Perhaps a distant force is unlocked and the necessary ripples in time and luck and destiny converge and deliver to your door a hint about the next step—a treasure map of sorts, unearthed by your own courage.

This habit doesn't take shape by a single momentous conversation with everyone you know. You don't have to sit everyone you love down and tell them all the reasons you've been holding back from them and from life. You don't have to shoot a video explaining your entire life and philosophy. Instead, just make it a daily practice to be sharing your thoughts and goals and feelings with others. Every day, share *something* with someone about what you *really* think and want in life. You could say, "You know, honey, today I was thinking about starting X because I'd love to Y." For example:

- I was thinking about researching how to write a book, because I think I have a story worth telling.

- I was thinking about starting to hit the gym every morning, because I'd love to feel more vital and alive.

- I was thinking about starting to look for another job, because I'd love to feel more passionate and appreciated.

- I was thinking about starting to cold-call some new coaches, because I'm ready to compete at a higher level.

These are simple statements. It's a simple formula. What do you want to share? Whatever it is, share it. Then take bold action each day to bring it to reality.

Performance Prompts

1. Something I really want to do that I haven't shared with enough people is . . .

2. If I were going to be more "me" in my everyday life, I would start to . . .

3. When I put myself out there and someone makes fun of me, I'm just going to . . .

4. A major dream I'm going to start telling people about and asking for some help with is . . .

PRACTICE THREE

FIND SOMEONE TO FIGHT FOR

"I don't know what your destiny will be,
but one thing I know: The only ones among you
who will be really happy are those who will
have sought and found how to serve."

—Albert Schweitzer

In 2006, I was broke. I had done what I have been trying to inspire you to do: I took action. I had quit my job to be a writer and trainer. I told everyone about my dream.

Plenty of people thought I was crazy—including, at times, me. I didn't know how to write or publish a book. No one knew me, and I had no supportive connections. Facebook, YouTube, and iTunes were still in their infancy. Getting your voice out there was hard.

I just wanted to share with people what I had learned from my car accident: that at the end of our lives, we will ask ourselves questions to evaluate whether we were happy with our lives. If you can figure out the questions you'll ask, then you can wake up each day and live intentionally so you'll be happy with the answers at the end. I learned that those questions for me were "Did I live? Did I love? Did I matter?"

I stayed up late each night, teaching myself to build websites and do online marketing because I wanted to reach a lot of people with that simple message.

I was living in my girlfriend's apartment because I was so broke. I wrote on a foldout "desk" borrowed from my mother's old sewing room. The apartment was so small that I used the bed as a credenza, where I stacked all my bills and notes and fears.

It was a tough time for me personally. The guy who would become the guy on motivation and high performance habits had very little of either. I knew what I wanted: to write, to train. I had that quote from Horace on my fridge: "In times of stress, be bold and valiant." And yet, many days passed while I did nothing to move forward on either desire.

I remember days sitting in a café, watching other people type on computers and thinking, *What a phony I am. Look at them work. I'm barely doing anything.* I would get up and walk around the park telling myself I needed to get in more inspired settings, telling myself that a walk would clear my head and make me write better. I circled that park for weeks and months, and my head was as muddled as ever. My motivation hadn't risen to the level of my dreams.

Nor had my habits. I was going to set all these alarms and mental triggers to wake up at precise hours each day and begin writing—after, of course, boiling the perfect cup of green tea, cooking the best omelet, activating the perfect state to write in. I followed the habits, sometimes, and they led to more dirty plates than written pages. Not all good habits lead to impressive results—especially when a key ingredient is missing.

And then, a very simple moment changed everything.

One night, I watched my girlfriend walk into the bedroom and, trying not to disturb me or the bills or notes I had strewn all over the bed, slip quietly beneath the covers.

I saw the love of my life sleeping under the weight of my bills. It broke my heart.

I gazed around the tiny apartment that I was contributing no money for because I had none—a space that had nothing but the love between us. An apartment where I sat useless, sad, unable to finish pages and chapters and the mission I dreamt of. And I thought, *This is not the life I want for us. She deserves better.*

At that moment, something inside me snapped or opened up or fell into place. Maybe my level of performance up to that point was okay for my preferences or needs in life. But I wasn't going to let my weak motivation or bad habits diminish the life of this woman who believed in me when everyone else thought I was crazy, the woman who bought me groceries, the woman who, too early in our relationship, admitted shyly, "I love you."

You know when it's courage, because somehow there is an all-in decision. Often, it doesn't come from you. It comes from wanting to serve another, to love another, to fight for another.

Either I was going to become a successful writer and trainer, staying focused on helping people whatever the obstacles, *fighting for this woman*, until I ended up successful, or . . . Or what? There was no other choice.

From that moment, I decided to follow my dreams with more focus and intensity. I was not going to waste my days meandering about, lost in distractions. I decided to think bigger, to stop letting my small business make me small-minded. I decided to fight for my art and amplify my voice so that I might make a greater difference. I decided not to worry about the critics and instead give my whole heart and effort to those who wanted positivity and progress in life. And I decided to marry that girl. Fighting for the life I wanted for us has kept me driven and contributing at the highest levels ever since.

My story isn't all that unusual. While writing this chapter, I went back through my interviews with the highest level of high performers (those with the highest average scores across the HP6). I found that a common theme was similar to the story I just shared:

We will do more for others than for ourselves.
And in doing something for others, we find our reason
for courage, and our cause for focus and excellence.

Each of the highest performing people I interviewed told me about *someone* who inspired them to excel. They all had a reason, and that reason was often a person, not always a purpose or a group of people. Most often, *just one person.* Sometimes, it was more than one: their kids, their employees, their extended family, their community's need. But more often than not, it was just *one.*

I share this because our culture today often emphasizes finding your life's purpose. And it's always this great, monumental cause that is destined to "change the world" and "benefit millions." A lot of people search, and some find that high purpose in life. And surely, that's a wonderful thing to have.

The historical research on courage, in general, suggests that people do things for noble causes beyond themselves. For high performers, that noble cause usually happens to be just one person or a few people.

And so, if you are a young person being told to find your purpose right now, don't feel that you have to look too far. Perhaps someone around you needs you to show up for them, and in doing that you'll bring to light some of your own powers. And if you are an older adult, remember those around you even as you seek that next mountain to climb.

What I found in my research was something so obvious that it's beautiful: No matter what pulled courage from these high performers, it was something noble. *You would admire their reason for doing it.* There was human goodness there. Some answers from their interviews make this clear:

- "She needed me. There was no other choice I could live with than to help her."

- "I didn't want them to suffer."

- "No one seemed to care, and there I was."

- "I wanted to do it for him; he would have wanted that."

- "Everyone else seemed to look the other way, so I stepped up."

- "I want to leave a legacy, so I decided to get out of my own way and go for it."

- "This action was a way to leave things better than I found them."

- "Love had to win, so I went back in."

Sometimes, courage appears to be a spontaneous act. But what I have found is that it's usually an expression or action built up from years of caring deeply about something or someone. So begin seeking things and people you care about. *Give.* Care deeply about something now. Stand up for something now. And then you will be more likely to find courage when it matters.

Performance Prompts

1. A courageous action I will take this week because someone I love needs me to take it is . . .

2. Another courageous action I will take this week, because a cause I believe in needs me to take it, is . . .

3. Another courageous action I will take this week, because my dream requires it of me, is . . .

COURAGE THROUGH COMPLEXITY

"Courage and perseverance have a magical talisman,
before which difficulties disappear and obstacles vanish into air."

—John Quincy Adams

Just as the universe doesn't become less complex, life doesn't tend to get easier. But *you* get stronger. You learn to show up more, cope better, and be truer and more conscious amid the judgment and hardship. Soon, the obstacles do begin to seem smaller and the path seems more your own. So no matter what happens, trust in yourself and lean forward. The next level opens after your next courageous step.

After more and more of those steps, you will look back with self-respect. Allow me to return to something I shared in the opening story of this chapter:

The kinds of courageous acts that you are proud of at the end of your life are those in which you faced uncertainty and real risk, with real stakes, when doing something for a cause or person beyond yourself, without any assurance of safety, reward, or success.

I know this to be true because I've faced the end of my life before—twice. I know this because I've sat with people dying in hospice and I know what they talk about. How they reminisce. What they wish they had done. What mattered to them. Where their self-respect and pride and legacy came from.

And here's what I've learned: For most people, courageous acts are indeed rare events. But we remember those acts, and they shape our sense of ourselves and our lives as much as the small stuff. And so I ask you to consider the questions below often, to ready your mind for even more courage. Only by conditioning ourselves now will we truly serve with grace and courage when called.

287

- What in my personal life have I avoided doing, which might involve hardship but just might improve my family's lives forever?

- What could I do at work that would require stepping out on a limb but would also truly change things for the better and help people?

- What decision could I make that would demonstrate a moral commitment to something higher than myself?

- How could I bring myself to face a situation that usually makes me nervous or anxious?

- What change could I make that scares me but will help someone I love?

- What good thing could I walk away from to advance my life?

- What have I wanted to say to those close to me, and when and how will I courageously declare that truth?

- Who needs me, and who will I fight for the rest of this year?

These questions might spur some brave thinking and action today. Ask them enough, and practice the habits in this chapter, and you'll come to this truth: Deep down, away from all the noise, where love blankets your heart and your dreams lie in wait, you are not afraid.

SECTION THREE

SUSTAINING SUCCESS

HIGH PERFORMANCE KILLERS
BEWARE THREE TRAPS

"The fault, dear Brutus, is not in
our stars but in ourselves."

—William Shakespeare, *Julius Caesar*

BEWARE SUPERIORITY

BEWARE DISSATISFACTION

BEWARE NEGLECT

"That's him, over there," Andre tells me. "Dreadful Don."

I look across the bar to the well-dressed executive Andre is pointing to. "Why do you call him that?"

Andre furrows his brow. "We *all* call him that. They called him that long before I got here. He's the VP of sales. Miserable to work with. Everyone hates him."

"But I thought you said he's the star performer in your company?"

"For the moment, yes. He's successful but a total jerk. This party tonight is happening only because he crushed it so hard the whole sales team made its numbers two months early. When you talk to him tomorrow, I'm sure he'll be delighted to tell you how awesome he is."

I'm surprised to hear Andre talk like this. He's a very centered, solid, likable CFO of a manufacturing company. I coached him at another company for years and never heard him speak ill of anyone. He's been at this new job for just six months, and it's hard to imagine that someone has gotten under his skin so quickly.

Something isn't computing. I see Don surrounded by his coworkers, and they all seem to be having a good time. "I don't get it," I say to Andre. "If he's a total jerk as you say, then how does he keep getting ahead? Won't people stop supporting him at some point and then he'll crash and burn?"

Andre takes a sip of his single malt and laughs. "Oh, they already have. He just doesn't know it yet."

The next morning, Andre brings me into the company head-quarters. He's getting paid twice what he did at his old job, but as we enter the building, I can sense he isn't happy to be here. "You'll see why today," he tells me.

We walk into the conference room, where Don is checking his PowerPoint. Today, he's leading the quarterly sales meeting, where he sets the tone and path to make the company's goals. His entire sales team of 144 people is here. The C suite, who Andre has brought me in to coach, is also here—CEO, CTO, CMO. I've worked with them all for just a few weeks, and all of them asked me to work with Don. They've arranged for me to meet with him after his presentation and assess whether I can help.

I watch Don give what many would consider a stellar ninety-minute presentation. He's strategic, organized, and articulate. He has that sort of forward lean and swagger that makes you want to go charge onto the battlefield with him.

After the presentation, I meet with Don privately. I ask, "How did you think your talk went?"

"It was good enough. You're never really satisfied with a speech, you know? You always think of something else you could tell them."

"Yeah, I know the feeling. How do you think the audience received it?"

"Most of it probably went over their heads. But it's just a meet-ing. It's my job to stay on top of them and really push them to exe-cute from here. It takes a lot of follow-up. You know how it is."

"It seemed pretty straightforward to me," I say. "You think it went over their heads?"

"Hey, man, you know. It's lonely at the top, so you just hope you can explain your point of view well."

"Lonely at the top?"

"You know what I mean. Not everyone gets us, you know? The best? I'm sure you've learned that working with so many winners. Maybe you can help me turn these guys into champions. They just don't get it, you know?"

I say nothing and just wait for him to share more.

He looks at me quizzically. "You do know what I mean, right? You know?"

I debate whether we have enough of a relationship that I can tell him the truth. He doesn't know that his attitude and the phrase "lonely at the top" are reliable omens for every great downfall I've ever seen.

"Hey, man, you can tell me what you're thinking. Say it straight. I don't have a lot of time today. I can handle you, I promise," he says, laughing. "Nothing you'll say will hurt my feelings. Promise."

"Okay, good. I think you have six months, tops, before you destroy your career."

#

This is a chapter about failure. But not just any kind of failure. It's about the calamitous fall from grace that high performers can experience when they get *so good* that they forget what made them successful.

This chapter is, in effect, the "antipractices" of high performance. It's about how people like Don start thinking they are separate from others, better than others, more capable than others, and more important than others—and how those attitudes destroy performance (and careers). It's also about the problems that come from the never-be-satisfied, hustle-and-grind approach that sucks passion and leads to overcommitment. This is a chapter about the warning signs—the thoughts, feelings, and behaviors that knock high performers out of the sky.

Long before I met Don, I had surveyed high performers about what brought an end to previous winning streaks. I surveyed five hundred people who had scored in the top 15 percent, looking for clues. I wanted to know how long they felt they had sustained their success, whether they had ever fallen hard, and whether they ever felt they had risen to such heights again. I asked them open-ended questions such as "When was a time you had an initial period of success—say, three to five years—then suddenly failed?" I asked more questions to find out what caused them to fail, how long they were down, how fast they achieved success again, and what factors led to the bounce back.

The stories were astoundingly similar to those I had heard working with high performers from all walks of life. I collected the five hundred surveys and stories, then did another twenty interviews to learn more. Then I compared all those findings to my own experiences coaching high performers over the past ten years. Obvious patterns emerged:

1. When high performers fell from grace, the most frequent culprits (aside from failing to practice the habits you've learned in this book) came down to three things.

2. When high performers rose back up, the habits in this book were the vehicle for that ascension.

3. When high performers describe such an up-and-down journey, they clearly *never* want to make the same mistakes again. The fall was *that painful*. When you fail at the beginning of a journey, it's frustrating. When you fail hard after making it for so many years, it feels immeasurably worse.

So what were the three things that caused high performers to fall out of prolonged success? Let's start with what *didn't* cause them to fail:

- *Fear was not the issue.* To become high performers, people have learned to get comfortable with the uncomfortable. The people I surveyed didn't report failing because of fear, worry, or holding back.

- *Competence was not an issue.* To succeed in the first place, you have to be good at your craft. No one said, "Gosh, Brendon, I just wasn't skilled enough to stay on top."

- *Other people were not the issue.* Of five hundred people who responded to my survey, only *seven* blamed other people for their stumbles, but even in those cases, the respondents ultimately reasoned that it was their own fault. High performers, especially those who have fallen down and got back up, take personal responsibility for their journey.

- *Creativity was not the issue.* I had expected some high performers to say they were passed up because they ran out of good ideas. That didn't happen.

- *Motivation was not the issue.* If anything, these high performers were deeply, if not desperately, motivated to climb back up. You could say they had extreme performance necessity.

- *Resources were not the issue.* Only thirty-eight of five hundred people blamed money or insufficient support as the reason they failed. I spoke with fourteen of those thirty-eight, and certainly lack of money or support was a ready excuse. But behind that excuse, they accepted a colder, harder truth: They messed up.

These issues could certainly be fair and understandable reasons for people to fail. But what I've learned from high performers is that these just aren't the real failure points of sustained performance. The real traps are *internal*—negative patterns of thinking, feeling, and behaving that slowly kill our humanity, zest, and well-being. The traps are **superiority**, **dissatisfaction**, and **neglect**.

If you're going to maintain high performance, you need to maintain your high performance habits and avoid these three traps.

TRAP #1: SUPERIORITY

"There are two kinds of pride, both good and bad. 'Good pride' represents our dignity and self-respect. 'Bad pride' is the deadly sin of superiority that reeks of conceit and arrogance."

—John Maxwell

High performers face a unique set of character traps because they are, by definition, outperforming so many around them. When you are succeeding beyond others, it's easy to get a big head. You can begin to think you're special, separate from, better than, or more important than other people. That was obvious in my conversations with Don, and it's what others were sharing about him. This is a way of thinking that you must avoid at all costs.

Of course, you probably would never say to yourself, "One day, I want to start feeling that I'm better than other people." No one wants to join the ranks of the egomaniacs, narcissists, braggarts, or elitists. You sense that this is true because you've likely met someone who truly believed they were superior to you or others. You can probably think of five people like that right now, and I bet you don't have a positive association with any of them. Superiority has no positive connotation in a healthy mind.

But I'm not here to talk about "those" people. I'm here to caution *you* that as *you* get more successful, *you* can quickly fall prey to the same fatal error. In fact, I'm here to suggest that you, like all humans, are *already* guilty of subtle thoughts and actions that point to feelings of superiority. You might not be demonstrating a bombastic ego, but there are a hundred shades and degrees of superiority. Have you recently thought that some of the people you work with are idiots and that your ideas are always better? Yes, that qualifies. Not asking your team to review your big presentation and find its errors or omissions because you "got this"? Uh-oh. Getting cut off in traffic, then racing ahead to cut that guy off just to show him who's boss—yep. Arguing your point over and over to your spouse even though they have been clear about their position and are not budging? Check. Failing to review your work because it's *always* good enough? Dang. Minimizing someone else so you look better? Oops. Discounting another person's ideas because they haven't put in the time you have? Anything here seem familiar?

See? Superiority draws us off track a quarter inch at a time. When it has a firm hold on us, we begin acting out like jerks. We stop asking people for their input or help because we think we're always right. We lose awareness of others' contributions and powers. We end up soloing and we destroy the sense of connection and camaraderie that makes high achievement fun and worthwhile. We dismiss people and we speak in tones of condescension. We start falling prey more often to confirmation bias—interpreting what we see as confirmation of our own beliefs, while neglecting or discounting the evidence against it.[1] We lose ourselves to thoughts of superiority that ultimately destroy our relationships and our performance.

The good news is, you can learn to spot exactly *when* and *how* these thoughts arise in your mind, and with that knowledge, you can avoid buying into them. *When* is the easy part. The roots of superiority always begin to grow in the soil of separateness and certainty. It's that moment when you begin to think you are separate from others, or certain about anything, that you are in greatest danger.

Here's how to know when superiority has infiltrated your mind:

1. You think you are better than another person or group.

2. You're so amazingly good at what you do that you don't feel you need feedback, guidance, diverse viewpoints, or support.

3. You feel that you automatically deserve people's admiration or compliance because of who you are, what position you hold, or what you've accomplished.

4. You feel that people don't understand you, so all those fights and failures are surely not your fault—it's that "they" just can't appreciate your situation or the demands, obligations, or opportunities you have to sort through daily.

When any of these realities is a constant in your life, you've begun the decline, even if you don't know it yet. What these thoughts have in common is a sense of separateness. You just feel so much more capable or accomplished than others that, in your mind, there is you at the top and then everyone else.

It's this separateness that fueled Don's belief that "it's lonely at the top." Yet Don isn't alone. A lot of people believe this bizarre idea. People say it because they think others can't possibly comprehend their lives. The problem is, this thought is inaccurate and obscenely destructive. If you ever feel as if the world can't understand you, then—and I won't bother looking for a gentler way to say this—it's time to pop the bubble you've been hanging out in. We have thousands of years of recorded human history, and over seven billion people walk this earth today. The odds are pretty good that someone, somewhere, has gone through what you're going through, and can easily understand your situation and advise you through it.

All isolation is ultimately self-imposed. This is a difficult truth to relay to people who feel that no one can understand them or their situation. I can't tell you how many times I've had to kindly tell someone to abandon their sense of separateness in truly difficult situations:

- You are not the first entrepreneur to face financial ruin.

- You are not the first parent to lose a child.

- You are not the first manager to be cheated by an employee.

- You are not the first lover to be cheated on.

- You are not the first striver to lose your dream.

- You are not the first CEO to run a large global company.

- You are not the first healthy person to find yourself suddenly battling cancer.

- You are not the first person to deal with depression or addiction in yourself or a loved one.

When we're facing any of these difficulties, it's easy to *feel* that we're the only one going through the struggle. But that feeling is pure illusion. There is no human emotion or situation you are contending with that someone, somewhere, cannot understand if you are vulnerable and real and open enough to share your thoughts, feelings, and challenges. Yes, you can keep telling yourself that your spouse can't possibly understand, and if you never try, that will be a self-fulfilling prophecy.

Their lack of understanding only grows in your silence.

Yes, you can tell yourself that no one on your team "gets it," but that's just your ego blinding you to the value that others can ultimately add. Discounting others doesn't make you a greater person; you are just choosing to be more separate, ultimately making yourself more vulnerable to failure.

I know that when you're trapped in hardship, these statements can feel judgmental or oblivious of your reality. But I respectfully share these ideas with you because I've seen so many good people lose it all, not through ill intent but through a sense of separateness that soon makes them dismiss others or fail to ask for help. It never hurts to remind strivers that we all are one human family and that there are really only two stories in the human narrative, both of which we all can know and connect to. You might recall these two stories are *struggle* and *progress.*

People can understand your struggle. They can understand your wins. And they can understand tough choices even if they themselves have never had to make them. If you don't believe it, then you are telling yourself a story that is not natural—that is disconnected from the reality of seven billion people who all have hearts and hurts and dreams.

Often, when I meet high performers who are so good that they are indeed at the top of their particular food chain—the CEO, the world champion athlete, the most popular person in school, the smartest woman in the room—I'll have to go further than this oneness argument. I'll have to remind them that someone, somewhere, is smarter, earns more, serves better, trains harder, and positively affects more people than they do. I don't say that to diminish these paragons, but to connect them to another reality: that whoever you are, what seems a big issue to you, what might be separating you from others in your circle of influence, might be child's play to a bigger fish in another pond. That perspective can prove hopeful. Someone out there has already solved the dilemma, mastered the thing that you believe makes you so different from others. If you can find them, you can find a mentor, a solution, and a path back to reality and humility.

A few more points about the lonely-at-the-top syndrome, just because it's just so corrosive:

> **First, I've rarely met a high performer who thinks they're "at the top."** *Most feel like they're just getting started.*

They understand they're still students of life, and no matter how stellar their success, they feel that they're just a few steps in on the path of mastery. This is a widely held attitude with the top scorers of our assessments whom I interviewed.

Second, here's a special reminder if you have begun dismissing other people's capabilities. You can't maximize your potential while minimizing others. What you have attained in life isn't because you're all that special, but because you're all that blessed.[2] The reality is that a large part of the differentiation in performance at your level comes down to the habits we've discussed—which anyone can begin implementing—augmented by exposure, training, practice, and access to excellence-driven mentors, coaches, or role models. That's why I often have to remind the superior minded: You are not better than anyone. You likely just got more exposure to your topic; you had more information or opportunity available to you; you got trained better; you had the opportunity to put in more passion or deliberate practice over more time; you had the opportunity to receive good feedback and guidance. These things are not inherent to who you are. These things, if given to another person, would help them rise to your level. True? (If you don't answer yes, please shake hands with your ego.)

This isn't just my opinion. In almost all studies on expert performance, the major thing that made the difference was not a person's innate talents, but the hours of exposure and deliberate practice. In the world of talent, expertise, or sustained world-class performance, there is no longer a debate of nature versus nurture. The myth of the naturally superior human has been deconstructed and obliterated by research across dozens of fields.[3]

This warrants the simplest of reminders: *Don't judge others as below you or separate from you.* Your frustration with people is coming from a *forgetfulness* that almost everyone could succeed at a higher level if they had more exposure, training, practice, and access to excellence-driven mentors, coaches, or role models. Remember, *everything is trainable.* That doesn't mean everyone will request the training, put in the hard work, reach number one, or have as much grit as you. But everyone is capable of success. Everyone can win at life. So let's be honest: *You were once a mess, too, or did you forget already?* But you improved. Give others that same opportunity. When you remember that you, too, struggled, and you remind yourself that others can dramatically improve themselves, that's when you start to be more compassionate. That's when you start to beat back any hint of a superiority complex.

But even knowing this, we haven't won the fight just yet. Thoughts of separateness are just seedlings of superiority. If you want to watch the complex bloom, just till those thoughts in the soil of *certainty.* Imagine how much more insufferable a person becomes when they are *certain* of the things we've discussed so far:

1. They are *certain* they are better than another person or group.

2. They are *certain* they are tops at what they do, so they are *certain* they don't need feedback, guidance, diverse viewpoints, or support.

3. They are *certain* they deserve people's admiration or compliance because of who they are, where they came from, or what they've earned or accomplished.

4. They are *certain* that people don't understand them, and any fights and failures are *certainly* not their fault.

My guess is, you wouldn't exactly be inspired by working with a person like this. People like this aren't only separate from others and, thus, dismissive of their ability to understand or help; they also become *condescending* toward others. You know that your mind has tipped into condescension the moment you start hearing yourself say, "What's wrong with these idiots?" When someone makes a mistake and you think, *What a moron!* before asking whether they had sufficient clarity, information, or support. When someone doesn't work as hard as you and you think, *Why are they so lazy? What is wrong with them?* When you start seeing others as wrong or inadequate for life, then you've fallen so far into the trap of superiority that you are in danger of destroying your connection with others, and your ability to lead.

Superior-minded people are certain they are better, more capable, more deserving.[4] And it's that certainty that closes their minds to learning, connection with others, and, ultimately, growth. The more you absolutely believe anything, the more likely you are to become blinded to new perspectives and opportunities. The moment someone becomes absolutely certain is the moment that superiority has won. For all these reasons, we must beware of separateness and certainty.

So what's the solution? I've found that the first step is always awareness. You have to be alert and catch yourself when you start thinking you are separate from others for any reason. Second, you need to develop habits that will help you *stay humble* and open even as you get better at what you do.

Humility is a foundational virtue that enables many other virtues to grow. It is associated with positive outcomes like marital fidelity, cooperation, compassion for others, strong social bonds, general group acceptance, optimism, hope, decisiveness, comfort with ambiguity, and openness to experience. It's also tied to our willingness to admit gaps in current knowledge and the tendency to feel guilty after wrongdoing.[5]

How do you stay humble?

You begin developing a more open and test-oriented mindset by flipping the earlier examples:

1. To avoid thinking you're superior to others, deliberately seek others' ideas for improving anything you do: *If you could improve on my idea, how would you go about it?* Ask this question enough, and you'll discover so many holes in your thinking, any sense of superiority begins to melt away in the harsh light of truth. Learning is the anvil on which humility is forged.

2. If you find that your thinking is not being challenged enough or your growth has topped out, hire a coach, trainer, or therapist. Yes, *hire* someone. Sometimes, your immediate peer group can't see beyond their knowledge of you. Sometimes, they're not qualified or available to help you through a specific challenge or period of life. Professionals can help you explore issues, find clarity, and leverage proven tools for growth. If you'd like a listing of certified professionals in this topic, visit HighPerformanceInstitute .com. If you can't hire someone, find a mentor and call or meet with them at least twice each month. Consistency in receiving feedback is the hallmark of consistent growth.

3. To avoid thinking you automatically deserve people's admiration or compliance just because of who you are, where you came from, or what you've accomplished, remind yourself that trust is earned through caring for others, not bragging about yourself. Challenge yourself to ask people more questions about who they are, where they come from, what they want to achieve. Before interacting with others, tell yourself, "I'm starting from scratch with this person. If this were my first date or interaction with them, what questions could I ask to learn more about them?"

4. Instead of believing that people don't understand you and that they are to blame for the fights and failures in your life, take ownership of your actions by reflecting on your role. After a conflict, ask yourself, "Am I distorting this situation in any way to make myself feel like the misunderstood hero? Am I spinning a story to make myself feel better? Am I trying to make excuses or play the victim to protect my ego? What were my actions that contributed to the issues at hand? What might I not know about this person or their situation?"

5. Keep a practice for reminding yourself of your blessings. Gratitude and humility have been shown to be "mutually reinforcing," meaning the more grateful you are, the more humble you feel. And the more humble you feel, the more grateful you are.[6]

These suggestions will help keep you humble, effective, and respectful. That's how you sustain success, and that's how you build a life you can be proud of.

One last point on superiority, from a leadership point of view. Not all high performers who spoke of failing to maintain their degree of success blamed an internal perception of superiority. They didn't all say they began thinking they were separate from or better than others. The issue for them was that *other* people started viewing them as acting superior. The high performers got so good, they simply disengaged from others because they truly didn't think they needed help. They didn't engage, and an assumption of aloofness and superiority grew to fill that attention vacuum. Never forget, people can perceive you to be superior minded when you don't engage with them, even if it's not your true intent or spirit. That's just one more way the above suggestions will help you maintain the truth and the perception of being a humble and engaged leader.

Performance Prompts

1. A recent situation where I found myself being overly critical or dismissive of others was . . .

2. The thoughts I had about myself in that situation and the others involved were . . .

3. Had I reimagined the situation from a more humble and appreciative view, I would probably have realized that . . .

4. The best way I can remind myself that everyone is dealing with difficulties in life and that we're all more alike than we are different is . . .

TRAP #2: DISSATISFACTION

*"Be satisfied with success in even the smallest matter,
and think that even such a result is no trifle."*

—Marcus Aurelius

I was standing alone in the dark backstage, and a terrible anxiety set in. A famous musician was out front, repeatedly telling the audience of thousands, *"Never be satisfied!"* He said this phrase perhaps ten times in fifteen minutes. He credited his dissatisfaction with giving him the "emotional fuel" needed to keep dreaming, innovating, outhustling his peers.

Oh, dear, I thought, my heart racing. *What am I going to do?*

I was the next speaker. The second slide in my presentation, which soon would be projected onto the jumbo monitors, had just two words blazoned across it: **BE SATISFIED**.

The musician was literally delivering the antithesis of what I was about to teach! Not that his message was wrong. If he credited his dissatisfaction with his successful career, who was I to argue? However someone explains their performance is true for them.

The issue for me was that he was saying *everyone* should refuse to be satisfied in life and career, because that dissatisfaction will lead to greater success. This, we know, is incorrect. High performers in general aren't dissatisfied with themselves, their lives, or their work. Remember just a few findings I've shared in this book: High performers are, in fact, happier than most people. They feel satisfied and well rewarded in their careers, and they cultivate experiences that are more positive than negative, with joy often at the heart of their endeavors.

As I was thinking through this, the event host started introducing me as the next speaker. There was no time to change my presentation. I would have to do what I've had to do many times in my career: bust a powerful and popular myth about performance.

There is a long-standing cultural sensibility that says we should never be satisfied with our work, because satisfaction would somehow lead to complacency. But does satisfaction really drain our motivation or weaken our resolve for excellence?

Having surveyed and coached so many of the world's top performers, I've found the answer is no. Satisfaction *must* accompany striving for optimal performance.[7]

Those who are never satisfied are never at peace. They can't tune in to their zone—the noise of a dissatisfied mind prevents them from finding a rhythm that makes them feel alive and effective. If I cannot sense satisfaction in the moment, then I am not feeling connection or gratitude for the moment. Dissatisfaction is disconnection, so people who feel it do not experience the full levels of engagement and joy that high performers so consistently talk about. Dissatisfaction causes them to obsess about the negative, leading in turn to a habit of missing what's working, and failing to praise or appreciate others. This negative focus prevents the kind of gratitude that makes life magical and leadership with others possible. The nothing-is-good-enough, never-settle mentality also compels them to discard too quickly what's in front of them and move on to the next iteration or thing. And with that, no real appreciation or memory of achievement is forged in their mind, and so they are just busy and empty ghosts on a hunt for some dream day when they might have perfection.

Ultimately, the dark, exhausting, negative emotional prison that is constant dissatisfaction saps performance. Perennial dissatisfaction is the first step on the path to misery.

The never-settle, unhappy striver mentality is akin to what researchers call *maladaptive perfectionism*.[8] This is the kind of perfectionism in which you have high standards—often a good thing—but are always beating yourself up for any imperfection (a bad thing). This can cause such high cognitive anxiety over making mistakes that optimal performance is all but impossible. Obsessive concern over mistakes has been associated with several negative outcomes, including anxiety, low confidence, a failure orientation, and negative reactions to basic mistakes during competition.[9] And the kicker is that no matter what you do or what you achieve, you'll always be dissatisfied. It's a miserable loop to be caught in, and that's why, as the research shows, it is often related to depression.[10]

If dissatisfaction is so detrimental to performance, why do so many people think you have to be dissatisfied to succeed? Because it feels natural and automatic. It's *easy* to be dissatisfied, because noticing what's wrong in a situation is a habit of evolution. Often called the negativity bias, this never-ending scouting for errors and anomalies helps our species survive.[11] When our distant ancestors heard a rustling in the thicket and the crickets stop chirping, an alarm went up telling them something was off. That's a good thing. But if overapplied in modern daily life, this same impulse doesn't help us survive—it causes suffering.

Some may argue that our brain defaults to seeking errors, but that isn't the only default setting. Your brain is hardwired just as much for happiness as for negativity or fear.[12] If this were not true, then how to explain the fact that, worldwide, most people are moderately happy most of the time?[13] Our natural tendency is to seek positive emotions and experiences. When we do, it enhances our learning and our ability to see new opportunities.[14] It also leads to flow states that make for superior objective performance outcomes.[15] That tendency should be encouraged and amplified. When it is, life blooms and high performance is more likely.

The reason I push so hard against the "never be satisfied" credo extends beyond the empirical research. Simply, this thinking has little to no practical value, because the emphasis is in the wrong area. It's pointing in a statement rather than a positive direction. When you speak to people who are fond of that instruction, and ask them to turn it into a positive takeaway, they say such things as "Stay motivated"; "Notice what's not working and improve it"; "Care about perfecting the details"; "Set your sights on bigger goals as you grow"; "Keep moving forward." The truth is, you can do all these things and *still* be satisfied. Seeking excellence and experiencing satisfaction are not mutually exclusive.

Being satisfied, then, doesn't mean "settling." It simply means accepting and taking pleasure in what *is*. It's allowing yourself to feel contentment whether or not a thing is complete or "perfect." For example, as I write this book, I'm satisfied even though I'm trying to make it better, even though I'm just weeks from deadline, even though I'm not sure how it will turn out. As I shoot my videos, I'm satisfied even though I know I could do better with more time or practice and that no matter what I do, plenty of people won't like the result. As I serve my clients, I'm satisfied even though we might not get a perfect solution. This sense of satisfaction doesn't mean I have everything figured out. It doesn't mean I don't care about the details or push the boundaries and cheer everyone on to get better and better. I've just made what I consider a simple choice in life: to be a satisfied striver rather than a dissatisfied curmudgeon. Whistle while you work, or grit your teeth and huff and puff? It's a choice.

But how to respond to those who say, "Brendon, I've become pretty successful even though I'm perennially dissatisfied"? I say simply this: Your path ahead doesn't have to feel so negative anymore, and if you allow dissatisfaction to be your approach, your cross, your brand, then the odds are, you will soon see your performance lag. We all need the payoff of satisfaction and fulfillment at some point. If you keep cheating yourself of it, then that neglect will be your Achilles' heel.

And let's be honest: Perhaps dissatisfaction wasn't *really* what made you good in the first place. What you are correlating with your success may not be the cause. What if it was an eye toward detail, a deep passion, or hunger to inspire others to grow that really drove you all those years? What if you were simply practicing one of the high performance habits without knowing it? I ask this because too often we give credit to the forefront negative emotions and experiences in life and miss the real causes of success. It's like when someone says, "I'm successful because I sleep only four hours a night." No, the lack of sleep isn't what made you successful—fifty years of sleep science proves that you were cognitively *impaired*, not optimized.[16] You succeeded *despite* being sleep deprived, because other positive attributes compensated for the deficit. In the same vein, I suggest that dissatisfaction was not the strength that helped you climb.

I know that no matter what I do, I can't win an argument here if you believe that dissatisfaction has helped you succeed. But maybe I can invite you to consider the possibility that it might feel better if, once in a while, you let yourself enjoy more moments, pat your-self on the back, high-five the team for a good effort, recognize that you're okay and things are going your way. When you can be in the moment and satisfied with what you're doing, you can access greater flow and potential. People around you will enjoy and appreciate and recommend you more. Soon, in the place of all that dissatisfaction will be a sense of real connection and play, and when that happens, you'll reach an entirely new level of mastery and performance. People who feel a sense of play, not dissatisfaction, perform better in almost every field of endeavor. Play is not indulgent; it's crucial to creativity, health, healing, and happiness.[17] Flow and play are gateways to mas-tery. So don't fret. *You won't lose passion by feeling better.*

All these points are even more important if you are a leader. Allowing greater satisfaction as you strive isn't just about how much better *you* can feel. It's also about how *others* feel around you. No one wants to work with someone who is perennially dissatisfied with themselves or others. We've found that leaders who are always stuck in error-detection mode and forget to celebrate the small wins also consistently fail to acknowledge progress, praise the team, encourage reflection, and champion other people's ideas. In other words, they're not exactly a joy to be around. That's why I warn high performers: If you become habitually dissatisfied, it's going to destroy your influ-ence with others, and as you now know, influence is critical to your long-term success.

So how can you avoid performance-sapping dissatisfaction? I suggest a big-picture reminder: Life is short, so decide to enjoy it. Instead of discontent, bring joy and honor to what you do. I promise you'll start feeling more alive, motivated, and fulfilled.

If it's hard to imagine a life free from dissatisfaction, you can at least start edging it out with tactical daily and weekly practices that help you appreciate life's blessings more often. This is especially true if you've slid from performance dissatisfaction into self-loathing. If that's the case, it's time to make peace with yourself. You've been through enough. Yesterday did not make it through last night, and this morning's sunlight belongs to a fresh new day.

In this moment now, you can breathe deep and finally, after all this time, give yourself love and appreciation.

To help you on this journey, try this:

- Start journaling at the end of each day. Write down three things that went well or better than expected that day. Write about any progress or blessings that you feel grateful for. It's such simple but essential advice to keep a high performer performing high: Start noticing what's going well, appreciate your blessings, enjoy the journey, and record your wins.

- Get your family or team together once a week for no other reason than to talk about what's working, what people are excited about, what difference your efforts are making in real people's lives.

- Start meetings by asking others to share one great thing that has happened that can give the team a sense of joy, pride, and fulfillment.

These are simple steps, but they will matter to the people you love and lead.

I remember finishing my presentation that day—the one where I had to carefully correct the famous musician's assertion that "never be satisfied" was a mentality the entire audience should adopt. I cautiously walked backstage, imagining that, if he was still there, he would be upset. And he was. There the musician stood, arms crossed. He said, "I heard your talk. I'm sure you're quite satisfied, then!"

I laughed sheepishly. "Yes, I try to be, but I hope that doesn't upset you. I tried not to negate your message about how it's so important to always strive to keep getting better. Were you at least satisfied with your talk? The audience seemed to like it."

"No," he huffed. "I'm not satisfied, and I don't think I should be or you should be. I have the humility to know I can do better."

I replied, "I agree. We all can do better. The only path I've seen that works long term is to begin enjoying what you are doing—which you seem to. You love what you do, right?"

"Yes, I do."

"And you told the audience that you feel you're on the path you were meant to walk in life?"

"Yes."

"Okay. Then don't you feel fulfilled?"

He thought about it for a moment and said, "I suppose not yet."

"Then when?" I asked. "If you love what you're doing and you feel you're on your right path, when do you get to just feel good about that for a moment?"

He unfolded his arms. "Good question. Who knows? Soon, maybe."

Three months later, the tabloids reported he had checked himself into a depression treatment center.

If your aim is to maintain high performance, please, allow yourself to feel the wins again.

Don't just hope to arrive somewhere someday and finally feel satisfied. *Strive satisfied.*

Performance Prompts

1. The areas of my life I've felt consistently dissatisfied with include . . .

2. Some good things that have also happened in those areas include . . .

3. Something I can say to myself the next time I feel dissatisfied, to get me to notice the good things and continue moving forward, is . . .

4. Someone who probably sees me dissatisfied more than I want them to is . . .

5. If I were going to inspire that person to believe you can enjoy life as you work hard and succeed, I would have to change these behaviors . . .

TRAP #3: NEGLECT

"If things are not going well with you, begin your effort at correcting the situation by carefully examining the service you are rendering, and especially the spirit in which you are rendering it."

—Roger Babson

Neglect, like the other traps of superiority and disappointment, sneaks up on you. You don't say to yourself, "I'm going to neglect my health, my family, my team, my responsibilities, my real passions and dreams." It's more that passion or busyness blinds you to what's important, just long enough for things to fall apart.

Often, then, it's not what you do that unseats you from high performance, but what you *don't* do. In single-minded pursuit of achievement and mastery in one area of life, you take your eyes off the other areas. Soon, those areas fight back for more attention. This is the story of those who work so hard in their career that they keep forgetting their spouse's needs. Soon, the marriage is in turmoil, the high performer feels awful, and performance declines. Switch this example out with neglect of one's health, children, friendships, spirituality, or finances, and you still have the same story: Obsession in one area of life hurts another area, setting off a negative cascade of events and feelings that eventually unseats the high performer.

Again, no one *intends* to neglect important parts of their life over the long term. At least, not the high performers I've interviewed who failed to maintain progress. In fact, most shared a sense of surprise that things ever got so out of hand. "I knew I was juggling too many balls," they'll often say, "but I hadn't realized it was so bad until . . ." It's that last word: *until*. I can't describe how many times I've heard that word emphasized with a tone of pain and regret.

I want you to avoid this fate. The good news is, it's tactically easy to avoid neglect. The bad news is, it requires a difficult and often dramatic mental shift. Before I share the *how* part, let me share two distinctions about *why* high performers neglect something important to them in the first place.

In conducting my interviews, what I found fascinating was that high performers don't blame their neglect on the same things as underperformers. Underperformers often blame other people or lack of time. "I didn't have enough support, so I couldn't do everything, and something had to give." Or "There just aren't enough hours in the day to do it all." No doubt, we could all justify neglecting parts of our lives for these reasons.

It's just that high performers rarely do. Instead, when they reflect on a time when they neglected something and it hurt their performance, they place most of the blame on their own shoulders. They take personal responsibility. Neglect was a shortcoming of their own. Their explanations for neglect, I found, can be categorized into two areas: obliviousness and overreaching.

Obliviousness

Obliviousness is the less used excuse of the two, but a destructive culprit nonetheless. It means you are so focused in one area that you are *completely unaware* of the growing problems in another. High performers who started losing explain it by saying, "I was so obsessed with work, I honestly didn't realize I was getting so fat." Or "She just up and left one day. I was blindsided and hated myself for it." Or "That's when I realized my team had been telling me the same things for months, but I was too busy to pay attention."

To hear high performers describe neglect due to obliviousness is always painful. They have an unmistakable tone: They *hate* that they took their eye off other things that mattered. Hindsight is painfully clear, especially for a neglectful former high performer staring into self-loathing and regret.

Part of the reason it's so painful is that the things that they believe helped them climb to success—hard work, focus, and persistence—became the very things that caused their demise. Researchers have noted how sometimes tenacity and grit, held for too long, can actually undermine well-being and good health, make us miss alternative paths to a goal, and even cause us to neglect opportunities for collaboration.[18] Intense hard work sustained for too long becomes workaholism, creating work-home conflict, which hurts the well-being of the workaholic and the family members.[19]

That's why I'm so passionate about alerting you so you don't fall prey to obliviousness. You don't want to be that person who is blindsided by what should have been obvious. There are always warning signs along the road to disaster. We just have to pay attention.

The chapters on clarity and influence will help you avoid obliviousness. Also, you might want to recall and implement the life arenas activity from the chapter on productivity:

> The solution is to keep perspective in life by keeping an eye on the quality or progress of the major life arenas. A simple weekly review of what we're after in the major areas of our life helps us rebalance or at least plan for more balance.
>
> I've found it useful to organize life into ten distinct categories: health, family, friends, intimate relationship, mission/work, finances, adventure, hobby, spirituality, and emotion. When I'm working with clients, I often have them rate their happiness on a scale of 1 through 10 and also write their goals in each of these ten arenas every Sunday night.

There may be other areas you want to self-monitor, or different descriptions or goals you are aiming for, so I encourage you to create your own categories, scoring, and thinking prompts. The goal is to review consistently, at least once a week. Our clients have found it enormously helpful, not only in avoiding neglect in one area, but in achieving greater overall life balance as well.

Overreaching

Now you have a new tool to avoid becoming oblivious as you continue to rise. The next issue, overreaching, is a little trickier to deal with.

One reason high performers become so effective is that they are more disciplined at setting priorities for what to focus on. As you learned in the productivity chapter, they discern their primary field of interest and then focus on prolific quality output. That's what gets them to the next level and keeps them growing and adding value. But when that focus wanes due to overreaching, so, too, does their performance.

According to the high performers who failed to maintain their success, overreaching was a problem that stemmed from an insatiable desire for more, coupled with an unrealistic sense of what is possible in a short time frame, which led to overcommitment. In other words, it was an issue of *going for too much, too fast, in too many domains.*

Their lesson learned was clear: When you're good, you want to take on more. But beware the impulse. High performance isn't about more for the sake of more, just because you can. It's often about less— zeroing in on just those few things that matter and protecting your time and well-being so you can truly engage those around you, enjoy your craft, and confidently handle your responsibilities. Focus on just a few things and the people and priorities you really care about, and you won't fall prey to overreaching. Broaden your ambitions too widely, and your appetite soon outstrips your abilities. Hence the importance of reminding yourself that the main thing is to keep the main thing the main thing.

I can usually tell whether someone is about to fail, by asking a simple question: "Do you feel seriously overcommitted right now?"

New achievers, I've found, *almost always* agree. Their initial success came from saying yes to almost everything that came across the plate, because they were still testing their capabilities, learning their strengths, trying to find the right thing, hoping to strike while the iron was hot. They feared they would miss out on something, and at some point, they overestimated their ability to handle things. The other group who say yes to the question? High performers on the decline.

Here's the difficult mindset shift you'll have to make once you hit high performance. It will feel in some ways like the antithesis of what you've been doing, like a dangerous and opposite approach, but it's vitally important:

Slow down, be more strategic, and say no more often.

I know, telling someone with the wind at their back to slow down seems disempowering. But do yourself a favor and read that sentence again. Then give yourself a gift and read it again *out loud*. It's important that the line really land for you.

Naturally, there's a wonderful lift and momentum that comes with high performance. You can start to feel as though you've got it all going for you, especially when all the new attention and opportunities propel new ambitions and confer new freedoms. The hustle and grind that enabled your hard-earned success feels rewarding and still necessary. But the hustle-and-grind mentality will burn you out, and if you continue taking on too much, you risk losing it all. Yes, you can do amazing things. Yes, you want to take on the world. Yes, you are a badass. But don't overcommit yourself just because you're good at what you do. It's a short hop from badass to burnout.

So *slow down*. Be patient. You have plenty of skill and plenty of time to keep building, adding value, innovating. You can scale up in your primary field of interest deliberately and patiently. Play the long game, and life feels less like a slog and more like play.

While slowing down sounds less sexy than "don't settle" or "strike while the iron is hot," it is nonetheless the advice of over *three-quarters* of the former high performers I spoke to. Trying to go faster and do more things seems so right when you're good and you're certain, but it can knock you for a serious tumble.

So what, exactly, do we mean by "slow down"? First, rather than live a reactive lifestyle, you take ownership of your day. When the successes pile up, it's easy to spend time responding to invitations and calls and well-wishers' requests. Suddenly, the day has cruised by and you haven't done anything. You feel successful, but nothing is really happening except new meetings. Slowing down means taking the time to care about your schedule—doing what you've learned in this book about reviewing your calendar and to-dos each night, each morning, each week.

It also means saying no to the good things that would stretch your day too far. If a good opportunity comes up but it's going to rob you of a few nights' sleep, force you to cancel strategic moves you planned long ago, or knock you out of time with your family, then just say no. Cramming your day so full that you have no time for thought or rejuvenation just makes you tired and irritable. And no one credits fatigue and a bad mood for their world-class performance.

That's why I encourage all high performers who want to keep rising to say *no* to almost every opportunity in their mind *first*, then force themselves to justify it before ever giving a yes. "Yes" got you into the game. Taking on a lot and pursuing a lot of interests helped you figure out your "thing." But now that you're succeeding, more yeses can start hurting you. "No" keeps you focused.

To help you discern between the yeses and nos, you have to start thinking much more strategically. Strategic thinking means stripping things down to the essentials and planning their accomplishment out over months and years. This is hard, but you have to weigh opportunities differently now, measuring them against a much longer horizon. You can't think just about how flashy something is this month. You have to be executing against a plan—your five moves—that's already in place for the next several months. If the new thing you want to commit to doesn't strategically move you toward your end goals, it must be delayed. Most opportunities in life that are really worthwhile and meaningful will still be here six months from now. If that's hard to believe, it's just because you're new to success. So slow down; say no more often; be more strategic. Don't let obliviousness to what really matters, or reaching for what doesn't, slow down all your hard-won momentum.

DON'T FORGET WHAT GOT YOU HERE

"Sometimes, we're so concerned about giving our children what we never had growing up, we neglect to give them what we did have growing up."

—James Dobson

One last simple reminder: Don't forget the positive habits that brought you to this level of success, and do not neglect the habits that you now know will take you to the next level. Too often, we think of neglect as overlooking our problems. But it's also forgetting to continue what was working for us. You might find it useful to ask, "What are the five main reasons I've succeeded so far in life?" Put those five things on your Sunday review list, too. Ask, "Am I continuing to do the things that have made me successful?"

One high performer told me that the best way to avoid neglecting something important to us is to teach others to value that very thing. If you are teaching your children the value of patience, for example, then you tend not to neglect that virtue (or your children). What might you begin teaching others so they keep you accountable for it?

Performance Prompts

1. An area where I am neglecting someone or something important in my life is . . .

2. An area where that neglect will cause me regret later on is . . .

3. An area where I can now return my focus, reallocating my attention to things that matter, is . . .

4. Some areas in my life where I feel overcommitted right now are . . .

5. The things I need to learn to say no to more often are . . .

6. An opportunity I really want to chase right now that I could schedule to revisit in few months is . . .

7. The main things moving the needle toward my success that I should be focused on right now, despite all the other exciting interests and opportunities I could chase, are . . .

8. The way I'll remind myself not to take on too much is . . .

TOUGH TRUTHS

The culprits that steal your success are not lack of values or intelligence. The culprits are ultimately *allocations of attention*. You feel separate from others, so you stop paying attention to feedback, diverse viewpoints, new ways of doing things. You get so good that you start noticing only what's wrong, and a constant state of disappointment drains your passion. You rationalize neglecting one area of life so you can get ahead, saying it will be "worth it," so you stop focusing on what really matters in life.

None of these things has to be your reality.

Superiority, dissatisfaction, and neglect are your enemies. Let them invade your life, and you lose. Be vigilant, avoid them, and practice your HP6, and all will be well.

It's always a difficult truth when we notice ourselves behaving in the negative ways we've discussed in this chapter. But if sustaining success is important to you, I encourage you to revisit this chapter often. It will keep you humble, satisfied, and focused. And it will allow you and others to enjoy what should be an extraordinary life and a joyous ascent to high performance.

THE #1 THING

"They are able who think they are able."
—Virgil

"Are you always this *on?*" Aurora asks.

"What do you mean?"

"You know, this . . . energized. Happy?"

I think for a moment and laugh. "Yes, I really am this annoying. Why?"

Aurora peers out at fifteen thousand people gathered in the arena. We're standing at the very top row, looking down to the stage. Within the hour, we'll both have the blessing of speaking here.

"But aren't you nervous?" she says. "I feel like I'm going to be sick. I can't keep my thoughts in order."

A production assistant interrupts and asks to escort us down to the green room beneath the arena. As we walk, Aurora continues. "You look so relaxed. How do you get so confident?"

I'm surprised by her questions because I, too, feel the nerves, and imagine they are showing. It's not only my first time speaking to this many people, but it's also my first time giving this specific presentation. I explain this to Aurora and say, "Honestly, I don't really have a gauge on how they'll react to my speech."

"Then why do you look so calm?"

"I definitely wouldn't say I'm calm! I feel plenty of nerves, too, but I'm not really thinking about it. I'll worry about the fifteen thousand when I get to them. I was just enjoying my conversation with you."

"That's nice of you to say, Brendon. I'm sorry, I just feel like I'm going to bomb."

"Why? Have you bombed in front of this many people before?"

She laughs. "No, you know that."

Aurora has actually never addressed a large crowd before. As a world-class gymnast, she has been in front of thousands of people—she just hasn't delivered a formal paid presentation. She got the speaking slot here because she's a hometown hero and recently medaled at the Olympics.

We arrive at the green room, and Aurora sits down in a makeup chair. She chitchats for a while with Lisa, the makeup artist, then asks, "So what should I be thinking, Brendon. This is your world, not mine."

"Well, what are you thinking now?"

"That I'm going to bomb!"

"But again, you've never bombed in front of this many people speaking before, right?"

"Right."

"So why tell yourself that story?"

"I don't know. It's just what I'm feeling."

"I hear you. But you already know that's not going to serve you. Let me ask a different question. *Why* do you even want to be here?"

"I just want to share my story with them and maybe inspire someone."

"Beautiful. Well, you know your story, right? You've only told it during interviews, like, a million times, right?"

Before she can answer, Lisa shares that she heard Aurora's story on ESPN.

"We all know your story, Aurora," I tell her, "and so do you. You already know what to say, so now it's just about *who you want to be* out there and *how you want to connect.* When you're at your best on the gym mat, how would you describe yourself?"

"Happy. Confident. I'm excited."

"When you were competing, did nerves accompany any of those emotions?"

"Sure."

I smile. "Then you've been here before. You know what to do and how to be. I guess the only real question that matters is how you want to connect with this audience . . ." I lean in and speak almost mockingly. "As the *nervous little gymnast* who feels as if she couldn't do a basic cartwheel, or as the woman who just showed the world her superpowers at the Olympics."

My tone catches Aurora off guard, but it makes Lisa laugh.

"You have to be congruent with who you are," I say. "You're not some little wide-eyed girl lost on a stage. You're a champion. Now, how does this champion sitting right here in front of me want to connect with her people today?"

"I want to love on them. I want them to know I got a medal because of their support."

"Then go love on them. Let *that* be your emotion. Let that be your message. Does that feel true to you?"

Aurora stands up and kisses me on the cheek. "You're right, Brendon. I'm a hundred pounds of love. Let's go love up on these people."

#

We've measured over a hundred variables in search of which habits matter most to high performance. We've asked high performers almost every conceivable question about how they got so extraordinary. We've also sought to find out what matters most in increasing overall HPI scores and scores in each habit area proven to correlate with high performance. And so far nothing we've found correlates with high performance scores across the board more than *confidence*. Confidence is the secret ingredient that makes you rise to the challenge.

You already know how important confidence is because I've shared that, along with *engaged* and *joyful*, *confident* is one of the three words high performers use most to describe their consistent emotional state. Their descriptions align with the data, too, since high performers worldwide strongly agree with this statement more than their peers: *I'm confident I can achieve my goals despite challenges or resistance.* It turns out that this kind of confidence correlates significantly and meaningfully with overall high performance, as well as with each of the six high performance habits individually. When someone is more confident, they consistently have greater clarity, energy, productivity, influence, necessity, and courage.[1]

We've also found that individuals who have high confidence also tend to have higher life happiness overall, a love for taking on new challenges, and a feeling of making a difference in the world.[2] Think about that for a moment. Confidence is a powerful gateway to so much of what we want in life.

These findings also align with nearly forty years of research stating that this kind of confidence—often called *self-efficacy*—predicts exceptional performance and happiness.[3] But it goes beyond excelling and feeling good. One meta-analysis across 57 cross-cultural studies involving over 22,000 individuals suggests that the more confident you are, the less likely you are to feel burnout from work.[4] In a world fraught with concerns about overwork, it turns out that working on our confidence might just be the save. Why would confidence help us avoid burnout? High performers tell me it's because when you are more confident, you are more willing to say no and more sure of what to focus on, which makes you more efficient and less prone to distraction.

Another study, with results across 173 studies spanning over 33,000 individuals, suggests that self-efficacy correlates strongly with positive health-related behaviors. The more you believe in your ability to perform well, the more likely you are to do things that protect, restore, and improve your health.[5] You've probably sensed this truth in your own life. When you feel good about yourself, you are more likely to work out.

These findings all lead to a dramatic conclusion in human performance: Becoming more confident is good for your health; it decreases burnout; and it makes you feel happy, willing to take on new challenges, and more fulfilled. For these reasons, I like to say that *nothing correlates like confidence.*

But this doesn't mean confidence alone *causes* high performance. You can have all the self-confidence in the world, but if you don't practice the high performance habits, the odds of long-term success aren't so good. It's clear from our research that to become extraordinary, you need strong confidence *and* high performing habits.

But where does the kind of confidence that improves performance come from? What, specifically, do high performers do to gain and maintain confidence as they deal with life's challenges and take on ever greater goals?

THE 3 C'S OF CONFIDENCE

"Self-confidence is the first requisite to great undertakings."

—Samuel Johnson

Once we found that confidence was so critical to high performance, I sought out thirty people with the highest overall HPI scores out of over 20,000 surveyed who also strongly agreed with the statement "I'm confident I can achieve my goals despite challenges or resistance." I had already studied much of the academic literature on confidence, and we had loads of data from the surveys, so I wanted to hear how the top high performers actually talked about it. I wondered whether they felt somehow super-human, as if they had an inborn and unstoppable kind of confidence that we mere mortals lack.

As you can probably guess, the answer was no. High performers *do* have more confidence than most people, but not by birthright, luck, or superhuman skill. What I found was that high performers simply *thought* about things that gave them more confidence than others, more often *did* things that gave them more confidence than others, and *avoided* things that drain confidence more often than others did. They almost universally reported that their confidence came from purposeful thinking and action. No one in the interviews, nor any other high performer I have ever trained or worked with, ever said, "I was just born confident enough to handle the enormous challenges and responsibilities I face in my life now."

So what did high performers think, do, and avoid to develop such strong confidence?

I can bucket my findings in three areas: *competence, congruence,* and *connection.* Because these are such important topics for developing high performance confidence, I'll treat them as practices, as we did in earlier chapters.

PRACTICE #1: DEVELOP COMPETENCE

"As is our confidence, so is our capacity."

—William Hazlitt

While most people think of confidence as a general belief in oneself, the kind of confidence that is most tied to performance improvement comes from belief in one's abilities in a specific task.[6] This means that the more knowledge, skill, ability, or talent—that is, competence— you have at a given task, the more likely you are to be confident and perform well. I've been teaching about this "confidence-competence loop" since 1997, and I'm continually surprised at how much it comes up in conversations with high performers.

The idea here is that the more competence you get at any given task, the more confident you'll become in trying it more often—and the more you'll stretch yourself. That repetition and stretching leads to more learning, which gives you more competence. More competence, then, begets more confidence, and round and round it goes. You can see how this plays out if you've ever gone to the gym. The first time you're there, you don't really know what to do with all the weights and machines. So you're uncertain and perhaps even awkward in your workout. But the more you go, the more you know. Soon, you're confident in your ability to use the weights and machines, and the more you know how to use them, the more you start pushing yourself. You weren't "born confident" in the gym; you *got* confident. Confidence is not a fixed personality trait. It's a muscle you build through exertion.

In one way or another, all the top thirty high performers spoke about the competence-confidence loop. They credited their current level of confidence to their *years of focus, learning, practice, and skill development*. In fact, twenty-three of the thirty referenced these types of things *first* when discussing confidence. And not one mentioned hitting the lottery at birth with tons of confidence. They didn't talk about general self-esteem as in "I like myself," or "I feel good about me." They talked about how they had run the miles and earned the confidence to do well in life. They think, *I know what to do and how to add value here.*

To my surprise, high performers attributed their confidence to this sort of competence even before mentioning character traits. I thought they would speak first to traits that gave them self-trust, then to those that fostered skill. I was wrong, which is why I say that the "loop" never fails to turn out more ahas.

In the chapter on productivity, I covered how to get supercompetent at any skill through practicing progressive mastery. So let me move on to another distinction in this area. High performers have confidence not only because of past skill acquired in a specific area, but equally from trust in their ability to gain *future competence*. That is, they reported that their confidence was not tied to one specific competency but rather to a belief that they could adequately handle things in the future—even if they had no experience. Their confidence came from belief in their power of *learning in general*.

High performers are learners, and their belief that they can learn what is necessary to win in the future gives them as much confidence as their current skill sets.

Having learned so many things in the past, they trust they can do it again. In this way, it became clear that the internal voice of a high performer is saying, "I believe in my ability to figure things out." It's a bit circular but no less true: The key competency that gives high performers confidence is the ability to quickly gain understanding or skill in new situations. In other words, the competency that matters is the ability to become competent.

That's why I knew that reminding Aurora of her superpowers would help her find a little more confidence before her speech. She had figured out a lot of things in her life, and simply acknowledging that could give her a small boost of confidence to handle this situation, too—even though she'd never done it before.

This idea is particularly important in sports. Every day on the field or in the arena, you're going to meet someone who has more experience and perhaps more talent and successes. You'll often feel as though you can't measure up, and often enough, that will be true. But just because you can't keep up doesn't mean you can't *show* up. Only by showing up consistently, even when you're the greenest novice, will you ever get that experience and confidence.

Besides a sometimes untethered trust in their ability to figure things out in the moment, high performers also gain more confidence by ruminating on past successes and learning more from them than others do.

High performers ponder the lessons from their wins. They give credit to themselves, and they allow those wins to integrate into their psyche and give them greater strength.

This is a vitally important distinction. Underperformers rarely reflect on their lessons learned, and if they do, they are too hard on themselves. And even when they win, they rarely *integrate* that win into their identity. They did well yet don't feel any stronger because of it. They just don't let themselves *feel the win*. They didn't get what gamers would call a "power-up." In conversations with them, it's obvious that they don't recognize how much they've learned, how far they've come, what they are capable of doing now or in the future. They lowball themselves even when they've put in the miles. And so they lack confidence.

That's why, as you strive, it's important that you begin a practice of reflecting on your progress and your new learning. Don't wait until New Year's Eve to think about all the great things you did and learned this year. I recommend you spend at least thirty minutes every Sunday reflecting on the previous week. What did you learn? What did you handle well? What do you deserve to give yourself a pat on the back for? As simplistic as this may sound, it can have a profound effect in helping you gain more confidence.

Performance Prompts

1. The competences—knowledge, skills, abilities, or talents—that I have worked hard to cultivate in my life include . . .

2. If I gave myself credit for learning all those things, I would start to feel more . . .

3. Something I've learned to do in the past few years that I have not yet given myself credit for is . . .

4. I feel that I can handle a big challenge in my life right now because I am good at learning how to . . .

5. A practice I'll begin doing every week to help me start feeling more confident is . . .

PRACTICE #2: BE CONGRUENT

"Self-trust is the first secret of success."

—Ralph Waldo Emerson

Living in congruence with the best of who we are is one of the primary motivations of humankind. I wrote an entire chapter about this topic in my book *The Charge*, and we'll use an excerpt here to begin the conversation:

> At the core of congruence are questions about how we are really living our life, not just imagining it. The drive for congruence forces you to ask yourself, "Am I being honest with who I am?" "Am I trustworthy—true to myself and others?" "Do I practice what I think and preach?" "Do I follow through on what I know of myself?" "Do I make a stand when the world challenges who I can become?" These questions, and our answers to them, define us and largely determine our destiny.
>
> It's hard to be congruent. Naturally, different parts of us are engaged at different times. Our identity, personality, states, and standards may vary from one context to the next. We might be a rock star at work but a janitor at home. We may be fun, exciting, and playful with our best friends but shy and reserved in bed. We can be aggressive in one situation, then fail to be assertive when it counts. Variance in who we are in any given context is natural and, despite what some would have you believe, healthy. Life would be terribly unhealthy (not to mention boring) if we were exactly the same all the time.
>
> To feel more congruent, though, we will have to be more conscious about who we are and what kind of life we want to live. We will have to be conscious in crafting and maintaining our identity.
>
> All this requires conscious choice and work. Maybe someone didn't light the candle of love for you when you were younger, so you've always had the identity of someone who isn't or could not be loved. Now, as an adult, you can consciously choose to light

that candle for yourself. Perhaps you were never given the attention or respect you desired. Now is the time to give it to yourself. Maybe no one ever instilled in you the confidence that made you feel you could shape or shake the world with your power. Give that confidence to yourself. This is the path to constructing your own identity.

From my interviews, it's clear that the last paragraph is how high performers have approached their lives. They didn't wait for others to define who they ought to be. At some point—often a major moment in their lives—they took control, defined who they wanted to be, and started living in accordance with that self-image.

> They shaped their identity by conscious will
> and have aligned their thoughts, feelings,
> and behaviors to support that identity.

The more days they live in congruence with who they have chosen to become, the more they feel a sense of general confidence in life. I heard it over and over again in interviews: "I decided to break free from my parents [or my job or my old relationships] and do what I really wanted to do." "I finally chose to seek work that was more *me*." "I started living with greater intention."

It's also clear that high performers no longer feel as if they were "faking it to make it." Though six of the thirty people I interviewed mentioned that phrase as something they did earlier in their lives or careers, none agreed that they were still "faking it." Instead, high performers seem to wake up each day and have a clear intention of who they really want to be, and then they go out into the world and give that intention real focus and energy. A sense of authenticity, pride, self-trust, and confidence comes from those congruent actions. When I spoke with Aurora in the green room, I made sure to remind her she was a champion so that her thoughts and actions would realign toward that truth. Sometimes, a simple challenge to how powerful we really are can give just the boost of confidence we need.

If you can understand the power of congruence, then you can understand why the habit of *seeking clarity* is so important to confidence. You can't be congruent with something you've never defined. No clarity, no congruence, no confidence. It's that simple. That's why I encourage you to revisit the chapter on clarity and remember to fill out the Clarity Chart™ each week. Enter each week with intention for who you want to be, then align your actions with that self-image, and you'll gain greater confidence.

Finally, I'll share something that a majority of high performers shared with me: Confidence comes from being truthful with yourself and others. You have to avoid the little lies that can easily tear at the fabric of your character. If you lie about the small things, you will cause a catastrophe when faced with the big things. Your heart and soul want to know you've lived an honest life. If you break that trust, you risk feeling incongruent and ruining your performance. Stand in your truth and tell the truth, and you'll feel congruent.

Performance Prompts

1. The person I really want to be in life could be described as . . .

2. Three things I could do each week to live more congruently with that vision for myself include . . .

3. Three things I should definitely stop doing in my life so I can live in greater congruence with my ideal image of myself are . . .

PRACTICE #3: ENJOY CONNECTING

"You can make more friends in two months by becoming interested in other people than you can in two years by trying to get other people interested in you."

—Dale Carnegie

As you know, high performers love to develop influence with others. They enjoy connecting with people and learning how they think, what challenges they face, and what they are trying to stand for in this world. They also like sharing those things with others. As a reminder, this doesn't mean all high performers are extroverts. An introvert is just as likely as an extrovert to be a high performer. A recent study of over nine hundred CEOs found that just over half of the highest performing were introverts.[7] With near fifty-fifty odds, it's not personality that's giving an edge.

Since high performance does not correlate strongly with personality, what, exactly, makes high performers so interested in other people? Why are they so curious about others? What gives them the confidence to talk with others, ask questions, engage?

Simply put, high performers have learned the tremendous *value* in relating with others. They've discovered that it is by connecting with others that they learn more about themselves and the world. It's their connection with others that inspires greater congruence and competence. You know this, too. The more you work with people, the more you learn about yourself. And the more you work with others, the more you learn new ways of thinking, new skills, new ways of serving. That hit of learning is what high performers told me gives them so much drive to engage.

This is an important distinction, especially if you don't consider yourself a "people person." It doesn't matter whether you are natural with others. What matters is this: "Do you want to learn from others? Will you take the time to do it? Will you genuinely try to engage someone and learn about how they think, what they need, what they stand for?" If you can summon that curiosity and talk to enough people with that intention, you will gain confidence. At least, that's what high performers have shared with us.

High performers' confidence, then, comes from a mindset that says, "I know I'll do well with others because I'll be genuinely interested in them because I want to learn." In my interviews, no one said the opposite: "I know I'll do well with others because I'll make them genuinely interested in *me*, because I want to teach them who I am." They are not thinking about their "elevator pitch" or what they have to tell everyone as much as about what they might learn or how they can serve. Confidence comes less from projection than from connection.

Performance Prompts

1. The main reason I want to become better with people is . . .

2. I know I'll become more confident with people when I . . .

3. To gain more confidence with people, from now on when I talk with them, I'll think to myself . . .

A FORMULA AND FAREWELL FOR NOW

"As soon as you trust yourself, you will know how to live."
—Johann von Goethe

As you reflect on these three confidence builders—competence, congruence, and connection—perhaps you've noticed an underlying theme. What drove the development for high performers in each of these areas was *curiosity*. It was curiosity that developed their knowledge, skills, and abilities. Curiosity drove their self-examination. You have to ask a lot of questions of yourself to see whether you're living a congruent life. Curiosity made them want to seek out others. Perhaps, then, there is a formula at play:

Curiosity x (Competence + Congruence + Connection) = Confidence

The promise of this equation is that you don't have to pretend to be superhuman. You just have to care enough to learn new things, to live in alignment with who you want to become, to take interest in others. You'll feel better about yourself, and research shows that curiosity itself can improve your well-being.[8] Curiosity is the electric arc for a life bright with joy and vibrancy. To get there, you just have to start conditioning the internal dialogue that says . . .

- *I know what to do and how to add value here (or at least I believe in my ability to figure things out and I'm willing to go for it).*
- *I know I'm living in alignment with the person I want to become.*
- *I know I'll do well with others, because I'm genuinely interested in learning about them and serving them.*

If these become your recurring thoughts and reality in life, the odds are you'll be confidently on your way to higher performance.

I don't pretend that becoming more confident or reaching high performance will be easy. Throughout this book, I've shared that the journey to becoming more extraordinary in life will always be fraught with struggle. But as I've also shared, *ease* is not the objective in personal development; *growth* is. So anticipate and honor the fact that it's going to be difficult to implement the habits and practices in this book.

While the journey will challenge you, at least you now have a map. You know the six habits required for high performance, and you know the practices to develop each. With the lessons in this chapter, you also know how to become even more confident on that path to higher performance. Get curious about your performance again, and seek to improve it through practicing the HP6:

1. *Seek clarity* on who you want to be, how you want to interact with others, and what will bring meaning into your life.

2. *Generate energy* so you can sustain focus, effort, and well-being. To stay on your A game, you'll need to care actively for your mental stamina, physical energy, and positive emotions.

3. *Raise the necessity* of your level of performance. This means actively tapping into the reasons you *must* perform well, based on a mix of your internal standards (e.g., your identity, beliefs, values, or expectations for excellence) and external demands (e.g., social obligations, competition, public commitments).

4. *Increase productivity* in your primary field of interest. Specifically, you'll need to focus on "prolific quality output" (PQO) in the area in which you want to be known and to drive impact. You'll also have to

minimize distractions (or opportunities) that steal your attention from creating PQO.

5. *Develop influence* with those around you so you can get them to believe in and support your efforts and ambitions. Without a positive support network, major achievements over the long haul are all but impossible.

6. *Demonstrate courage* by expressing your ideas, taking bold action, and standing up for yourself and others even in the face of fear, uncertainty, or changing conditions.

Seek clarity. Generate energy. Raise necessity. Increase productivity. Develop Influence. Demonstrate Courage. These are the six habits that you need to adopt to reach high performance and stay there. These are the habits that will make you more confident in life and even more extraordinary.

So what now? Keep the checklist of the six habits by you at all times. You can find the Summary Guide at the end of this book, and you can also get a separate daily planner at HighPerformanceHabits .com/tools. From now on, before every meeting you go into, before every phone call, before you start any new project or pursue any new goal, revisit the six habits.

Then, every sixty days, retake the High Performance Indicator to track your progress and identify the habits you need to continue focusing on. If you've already taken the HPI, you'll get a reminder to take it again in sixty days. If you haven't, or if you miss the reminder, just take the basic assessment anytime for free at HighPerformance Indicator.com. If you'd like to continue your research and learning in this area, consider attending one of my events or joining our High Performance Master's Program. When you're ready, just visit High PerformanceInstitute.com.

Twenty-odd years ago, I stood bloodied and in shock atop the crumpled hood of a car after my accident. I learned that at the end of our lives, we all will ask questions to evaluate whether we were happy with our journey. I learned that my questions were to be *Did I live? Did I love? Did I matter?* I didn't particularly like my answers to those questions, so I sought to change my life and looked for the best ways to go about it. I felt that striving to become my best self was a way to earn the great blessing of the second chance I was given. That striving led to a life of learning and, ultimately, to the discovery of these high performance habits.

I hope that as you close this book, you decide to live with similar intention and reverence for your life. I hope you wake each day and decide to practice the habits that will make you proud of your life. I hope that as you endeavor to live an extraordinary life, you bring the joy and honor the struggle and seek to serve others. I hope that as you look back one day, having reached a level of performance you could never have dreamed of, you can say that you wanted it, you worked for it, you willed it to happen—that you never gave up and you never will. *You became extraordinary because you chose to.*

That reality, I believe, is something available to each of us.

Now go *earn it.*

SUMMARY GUIDE

"Whatever you are, be a good one."

—Abraham Lincoln

PERSONAL HABITS

HABIT ONE: SEEK CLARITY

1. <u>Envision the Future Four.</u> Have vision and consistently set clear intentions for who you want to be each day, how you want to interact with others, what skills you must develop to win in the future, and how you can make a difference and serve with excellence. Never enter a situation without thinking through these four categories (self, social, skills, service).

2. <u>Determine the Feeling You're After.</u> Ask yourself frequently, "What is the primary feeling I want to bring to this situation, and what is the primary feeling I want to get from this situation?" Don't wait for emotions to land on you; choose and cultivate the feelings that you wish to consistently experience and share in life.

3. <u>Define What's Meaningful.</u> Not everything that is achievable is important, and so achievement is not the issue—alignment is. Look to upcoming months and projects and determine what might bring you enthusiasm, connection, and satisfaction— then spend more time there. Always be asking, "How can I make this effort personally meaningful to me?"

HABIT TWO: GENERATE ENERGY

1. <u>Release Tension, Set Intention.</u> Use transitions between activities to renew your energy. Do this by closing your eyes, practicing deep breathing, and releasing tension in your body and thoughts in your mind. Try to do this at least once every hour. Once you feel tension lift, set a clear intention for your next activity, open your eyes, and get to work with vibrant focus.

2. <u>Bring the Joy.</u> Be responsible for the energy you bring to your day and each situation in life. Focus especially on bringing joy to your activities. Anticipate positive outcomes from your actions, ask yourself questions that generate positive emotions, set triggers to remind you to be positive and grateful, and appreciate the small things and the people around you.

3. <u>Optimize Health.</u> If the demands of your life require you to learn quickly, deal with stress, be alert, pay attention, remember important things, and keep a positive mood, then you must take sleep, exercise, and nutrition more seriously. Work with your doctor and other professionals to optimize your health. You already know things you should be doing. Do them!

HABIT THREE: RAISE NECESSITY

1. <u>Know Who Needs Your A Game.</u> You cannot become extraordinary without a sense that it's absolutely necessary to excel, for yourself and for others. From now on, whenever you sit down at your desk, ask: "Who needs me on my A game the most right now? What about my identity and external obligations makes it imperative for me to deliver today?"

2. <u>Affirm the Why.</u> When you verbalize something, it becomes more real and important to you. Speak your "why" to yourself out loud often, and share it with others. This will motivate you to live in congruence with your commitments. So the next time you want to increase your performance necessity, declare—to yourself and others—what you want and why you want it.

3. <u>Level Up Your Squad.</u> Emotions and excellence are contagious, so spend more time with the most positive and successful people in your peer group. Then continue building your ideal network of supportive and empowering people. Ask, "How can I work with the best people as I embark on this next project? How can I inspire others to raise their standards?"

SOCIAL HABITS

HABIT FOUR: INCREASE PRODUCTIVITY

1. <u>Increase the Outputs That Matter.</u> Determine the outputs that matter the most in determining your success, differentiation, and contribution to your field or industry. Focus there, say no to almost everything else, and be prolific in creating those outputs with high standards of quality. Remember that the main thing is to keep the main thing the main thing.

2. <u>Chart Your Five Moves.</u> Ask, "If there were only five major moves to make that goal happen, what would they be?" Think of each major move as a big bucket of activities, a project. Break the projects down into deliverables, deadlines, and activities. Once you're clear on these things, put them into your calendar, and schedule the bulk of your time working on them.

3. <u>Get Insanely Good at Key Skills (Progressive Mastery).</u> Determine the five major skills you need to develop over the next three years to grow into the person you hope to become. Then set out to develop those skills with obsessive focus through the ten steps of progressive mastery. The most important thing is to always be developing the critical skills to your future success.

HABIT FIVE: DEVELOP INFLUENCE

1. <u>Teach People How to Think.</u> In every situation of influence, prepare by asking yourself how do you want other people to think about (a) themselves, (b) other people, and (c) the world at large. Then go communicate that consistently. Shape people's thinking by saying things like: "Think of it this way . . ." "What do you think about . . ." "What would happen if we tried . . ."

2. <u>Challenge People to Grow.</u> Observe people's character, connections, and contributions, and actively challenge them to develop those things even further. Ask people if they gave their all, if they could be treating those around them better,

and if they could give even more or serve with even greater excellence and distinction.

3. <u>Role Model the Way.</u> Seventy-one percent of high performers say they think about being a role model daily. They want to be a good role model for their family, the team, and the greater community. So ask, "How can I handle this situation in a way that will inspire others to believe in themselves, be their best, and serve others with integrity, heart, and excellence?"

HABIT SIX: DEMONSTRATE COURAGE

1. <u>Honor the Struggle.</u> When you have the opportunity to learn and serve, you don't complain about the effort involved. View struggle as a necessary, important, and positive part of your journey so that you can find true peace and personal power. Don't bemoan the inevitable hardships of self-improvement and chasing your dreams; have reverence for challenge.

2. <u>Share Your Truth and Ambitions.</u> The main motivation of humankind is to be free, to express our true selves and pursue our dreams without restriction—to experience what may be called personal freedom. Follow this impulse by consistently sharing your true thoughts, feelings, needs, and dreams with other people. Do not play small to placate others. Live your truth.

3. <u>Find Someone to Fight For.</u> We need a noble cause to rise for. High performers tend to make that cause just one person— they want to fight for that person so they can be safe, improve, or live a better quality of life. You will do more for others than for yourself. And in doing something for others, you will find your reason for courage, and your cause for focus and excellence.

These six habits and the three practices that strengthen each are your path to an extraordinary life. There are other basic strategies in the book, but these six meta-habits are the ones that most move the needle toward progress.

For even more resources, including checklists, posters, assessments, day planners, journals, and corporate training tools, visit HighPerformanceHabits.com/tools.

ABOUT THE AUTHOR

 **BRENDON BURCHARD** is the world's leading high performance coach and one of the most watched, quoted, and followed personal development trainers in history. *SUCCESS* magazine and *O, The Oprah Magazine* have both named him one of the most influential leaders in personal growth and achievement. He has trained and certified more people on the topic of high performance than anyone in the world.

After suffering depression and surviving a car accident at the age of nineteen, Brendon faced what he calls life's last questions: "Did I live fully? Did I love openly? Did I make a difference?" His intention to be happy with the answers led to dramatic personal transformations and, later, his life's purpose of helping others live, love, and matter. After graduating with a master's degree in organizational communication, he worked as a change management consultant for Accenture. In 2006, he began his career writing books, hosting seminars, coaching individual clients, and creating online courses.

Brendon is now a Top 100 Most Followed Public Figure on Facebook and the star of the most watched self-help show on YouTube. His personal development videos have been viewed over 100,000,000 times. Over 1.6 million people have taken his online courses or video series. For these results, Oprah.com named him "one of the most successful online trainers in history."

Brendon is a #1 *New York Times*, #1 *USA TODAY*, and #1 *Wall Street Journal* best-selling author, and his books include *The Motivation Manifesto, The Charge, The Millionaire Messenger, Life's Golden Ticket,* and *The Student Leadership Guide.* His first podcast, *The Charged Life,* debuted at #1 on iTunes across all categories and spent over 100 weeks in the top 10 of its category.

As CEO of the High Performance Institute, Brendon leads a team of coaches, creators, and researchers whose mission is to help people create and enjoy extraordinary lives. He travels the globe speaking and serves as the lead trainer at High Performance Academy, the famed four-day personal and professional development seminar. *Entrepreneur* magazine ranked his seminar for social media thought leaders, Experts Academy, as "one of the Top 5 Must-Attends for all entrepreneurs."

Recognized as a worldwide authority on both human motivation and business marketing, Brendon is the recipient of the Maharishi Award and sits on the Innovation Board at the XPRIZE Foundation.

Visit him at Brendon.com.

ACKNOWLEDGMENTS

This is the sixth time in my life that I've sat down to write the acknowledgments section after having just completed the last page of the manuscript. I feel blessed knowing that so many of the people who inspired and supported the last five books are still in my life. Long-term relationships are more important to, or perhaps the very meaning of, long-term success.

If you're familiar with my work, you know that I feel grateful to God first and always for the second chance I was given after my car accident. Every day I hope to earn that blessing—what I call life's golden ticket—by seeking to live more fully, love more openly, and make a greater difference.

My work would not have been possible without the love and strength of my parents, siblings, mentors, and wife. Mom, thank you for showing all of us how to honor the struggle and bring the joy to every moment of our lives. Dad, we miss you. I've never gone a day or written a page without thinking of you since you passed. David, Bryan, and Helen, thank you for inspiring me to be a better man and brother. I love you more than you know. Linda Ballew, you were an extension of my family and my first real mentor. Thank you for teaching me to create, write, film, and lead with excellence. Denise, my sunshine, thank you for believing in me through it all, and for showing me what it looks like to be a thoughtful, kind, loving, and extraordinary human. You are the most remarkable person I've ever met and the greatest gift of my life. To Marty and Sandy—thanks for the example and for cheering us on.

While I frequently disappeared over the course of two and a half years writing this book, my remarkable team at The Burchard Group cheered me on, protected my time, and kept the momentum serving our students and mission. To my team, thank you for your commitment, excellence, and creativity in amplifying my work well beyond these pages. Few will ever know the blessings and sweeping difficulties of serving millions of students and tens of millions of fans in this genre. But *you* know, and you make it happen every day. I'm so thankful and in awe of what we've built.

Denise McIntyre somehow manages to keep us all on track. Thank you, Dmac, for your extraordinary belief, trust, leadership, and friendship. You've been there through it all, and I can never say thank you enough. Mel Abraham has guided many of my big business decisions, introduced me on stage, kept away the bad guys, and become one of my dearest friends. Everyone should be so lucky to have such generous comrades as Dmac and Mel. This is the broader team whom I am privileged to serve with every day: Jeremy Abraham, Adim Coleman, Karen Gelsman, Michael Hunter, Alex Houg, Hannah Houg, Michelle Huljev, Maggie Kirkland, Jessica Lipman, Helen Lynch, Jason Miller, Terry Powers, Travis Shields, Michele Smith, Danny Southwick, and Anthony Trucks. Thanks, too, to the original B-crew, Jennifer Robbins, who supported my early career and set the bar for excellence that we continue to strive to meet.

There are other extraordinary people who made this book happen. Bringing a book to life and market takes a lot of hands. Scott Hoffman, my agent, believed in me from day one. Through six books, I've never felt alone knowing you're out there, buddy. I'm honored to have you as a friend and comrade on this incredible journey. Reid Tracy took me in at Hay House after another publisher failed to see the promise of *The Motivation Manifesto*. Reid, I will never forget your generosity and the honor that you've given me to be part of the Hay House family. You're the most important leader in the history of personal development publishing, and I hope you know the impact you've had on me and the world. Perry Crowe, my editor at Hay House, ushered this baby to completion with a patient hand and kind spirit. Thanks, Perry, for your excellence in editing and corralling. Constance Hale took a look at the first draft and provided great early edits and comments, and thankfully scared me enough to begin again. Thanks, Connie. If this book is in decent shape, it's because of Michael Carr, the best editor I have ever worked with. Michael has edited all my books, which has never been an easy task since I've written each in a new voice and generally failed to learn from previous mistakes. Thank you, Michael, for all the late nights on this one, and for making me appear a better writer.

To the many friends, psychologists, professional coaches, and mentors who shaped the thinking of this book and helped me with the surveys, research, and analysis, thank you. I must especially thank Danny Southwick, for being as passionate as I am about this topic, for helping lead some of our researchers, and for all the late nights of review. You're my brother from another, and you're a remarkable talent and gift in the positive psychology movement. Thanks also to Shannon Thompson, Alissa Mrazek, and Mike Mrazek for providing additional analysis and literature reviews. Alissa and Mike—thanks for the saves, reliability, and enthusiasm.

My team over at Growth.com also cheered me on, served our coaching clients with world-class professionalism, and taught me so much about organizational excellence. Thank you, Dean Graziosi and Ethan Willis, for leading Growth and for building something so magical. I can't count how many great life lessons and business insights I've learned from you both. You're my new mentors. To our first leaders at Growth, I'm so proud of you and thankful, including Dean's entire team and Damon Willis, Bryan Hatch, and Cary Inouye.

To our worldwide community of peers who are Certified High Performance Coaches, thank you for the dedication, heart, and leadership you bring to the personal and professional development coaching industry. You are truly the finest coaches in the world, and I'm honored to serve with you.

I am also deeply grateful for all my readers, online students, social media fans, and all their kind comments and support. Despite the recent and generous attention, I still feel like I'm just one small ripple in a long line of people who dedicated themselves to teaching personal development. I would have amounted to very little in life if I hadn't read so many books on psychology and self-improvement. Since I was nineteen, I have read at least one book every week. I've complemented that with at least one research article per day since I was twenty-eight and I still feel like a novice. This commitment to reading was, perhaps, the best habit I have ever begun. Since people always ask for my recommendations, these are the masters in my field who shaped my early thinking and life: Dale Carnegie, Napoleon Hill, Earl Nightingale, Og Mandino, Norman Cousins, Jim Rohn, John Wooden, Wayne Dyer, Marianne Williamson, Stephen Covey, Louise Hay, Marshall Goldsmith, Brian Tracy, Zig Ziglar, Harvey Mackay, Peter Drucker, Frances Hesselbein, James Redfield, Debbie Ford, Dan Millman, Tom Peters, Les Brown, Richard Carlson, Jack Canfield, Robin Sharma, Tony Robbins, Daniel Amen, and Paulo Coelho. And these are the brilliant minds and psychologists whose work inspired me to go even deeper and conduct this type of research: Abraham Maslow, Carl Rogers, Alfred Adler, Erich Fromm, Nathaniel Branden, Albert Bandura, Richard Davidson, Roy Baumeister, Barbara Fredrickson, Edward Deci, Richard Ryan, Mihaly Csikszentmihalyi, Martin Seligman, Daniel Goleman, John Gottman, Carol Dweck, Michael Merzenich, Angela Duckworth, and

Anders Ericsson. I'm just a coach, so if you truly want to understand the human condition and appreciate academic excellence at its finest, see their work.

If you heard about this book from any video-based online marketing, it's only because I learned something about that from Jeff Walker, Frank Kern, and another dozen or so great online trainers and marketers. To all who have helped me learn about sharing my message, and to all who have promoted my work and mission, I thank you. Who knew that online and social media marketing would become such a thing? To my friends and collaborators in the industry, thank you for your example, friendship, and leadership, especially Joe Polish, Tony Robbins, Robin Sharma, Peter Diamandis, Daniel Amen, Chalene Johnson, Nick Ortner, Marie Forleo, JJ Virgin, Gabby Bernstein, Mat Boggs, Mary Morrissey, Janet Attwood, Chris Attwood, Jack Canfield, Brian Tracy, Harvey Mackay, Lewis Howes, Kris Carr, Tony Horton, Larry King, Shawna King, Arianna Huffington, Stuart Johnson, and Oprah Winfrey.

To my coaching clients worldwide, thank you for the opportunity and for teaching me so much.

To my dear friends Ryan, Jason, Steve, Jesse, Dave, Nick, Stephan, and all the wild ones and Grizzlies from Montana, I love you and miss you. Thanks for believing in the scrawny loud kid when no one else did.

Finally, to all my friends, colleagues, students, and fans who may have felt neglected at any time during this writing project—the longest of my career—I hope you find the final output justified the absence. You've been in my mind and heart every day and every page.

ENDNOTES

INTRODUCTION

1. Several of my writer friends wondered why I made this choice. Books in this genre quickly become dated when they overly rely on company case studies to support their assertions. A few examples may help: Consider *Good to Great*, by Jim Collins. Among his celebrated company profiles were Circuit City, now bankrupt, and Fannie Mae, charged with securities fraud that contributed significantly to the financial meltdown of 2007–2008. Wells Fargo, another "great" company, was fined \$185 million, and fired over five thousand employees, for opening millions of fraudulent accounts. Gary Hamel's outstanding book *Leading the Revolution* lauded Enron, whose top officers were imprisoned for running one of the most corrupt companies of all time. Tom Peters's book *In Search of Excellence* profiled Atari, NCR, Wang Labs, and Xerox—all companies that were soon dogs. This doesn't mean that these authors' assertions were wrong at the time. It does mean that, inevitably, performance changes, and if you make your case by highlighting companies, you end up with a book that will become irrelevant. And besides, company "performance" is a misnomer—people are the performers, not companies. That's why I chose to avoid company profiles in this book. I chose instead to use the lens of a performance coach and researcher, looking for individual differences in behavior that help some people succeed more than others. I chose not to highlight contemporary individuals here for the same reason: Even though it makes for an engaging read in the short term, it can date the material. Individuals, like companies, can also fall from a high perch—and at some point, most of us do. This book pulls no punches. High performance isn't something everyone can sustain forever. That's why I've chosen to favor strategies that we

know work, rather than individuals who happen to be stars today. I've peppered in coaching vignettes and personal experiences so the vital how-to strategies and tactics don't become tedious. Again, this wasn't an easy call, but knowing that I can share stories, case studies, and timely examples in various online venues freed me to make the call. All my career, I have been compensated for getting results for people, not interviewing people about their backgrounds. That's reflected in this work. If you enjoy the lifestyle-based interviews of fascinating people, I recommend you check out podcasts or books toward that end. For more of my personal perspectives and stories, visit my podcast on iTunes. For more content related to the research, visit HighPerformanceInstitute.com.

BEYOND NATURAL: THE QUEST FOR HIGH PERFORMANCE

1. To mask identities and protect the privacy of all my clients and students, I have appropriately changed the names and details of these stories. Any resulting resemblance to persons living or dead is entirely coincidental and unintentional.
2. Dweck, C. S. (2008); Dweck, C. S., & Leggett, E. L. (1988).
3. Duckworth, A. L. (2016); Duckworth, A. L., et al. (2015).
4. Ericsson, K. A., & Pool, R. (2016a); Ericsson, K. A. (2014).
5. Munyon, T. P., et al. (2015); Goleman, D., et al. (2013); Goleman, D. (2007).
6. See Bossidy, L., et al. (2011); Seidman, D. (2011).
7. Reivich, K., & Shatté, A. (2002).
8. Ratey, J. J., & Hagerman, E. (2008).
9. To see our latest methodology report on the High Performance Indicator (HPI), visit HighPerformanceInstitute.com.
10. For a more academic discussion on these nine factors, visit HighPeformance Institute.com/research.

HIGH PERFORMANCE HABIT #1: SEEK CLARITY

1. Campbell, J. D., et al. (1996).
2. Locke, E. A., & Latham, G. P. (2002).
3. Gollwitzer, P. M., & Brandstätter, V. (1997).
4. Gollwitzer, P. M. (1999); Gollwitzer, P. M., & Oettingen, G. (2016).
5. Torrance, E.P. (1983).
6. Of course, one can argue that a shorter response time or a more confident tone doesn't necessarily indicate greater clarity. Perhaps that person never thought of these questions before but just happens to be more creative,

better at assimilating ideas on the fly. Maybe they're more extroverted and can quickly assert and articulate their ideas better. But that's not what I found when comparing their HPI scores to their responses in the interviews. (The HPI asks about creativity, confidence, and assertiveness, for example, and many people who reported low creativity or assertiveness on the assessment could still respond quickly and confidently.) In general, high performance scores do not strongly correlate with self-reported creativity or personality descriptors, so it makes sense that speed and tone of response might simply mean that people had considered this sort of question before. But we'll have to test that in a more controlled way in future research.

7. Goleman, D. (1998); Goleman, D., et al. (2001, 2013).

8. Boggs, M., & Miller, J. (2008).

9. Gottman, J., & Silver, N. (1995, 2015).

10. Empirical research supports this attitude. For example, one can interpret anxiety as stress or as excitement, and experience different benefits and consequences of that choice. See Crum, A. J., et al. (2013).

11. Kleinginna, P. R., & Kleinginna, A. M. (1981); Lang, P. J. (2010); Damasio, A. R. (1999).

12. I use the word *reaction* here to describe both a reaction from a real-world stimulus, meaning something we see or sense outside of us, and also a reaction from anticipation, something that happens within. When our mind anticipates something that is going to happen or could happen, emotion can stir. That emotion is a reaction or result of anticipation.

13. Emotions are often a result of how our brain anticipates situations, conceptualizes feelings, or remembers old situations. Despite my examples here, and common misconceptions, your emotions are not always the same as mine, and there is great variability in how our brain conceptualizes and generates emotion. See Barrett, L. F. (2017, 2017).

14. For a broader view of emotions, see Lewis, M., et al. (2010).

15. Ryff, C. D., & Singer, B. (1998); Markman, K. D., et al. (2013).

16. For a broader general discussion on meaning, start with MacKenzie, M. J., & Baumeister, R. (2014); Wrzesniewski, A. (2003); Rosso, B. D., et al. (2010).

17. Steger, M. F., et al. (2006).

18. Sun, J., et al. (2017).

19. Stillman, T. F., et al. (2009).

20. Debats, D. L. (1999); Lambert, N. M., et al. (2010); Markman, K. D., et al. (2013).

21. On the importance of security, see Yousef, D. A. (1998); on autonomy, see Herzberg, F., et al. (1969); on balance, see Thompson, C. A., & Prottas, D. J. (2006).

22. Martela, F., & Steger, M. F. (2016).

HIGH PERFORMANCE HABIT #2: GENERATE ENERGY

1. For further distinctions on this topic in general, see also Koball, H. L., et al. (2010).

2. This relationship is strong (r = .63).

3. Ogden, C. L., et al. (2015).

4. For the latest guidelines, visit https://www.cdc.gov/physicalactivity/basics/adults.

5. American Psychological Association (2015).

6. American Psychological Association (2016).

7. Seppala, E., & Cameron, K. (2015); Harter, J. K., et al. (2003); Danna, K., & Griffin, R. W. (1999).

8. Ghosh, S., et al. (2013). Issa, G., et al. (2010); Tafet, G. E., et al. (2001); Isovich, E., et al. (2000).

9. For more on anxiety and wellness, see Grossman, P., et al. (2004); Brown, K. W., & Ryan, R. M. (2003). For creativity see Horan, R. (2009).

10. Valentine, E. R., & Sweet, P. L. (1999).

11. Some have noted that the "Release Tension, Set Intention" approach is more of a relaxation technique than a meditative practice. I don't have an opinion on the matter, and both relaxation techniques and meditation techniques can be tremendously powerful. See Jain, S., et al. (2007) for a controlled trial between the two, which gives meditation a slight edge. For a look at the positive neural effects of meditation, especially on attention, see Hasenkamp, W., & Barsalou, L. W. (2012). For the serious student also wanting a critical view into the hype and poor science around meditation, see Sedlmeier, P., et al. (2012).

12. Miller, J. J., et al. (1995).

13. Lyubomirsky, S., et al. (2005).

14. Bryan, T., & Bryan, J. (1991).

15. Sy, T., et al. (2005); Staw, B. M., & Barsade, S. G. (1993).

16. Isen, A. M., et al. (1991).

17. Isen, A. M., & Levin, P. F. (1972); Isen, A. M., et al. (1976).

18. Davidson, R. J., et al. (2000).

19. Lemonick, M. D. (2005).

20. This is also a well-researched practice in goal-attainment science, called Mental-Contrasting and Implementation Intentions (MCII). It means you think about what you want, think about the obstacles that will stand in the way, and set up specific intentions about how you will handle those obstacles. Interestingly, just visualizing what you want (à la The Secret) is often negatively correlated with goal attainment. But visualizing success and thinking through a plan to deal with obstacles is highly associated

with goal attainment. See Duckworth, A. L., et al. (2011a) and Oettingen, G., et al. (2001). For a discussion of self-talk in the third person, see Kross, E., et al. (2014).

21. Lemonick, M. D. (2005).

22. Schirmer, A., et al. (2011); Hertenstein, M. J., et al. (2009).

23. Emmons, R. A. (2000).

24. Seligman, M. E., et al. (2005).

25. See Pilcher, J. J., & Huffcutt, A. J. (1996); Benca, R. M., et al. (1992); Cappuccio, F. P., et al. (2008).

26. For a more in-depth look into the science regarding the interactions of genes, behavior, and environment, start with Blazer, D. G., & Hernandez, L. M. (2006).

27. Cotman, C. W., & Berchtold, N. C. (2002).

28. Ibid.

29. Tomporowski, P. D. (2003); Tenenbaum, G., et al. (1993).

30. Foley, T. E., & Fleshner, M. (2008); Ratey, J. J., & Hagerman, E. (2008).

31. Castelli, D. M., et al. (2007); Kramer, A. F., & Hillman, C. H. (2006); Sibley, B. A., & Etnier, J. L. (2003).

32. Ratey, J. J., & Hagerman, E. (2008); Penninx, B. W., et al. (2002); Chen, C., et al. (2016).

33. Jacobs, B. L. (1994); Jacobs, B. L., & Azmitia, E. C. (1992); Ratey, J. J., & Hagerman, E. (2008).

34. Rethorst, C. D., et al. (2009); Jacobs, B. L. (1994); Jacobs, B. L., & Azmitia, E. C. (1992); Ratey, J. J., & Hagerman, E. (2008); Chaouloff, F., et al. (1989).

35. Anderson, E., & Shivakumar, G. (2015); Sparling, P. B., et al. (2003).

36. Obesity stats: Davis, C., et al. (2004). Excess consumption: McCrory, M. A., et al. (2002).

37. Davis, C., et al. (2004).

38. On the connection between nutrition and productivity, see Hoddinott, J., et al. (2008); Thomas, D., & Frankenberg, E. (2002); Strauss, J., & Thomas, D. (1998).

39. Behrman, J. R. (1993).

40. For plenty of reasons why, see Grawitch, M. J., et al. (2006); Wright, T. A., & Cropanzano, R. (2000).

41. Seen at http://www.apa.org/news/press/releases/2016/06/workplace-well -being.aspx.

HIGH PERFORMANCE HABIT #3: RAISE NECESSITY

1. Psychologists often call this "identification." See Deci, E. L., & Ryan, R. M. (2010, 2002); Koestner, R. (1996).

2. Locke, E. A., & Latham, G. P. (2002).

3. Self-monitoring and other feedback mechanisms are key to this result. See Bandura, A., & Cervone, D. (1983).

4. This is a common finding of successful and healthy people in general. See Bandura, A. (1991).

5. See Harkin, B., et al. (2016).

6. Teixeira, P. J., et al. (2015).

7. Frost, R. O., & Henderson, K. J. (1991).

8. This has been found to be true in lots of life situations, from sports to music to everyday life. See Beilock, S. L., & Carr, T. H. (2001); Wan, C. Y., & Huon, G. F. (2005).

9. Locke, E. A., & Latham, G. P. (2002).

10. Ryan, R. M., & Deci, E. L. (2000a, 2000b).

11. Ericsson, K. A., et al. (1993). Duckworth, A. L., et al. (2011a, 2011b).

12. See the full findings at HighPerformanceInstitute.com/research.

13. For example, Baumeister, R. F. (1984) defined pressure as "any factor or combination of factors that increases the importance of performing well on a particular occasion." Regarding high performance research, I define external forces more broadly than a particular occasion or event. I see them as complementing drives or activities that are already important. External forces might not increase a subject's sense of the importance of performing well at all, but may just make the already important activity more social or more personally meaningful.

14. In fact, that statement didn't meaningfully predict any high scores in any category or other predictor variable of high performance. The only two things that statement correlated with were things you don't really want. The strongest correlation was with "I deal with more stress than my peers"—a statistically significant but weak relationship. The next closest was "People don't understand how hard I work," which is still statistically significant though very weak.

15. I recognize the issues in using the terms *duty*, *obligation*, and *responsibility* in such broad strokes and interchangeably, so my apologies to linguists and philosophers everywhere. Especially Hume and Kant. For related philosophy on these topics, see Schneewind, J. B. (1992); Feinberg, J. (1966); Brandt, R. B. (1964); Wand, B. (1956). My aim in this section is to convey how high performers actually talk, how they describe that general sense of being "supposed" to do something and why they "must" succeed. To honor their descriptions, I'll use duty interchangeably with any social obligation or responsibility that makes high performers find it necessary to succeed consistently.

16. See Lerner, J. S., & Tetlock, P. E. (1999); Crown, D. F., & Rosse, J. G. (1995); Forward, J., & Zander, A. (1971); Humphreys, M. S., & Revelle, W. (1984). For a wide-ranging discussion on how individual judgment and choice can be shaped by accountability, see Tetlock, P. E. (1992).

17. For multiple perspectives and mechanisms on this, including pros and cons, see Rummler, G. A., & Brache, A. P. (1995); Dubnick, M. (2005); Frink, D. D., & Ferris, G. R. (1998).

18. Fuligni, A. J. (2001).

19. Cunningham, G. B. (2006); Sulsky, L. M. (1999).

20. In this case, high performers were defined as those who scored 4.4 in the category of productivity and a 4.2 or higher on the full HPI assessment. (Productivity is just one category of the HPI, but the full assessment includes over 100 more variables that add up to a total score.)

21. Leroy, S. (2009).

22. Csikszentmihalyi, M., & Rathunde, K. (1993); Csikszentmihalyi, M. (1975, 1997); Csikszentmihalyi, M., et al. (2005).

23. In the last five years of surveys, we've never seen a strong correlation between high performance and common personality descriptions (from the "Big 5" personality traits). Modern organizational research seems to confirm this. A recent study found high performing CEOs are as likely to be introverts as they are to be extroverts. See Botelho, E. L., et al. (2017). For a full discussion on why introverts get shortchanged, see Cain, S. (2013). More broadly, when it comes to success, personality traits have extremely limited predictive validity. See Barrick, M. R., & Mount, M. K. (1991); Duckworth, A. L., et al. (2007); Morgeson, F. P., et al. (2007). Observing meta-analyses on personality and achievement, Angela Duckworth, a psychologist at University of Pennsylvania and a MacArthur "genius" grant recipient, found that "at best, any given personality trait accounts for less than 2 percent of variance in achievement." See Duckworth, A. L., et al. (2007).

24. Schimel, J., et al. (2004).

25. Pury, C. L., et al. (2007); Pury, C. L., & Kowalski, R. M. (2007).

26. See Christakis, N. A., & Fowler, J. H. (2008b). On sleep, see Mednick, S. C., et al. (2010); on the food you eat, Pachucki, M. A., et al. (2011); on economic behavior, O'Boyle, E. (2016).

27. On smoking, see Christakis, N. A., & Fowler, J. H. (2008a); on obesity, Christakis, N. A., & Fowler, J. H. (2007); on loneliness, Cacioppo, J. T., et al. (2009); on depression, Rosenquist, J. N., et al. (2011); on divorce, McDermott, R., et al. (2013); on drug use, Mednick, S. C., et al. (2010).

28. On happiness, see Christakis, N. A., & Fowler, J. H. (2008b); on prosocial behavior, see Fowler, J. H., & Christakis, N. A. (2010).

29. Coyle, D. (2009); Chambliss, D. F. (1989).

30. Christakis, N. A., & Fowler, J. H. (2009).

31. Felitti, V. J., et al., (1998).

32. Danese, A., & McEwen, B. S. (2012).

33. Lee, T. (2016); Kristof, N. (2016); Dunlap, E., et al. (2009).

34. Dweck, C. S. (2014).

35. Claro, S., et al. (2016).

36. Duckworth, A. L. (2016); Seligman, M. E. P. (2012).

37. Beck, J. S. (2011); Begley, S., & Davidson, R. (2012); Butler, A. C., et al. (2006); Seligman, M. E. P. (1990).

38. It is perhaps tempting to say, "Well, that must just be because they're extroverts," but this is not the case. High performance does not correlate with personality, and these practices aren't necessarily tied to a personality of extroversion. Instead, prosocial behavior and attempts to work or network with more advanced groups of people is tied to desires for growth, achievement, and contribution, regardless of personality.

39. US Department of Labor (2016). Release available at https://www.bls.gov/news.release/volun.nr0.htm.

40. For perhaps the best book written on competition and its effects on winning, losing, and life, see Bronson, P., & Merryman, A. (2013).

HIGH PERFORMANCE HABIT #4: INCREASE PRODUCTIVITY

1. Our research found that people who feel like they give more than their peers are no more likely to be productive than the average respondent. Neither are those who feel they are making a difference. In other words, a sense of giving more or making a difference was not strongly correlated to productivity. Givers might feel a lot of heart, but they don't always finish what they start.

2. Csikszentmihalyi, M. (1996); Locke, E. A., & Latham, G. P. (1990).

3. Cerasoli, C. P., et al. (2014).

4. Weldon, E., et al. (1991); Locke, E. A., & Latham, G. P. (1990).

5. On nutrition, see Hoddinott, J., et al. (2008); on exercise, see Cotman, C. W., & Berchtold, N. C. (2002).

6. For nutrition and productivity connections, see Hoddinott, J., et al. (2008); Thomas, D., & Frankenberg, E. (2002); Strauss, J., & Thomas, D. (1998).

7. Lyubomirsky, S., et al. (2005).

8. Lyubomirsky, S., et al. (2005).

9. Sgroi, D. (2015).

10. See LexisNexis (2010).

11. See http://www.nytimes.com/2013/05/05/opinion/sunday/a-focus-on-distraction.html.

12. Lavie, N. (2010).

13. On optimal performance, see Ericsson, K. A., et al. (1993); on quality of work, see Newport, C. (2016).

14. Leroy, S. (2009).

15. Mark, G., et al. (2005).

16. Yes, the average American watches that much, as of June 2016 according to *The New York Times*. See Koblin, J. (2016).

17. Executives reported a 19 percent increase in their sense of well-being, and a 24 percent increase in their sense of work-life balance. We asked five questions related to both topics (well-being and work-life balance), and respondents rated themselves on each question, on a 1–10 scale. The percentage increased was an average of the group of 16 after six weeks. This was an informal survey, and we are working to validate the scale for a broader study on productivity.

18. Immordino-Yang, M. H., et al. (2012).

19. On the case for giving yourself more breaks during the day, see https:// www.fastcompany.com/3035605/how-to-be-a-success-at-everything/the -exact-amount-of-time-you-should-work-every-day.

20. Trougakos, J. P., & Hideg, I. (2009); Trougakos, J. P., et al. (2008).

21. Trougakos, J. P., et al. (2014).

22. Berman, M. G., et al. (2008).

23. Garrett, G., et al. (2016).

24. Carter, E. C., et al. (2015).

25. For a solid discussion on how the mind works in this modern era of information overwhelm, see Levitin, D. J. (2014).

26. Schwartz, T., & McCarthy, C. (2007).

27. See https://www.fastcompany.com/3035605/how-to-be-a-success-at -everything/the-exact-amount-of-time-you-should-work-every-day.

28. Ericsson, K. A., et al. (1993).

29. Simonton, D. K. (1988).

30. Chui, M., et al. (2012).

31. Whittaker, S., et al. (2011, May).

32. For how the experts industry functions, see my book *The Millionaire Messenger*.

33. Senécal, C., et al. (1995).

34. Wood, R., & Locke, E. (1990).

35. Weldon, E., & Weingart, L. R. (1993); Weldon, E., et al. (1991).

36. For the cognitive resources gained by having a plan, see Masicampo, E. J., & Baumeister, R. F. (2011).

37. As an example, Tom Brady has his practices and workouts scheduled well into his forties. As I was editing this book, he led the New England Patriots to winning Super Bowl LI, in what many have called one of the greatest comebacks and sports performances in history. To read how obsessive he is about maintaining his system, see "obsessive" about maintaining his

system: https://www.si.com/nfl/2014/12/10/tom-brady-new-england
-patriots-age-fitness.

38. But not always. For an insightful and wide-ranging exploration of skills, see Grugulis, I., et al. (2017).

39. See Dweck, C. S. (2008); Duckworth, A. L. (2016); and Ericsson, K. A., & Poole, R. (2016a).

40. Ericsson, K. A., & Pool, R. (2016c).

41. My favorite compilation of the great speeches is Safire, W. (2004).

HIGH PERFORMANCE HABIT #5: DEVELOP INFLUENCE

1. As an example, in two separate surveys "I am more giving than my peers" failed to meet a significant, meaningful correlation with influence (higher than r = .20). These were not small samples: The first study involved 8,826 high performers (63 percent female) from 140 countries and the second involved 4,626 individuals (67 percent female) from 50 countries.

2. (r = .45).

3. In the same two surveys, "I am more creative than my peers" was correlated with influence at .17 and .19, failing to meet a significant, meaningful correlation.

4. We found this to be true for both the same two surveys.

5. A must-read for those interested in influence, especially those who claim they can't have it, is Munyon, T. P., et al. (2015). For research on how political skill leads to promotability, see Gentry, W. A., et al. (2012).

6. Flynn, F. J., & Bohns, V. K. (2012).

7. Savitsky, K., et al. (2001).

8. Jecker, J., & Landy, D. (1969).

9. Weaver, K., et al. (2007).

10. Marquardt, M. J. (2011); Kouzes, J. M., & Posner, B. Z. (2011); Kanter, R. M. (1999); Nanus, B. (1992).

11. Grant, A. (2013).

12. Cialdini, R. B. (2007); Regan, D. T. (1971).

13. Bolman, L. G., & Deal, T. E. (2003).

14. Access the full report at https://www.apaexcellence.org/assets/general/2016-work-and-wellbeing-survey-results.pdf.

15. Grant, A. M., & Gino, F. (2010).

HIGH PERFORMANCE HABIT #6: DEMONSTRATE COURAGE

1. Women, on average, were observed to score slightly higher on courage compared with men, but this percentage was so slight, and the sample so large, that this was not a significant difference. In our coaching interven-

tions, there is no measurable difference between men and women and their responses (or improvement ability) related to courage.

2. From one study: love mastering challenges, r = .45; perceive themselves as assertive, r = .45; perceive themselves as confident, r = .49; perceive themselves as high performers, r = .41; perceive themselves as more successful than their peers, r = .40; and are happy with their life overall, r = .41.

3. Rachman, S. J. (2010).

4. For "not fearlessness," see Rachman, S. J. (2010); for "taking action despite fear," see Norton & Weiss (2009).

5. Rachman, S. (1990); Macmillan & Rachman (1988).

6. On bomb-disposal operators and soldiers, see Cox, D., et al. (1983); on astronauts, see Ruff & Korchin (1964).

7. Rachman, S. (1990).

8. For a comprehensive review of how we conceptualize courage, see Pury, C. L., & Lopez, S. J. (2010).

9. This aligns with the components found in a comprehensive review of courage constructs by Rate, C. R., et al. (2007).

10. Pury, C. L., et al. (2015); Pury, C. L., & Starkey, C. B. (2010).

11. Pury, C. L., & Hensel, A. D. (2010).

12. Dweck, C. S. (2008).

13. Dweck, C. S., & Leggett, E. L. (1988).

BEWARE THREE TRAPS

1. Nickerson, R. S. (1998).

2. Not surprisingly, superiority-minded people are more likely to attribute their success (and others' supposed failures) to "permanent traits" such as personality, talent, IQ, or good looks. See Tracy, J. L., et al. (2009).

3. See Ericsson, K. A., & Pool, R. (2016a, 2016b & 2016c).

4. Ironically, people who are prone to feelings of superiority are less emotionally stable than others. And people who feel that they are better than others report feeling less supported and less connected to other people. See Tracy, J. L., et al. (2009).

5. Wright, J. C., et al. (2017).

6. See Kruse, E., et al. (2014).

7. You might recall the earlier reference about the meta-analysis spanning over 275,000 people that showed that happiness leads to a number of positive outcomes, such as longer life, less sickness, more financial success, more fulfilling marriages and satisfying relationships, more fulfilling and productive work, and greater social influence. See Lyubomirsky, S., et al. (2005).

8. See Grzegorek, J., et al. (2004); Rice, K. G., et al. (2003).

9. Frost, R. O., & Henderson, K. J. (1991).

10. Hewitt, P. L., & Flett, G. L. (2002).

11. See Rozin, P., & Royzman, E. B. (2001).

12. Hanson, R. (2013); Lykken, D. (2000).

13. Diener, E., & Biswas-Diener, R. (2011); Lyubomirsky, S., et al. (2005).

14. Fredrickson, B. (2004).

15. Csikszentmihalyi, M. (1997); Stavrou, N. A., et al. (2007).

16. For the impairments brought on by sleep, especially in performance-related outcomes, see Samuels, C. (2009).

17. Marano, H. E. (1999); Elkind, D. (2007); Gil, E. (2012).

18. For the costs of persistence on health, see Miller, G. E., & Wrosch, C. (2007). For issues with narrow-mindedness, and other personal issues, see Kashdan, T. (2017).

19. Bonebright, C. A., et al. (2000).

THE #1 THING

1. Confidence correlates significantly and meaningfully with overall high performance ($r = .59$). This means that confidence predicts 35 percent of the variance in high performance. Confidence also correlates significantly and meaningfully with all HP6s. Clarity $r = .53$ (confidence predicts 28 percent of the variance in clarity). Energy $r = .47$ (confidence predicts 22 percent of the variance in energy). Productivity $r = .44$ (confidence predicts 19 percent of the variance in productivity). Influence $r =. 41$ (confidence predicts 17 percent of the variance in influence). Necessity $r = .37$ (confidence predicts 13 percent of the variance in necessity). Courage $r = .49$ (confidence predicts 24 percent of the variance in courage).

2. "I'm happy with my life overall" ($r = .42$); confidence predicts 18 percent of the variance. "I love trying to master new challenges" ($r = .44$); confidence predicts 19 percent of the variance. "I feel as though I'm making a difference" ($r = .46$); confidence predicts 21 percent of the variance.

3. There is a distinction between general self-confidence and self-efficacy. Confidence is usually viewed as a general estimation of one's worth or abilities, whereas self-efficacy is belief in one's ability to perform well at a given task or in a given context. But since high performers don't speak in these distinctions, and it remains more of an academic distinction in general, we'll use the two interchangeably. For more on self-efficacy, see Bandura, A. (1980); Stajkovic, A. D., & Luthans, F. (1998).

4. Shoji, K., et al. (2016).

5. Duff, D. C. (2010).

6. Again, this is often referred to as self-efficacy. See Bandura, A. (1980, 1982, 1991); Bandura, A., & Cervone, D. (1983).

7. Botelho, E. L., et al. (2017).

8. Sheldon, K. M., et al. (2015).

REFERENCES

The following references served us greatly in our literature reviews for this project. Although not every resource is cited in the endnotes of this book, each informed the work and our supplemental research articles on High PerformanceInstitute.com. Anticipating that a new generation of students interested in this emerging field will look for additional gateways to learning, we have included all that we deemed relevant. The author wishes to thank all the researchers and practitioners, both here and elsewhere, who generously provided their expertise and insight for this book and for our other efforts inspiring the world to high performance. For additional resources, visit www.HighPerformanceInstitute.com.

Accenture (2009). *Untapped potential: Stretching toward the future. International women's day 2009 global research results.* Retrieved from https://www.in.gov/icw/files/Accenture_Research.pdf

Aggerholm, K. (2015). *Talent development, existential philosophy and sport: On becoming an elite athlete.* New York, NY: Routledge.

Amen, D. G. (2015). *Change your brain, change your life: The breakthrough program for conquering anxiety, depression, obsessiveness, lack of focus, anger, and memory problems.* New York, NY: Harmony.

American Psychological Association (2015). *Stress in America: Paying with our health.* Retrieved from http://www.apa.org/news/press/releases/stress/2014/stress-report.pdf

American Psychological Association (2016). *2016 Work and well-being survey.* Retrieved from http://www.apaexcellence.org/assets/general/2016-work-and-wellbeing-survey-results.pdf

Anderson, E., & Shivakumar, G. (2015). Effects of exercise and physical activity on anxiety. Progress in physical activity and exercise and affective and anxiety disorders: translational studies, perspectives and future directions. *Frontiers in Psychiatry, 4, 27.* Retrieved from http://journal.frontiersin.org/article/10.3389/fpsyt.2013.00027/full

Aronson, J. (1992). Women's sense of responsibility for the care of old people: "But who else is going to do it?" *Gender & Society*, 6(1), 8–29.

Artz, B., Goodall, A. H., & Oswald, A. J. (2016). Do women ask? *IZA Discussion Papers*. No. 10183. Retrieved from https://www.econstor.eu/bitstream/10419/147869/1/dp10183.pdf

Bandura, A. (1980). Gauging the relationship between self-efficacy judgment and action. *Cognitive Therapy and Research, 4,* 263–268.

Bandura, A. (1982). Self-efficacy mechanism in human agency. *American Psychologist, 37*(2), 122.

Bandura, A. (1991). Social cognitive theory of self-regulation. *Organizational Behavior and Human Decision Processes, 50*(2), 248–287.

Bandura, A., & Cervone, D. (1983). Self-evaluative and self-efficacy mechanisms governing the motivational effects of goal systems. *Journal of Personality and Social Psychology, 45*(5), 1017.

Barnwell, B. (2014, August 27). The it factor. *Grantland*. Retrieved from http://grantland.com/features/it-factor-nfl-quarterback-intangibles

Barrett, L. F. (2017). The theory of constructed emotion: an active inference account of interoception and categorization. *Social Cognitive and Affective Neuroscience, 12*(1), 1–23.

Barrett, L. F. (2017). *How emotions are made: The secret life of the brain.* New York, NY: Houghton Mifflin Harcourt.

Barrick, M. R., & Mount, M. K. (1991). The big five personality dimensions and job performance: a meta-analysis. *Personnel Psychology, 44*(1), 1-26.

Batty, G. D., Deary, I. J., & Gottfredson, L. S. (2007). Premorbid (early life) IQ and later mortality risk: Systematic review. *Annals of Epidemiology, 17*(4), 278–288.

Baumeister, R. F. (1984). Choking under pressure: Self-conscious and paradoxical effects of incentives on skillful performance. *Journal of Personality and Social Psychology, 46*(3), 610–620.

Bayer, A. E., & Folger, J. (1966). Some correlates of a citation measure of productivity in science. *Sociology of Education, 39,* 381–390.

Beck, J. S. (2011). *Cognitive behavior therapy: Basics and beyond.* New York, NY: Guilford Press.

Begley, S., & Davidson, R. (2012). *The emotional life of your brain: How its unique patterns affect the way you think, feel, and live—and how you can change them.* New York, NY: Penguin.

Behrman, J. R. (1993). The economic rationale for investing in nutrition in developing countries. *World Development, 21*(11), 1749–1771.

Beilock, S. L., & Carr, T. H. (2001). On the fragility of skilled performance: What governs choking under pressure? *Journal of Experimental Psychology: General, 130*(4), 701.

Benca, R. M., Obermeyer, W. H., Thisted, R. A., & Gillin, J. C. (1992). Sleep and psychiatric disorders: A meta-analysis. *Archives of General Psychiatry, 49*(8), 651–668.

Berman, M. G., Jonides, J., & Kaplan, S. (2008). The cognitive benefits of interacting with nature. *Psychological Science, 19*(12), 1207–1212.

Blackwell, L., Dweck, C., & Trzesniewski, K. (2007). Achievement across the adolescent transition: A longitudinal study and an intervention. *Child Development, 78*(1), 246–263.

Blazer, D. G., & Hernandez, L. M. (Eds.). (2006). *Genes, behavior, and the social environment: Moving beyond the nature/nurture debate.* Washington, DC: National Academies Press.

Bloom, B. S. (1985). The nature of the study and why it was done. In B. S. Bloom (Ed.), *Developing talent in young people* (pp. 3–18). New York, NY: Ballantine.

Bolman, L. G., & Deal, T. E. (2003). *Reframing organizations: Artistry, choice, and leadership.* Hoboken, NJ: John Wiley & Sons.

Boggs, M., & Miller, J. (2008). *Project everlasting.* New York, NY: Fireside.

Bonebright, C. A., Clay, D. L., & Ankermann, R. D. (2000). The relationship of workaholism with work-life conflict, life satisfaction, and purpose in life. *Journal of Counseling Psychology, 47*(4), 469–477.

Borjas, G. J. (1990). *Friends or strangers: The impact of immigrants on the US economy.* New York, NY: Basic Books.

Bossidy, L., Charan, R., & Burck, C. (2011). *Execution: The discipline of getting things done.* New York, NY: Random House.

Botelho, E. L., Powell, K. R., Kinkaid S., Wang, D. (2017). What sets successful CEOs apart. *Harvard Business Review,* May–June, 70–77.

Brandt, R. B. (1964). The concepts of obligation and duty. *Mind, 73*(291), 374-393.

Bronson, P., & Merryman, A. (2013). *Top dog: The science of winning and losing.* New York, NY: Random House.

Brown, K. W., & Ryan, R. M. (2003). The benefits of being present: Mindfulness and its role in psychological well-being. *Journal of Personality and Social Psychology, 84*(4), 822.

Bryan, T., & Bryan, J. (1991). Positive mood and math performance. *Journal of Learning Disabilities, 24,* 490–494.

Burt, C. (1966). The genetic determination of differences in intelligence: A study of monozygotic twins reared together and apart. *British Journal of Psychology, 57*(12), 137–153.

Butler, A. C., Chapman, J. E., Forman, E. M., & Beck, A. T. (2006). The empirical status of cognitive-behavioral therapy: A review of meta-analyses. *Clinical Psychology Review, 26*(1), 17–31.

Cacioppo, J. T., Fowler, J. H., & Christakis, N. A. (2009). Alone in the crowd: The structure and spread of loneliness in a large social network. *Journal of Personality and Social Psychology, 97,* 977–991.

Cain, S. (2013). *Quiet: The power of introverts in a world that can't stop talking.* New York, NY: Broadway Books.

Campbell, J. D., Trapnell, P. D., Heine, S. J., Katz, I. M., Lavallee, L. F., & Lehman, D. R. (1996). Self-concept clarity: Measurement, personality correlates, and cultural boundaries. *Journal of Personality and Social Psychology, 70*(1), 141.

Cappuccio, F. P., Taggart, F. M., Kandala, N., Currie, A., Peile, E., Stranges, S., & Miller, M. A. (2008). Meta-analysis of short sleep duration and obesity in children and adults. *SLEEP, 31*(5), 619.

Capron, C., & Duyme, M. (1989). Assessment of the effects of socio-economic status on IQ in a full cross-fostering study. *Nature, 340,* 552–554.

Carter, E. C., Kofler, L. M., Forster, D. E., & McCullough, M. E. (2015). A series of meta-analytic tests of the depletion effect: Self-control does not seem to rely on a limited resource. *Journal of Experimental Psychology: General, 144*(4), 796–815.

Caspi, A., Roberts, B. W., & Shiner, R. L. (2005). Personality development: Stability and change. *Annual Review of Psychology, 56,* 453–484. Retrieved from http://dx.doi.org/10.1146/annurev.psych.55.090902.141913

Castelli, D. M., Hillman, C. H., Buck, S. M., & Erwin, H. E. (2007). Physical fitness and academic achievement in third- and fifth-grade students. *Journal of Sport and Exercise Psychology, 29*(2), 239–252.

Center for Behavioral Health Statistics and Quality. (2015). *Behavioral health trends in the United States: Results from the 2014 national survey on drug use and health* (HHS Publication no. SMA 15-4927, NSDUH Series H-50). Retrieved from https://www.samhsa.gov/data/sites/default/files/NSDUH-FRR1-2014/NSDUH-FRR1-2014.htm

Center for Behavioral Health Statistics and Quality. (2016). *Key substance use and mental health indicators in the United States: Results from the 2015 national survey on drug use and health.* Retrieved from https://www.samhsa.gov/data/sites/default/files/NSDUH-FFR1-2015/NSDUH-FFR1-2015/NSDUH-FFR1-2015.pdf

Cerasoli, C. P., Nicklin, J. M., & Ford, M. T. (2014). Intrinsic motivation and extrinsic incentives jointly predict performance: A 40-year meta-analysis. *Psychological Bulletin, 140*(4), 980.

Chambliss, D. F. (1989). The mundanity of excellence: An ethnographic report on stratification and Olympic swimmers. *Sociological Theory, 7*(1), 70–86.

Chaouloff, F., Laude, D., & Elghozi, J. (1989). Physical exercise: Evidence for differential consequences of tryptophan on 5-HT synthesis and metabolism in central serotonergic cell bodies and terminals. *Journal of Neural Transmission, 78*(2), 1435–1463.

Chen, C., Nakagawa, S., Kitaichi, Y., An, Y., Omiya, Y., Song, N., . . . & Kusumi, I. (2016). The role of medial prefrontal corticosterone and dopamine in the antidepressant-like effect of exercise. *Psychoneuroendocrinology, 69,* 1–9.

Christakis, N. A., & Fowler, J. H. (2007). The spread of obesity in a large social network over 32 years. *New England Journal of Medicine, 357*(4), 370–379. doi:10.1056/NEJMsa066082

Christakis, N. A., & Fowler, J. H. (2008a). The collective dynamics of smoking in a large social network. *New England Journal of Medicine, 358,* 2249–2258. doi:10.1056/NEJMsa0706154

Christakis, N. A., & Fowler, J. H. (2008b). Dynamic spread of happiness in a large social network: Longitudinal analysis over 20 years in the Framingham Heart Study. *British Medical Journal, 337*(a2338), 1–9. doi:10.1136/bmj .a2338

Christakis, N. A., & Fowler, J. H. (2009). *Connected: The surprising power of our social networks and how they shape our lives.* New York, NY: Little, Brown and Company.

Christakis, N. A., & Fowler, J. H. (2013). Social contagion theory: Examining dynamic social networks and human behavior. *Statistics in Medicine, 32*(4), 556–577.

Chui, M., Manyika, J., Bughin, J., Dobbs, R., Roxburgh, C., Sarrazin, H., . . . & Westergren, M. (2012, July). The social economy: Unlocking value and productivity through social technologies. *McKinsey Global Institute.*

Cialdini, R. B. (2007). *Influence: The psychology of persuasion.* New York, NY: Harper Collins.

Claro, S., Paunesku, D., & Dweck, C. S. (2016). Growth mindset tempers the effects of poverty on academic achievement. *Proceedings of the National Academy of Sciences, 113*(31), 8664–8668.

Cole, J. R., & Cole, S. (1973). *Social stratification in science.* Chicago, IL: University of Chicago Press.

Columbia University, CASA. (2012, July). *Addiction medicine: Closing the gap between science and practice.* Retrieved from www.centeronaddiction.org /download/file/fid/1177

Connor, K. M., & Davidson, J. R. T. (2003). Development of a new resilience scale: The Connor-Davidson Resilience Scale (CD-RISC). *Depression and Anxiety, 18,* 76–82.

Cotman, C. W., & Berchtold, N. C. (2002). Exercise: A behavioral intervention to enhance brain health and plasticity. *Trends in Neurosciences, 25*(6), 295–301.

Cox, D., Hallam, R., O'Connor, K., & Rachman, S. (1983). An experimental analysis of fearlessness and courage. *British Journal of Psychology, 74,* 107–117.

Coyle, D. (2009). *The talent code: Greatest isn't born. It's grown. Here's how.* New York, NY: Bantam.

Crown, D. F., & Rosse, J. G. (1995). Yours, mine, and ours: Facilitating group productivity through the integration of individual and group goals. *Organizational Behavior and Human Decision Processes, 64,* 138–150.

Crum, A. J., Salovey, P., & Achor, S. (2013). Rethinking stress: The role of mindsets in determining the stress response. *Journal of Personality and Social Psychology, 104*(4), 716.

Crust, L., & Clough, P. J. (2011). Developing mental toughness: From research to practice. *Journal of Sport Psychology in Action, 2*(1), 21–32.

Csikszentmihalyi, M. (1975). *Beyond boredom and anxiety.* San Francisco, CA: Jossey-Bass.

Csikszentmihalyi, M. (1996). *Creativity: Flow and the psychology of discovery and invention.* New York, NY: Harper Collins.

Csikszentmihalyi, M. (1997). *Finding flow: The psychology of engagement with everyday life.* New York, NY: Basic Books.

Csikszentmihalyi, M., Abuhamdeh, S., & Nakamura, J. (2005). Flow. In A. Elliot (Ed.), *Handbook of competence and motivation* (pp. 598–698). New York, NY: Guilford Press.

Csikszentmihalyi, M., & Rathunde, K. (1993). The measurement of flow in everyday life: Toward a theory of emergent motivation. In J. E. Jacobs (Ed.), *Developmental perspectives on motivation: Volume 40 of the Nebraska Symposium on Motivation* (pp. 57–97). Lincoln, NE: University of Nebraska Press.

Culture. (2016). In *Merriam-Webster's online dictionary* (11th ed.) Retrieved from http://www.merriam-webster.com/dictionary/culture

Cunningham, G. B. (2006). The relationships among commitment to change, coping with change, and turnover intentions. *European Journal of Work and Organizational Psychology, 15*(1), 29–45.

Damasio, A. R. (1999). *The feeling of what happens: Body and emotion in the making of consciousness.* Boston, MA: Houghton Mifflin Harcourt.

Danese, A., & McEwen, B. S. (2012). Adverse childhood experiences, allostasis, allostatic load, and age-related disease. *Physiology & Behavior, 106*(1), 29–39.

Danna, K., & Griffin, R. W. (1999). Health and well-being in the workplace: A review and synthesis of the literature. *Journal of Management, 25*(3), 357–384.

Davidson, R. J., Jackson, D., & Kalin, N. H. (2000). Emotion, plasticity, context, and regulation: Perspectives from affective neuroscience. *Psychological Bulletin 126,* 890–909.

Davis, C., Levitan, R. D., Muglia, P., Bewell, C., & Kennedy, J. L. (2004). Decision-making deficits and overeating: A risk model for obesity. *Obesity Research, 12*(6), 929–935.

Debats, D. L. (1999). Sources of meaning: An investigation of significant commitments in life. *Journal of Humanistic Psychology, 39*(4), 30–57.

Deci, E. L., & Ryan, R. M. (2002). *Handbook of self-determination research.* Rochester, NY: University of Rochester Press.

Deci, E. L., & Ryan, R. M. (2010). *Self-determination.* Hoboken, NJ: John Wiley & Sons.

Demerouti E., Bakker, A. B., Nachreiner, F., & Schaufeli, W. B. (2000). A model of burnout and life satisfaction amongst nurses. *Journal of Advanced Nursing, 32*(2), 454–464.

Diener, C. I., & Dweck, C. S. (1978). An analysis of learned helplessness: Continuous changes in performance, strategy, and achievement cognitions following failure. *Personality and Social Psychology, 36*(5), 451–461.

Diener, E., & Biswas-Diener, R. (2011). *Happiness: Unlocking the mysteries of psychological wealth.* Hoboken, NJ: John Wiley & Sons.

Diener, E., & Seligman, M. E. (2004). Beyond money: Toward an economy of well-being. *Psychological Science in the Public Interest, 5*(1), 1–31.

Diener, E. D., Emmons, R. A., Larsen, R. J., & Griffin, S. (1985). The satisfaction with life scale. *Journal of Personality Assessment, 49*(1), 71–75.

Doidge, N. (2007). *The brain that changes itself: Stories of personal triumph from the frontiers of brain science.* New York, NY: Penguin.

Doll, J., & Mayr, U. (1987). Intelligenz und schachleistung – Eine untersuchung an schachexperten [Intelligence and performance in chess – A study of chess experts]. *Psychologische Beiträge, 29,* 270–289.

Drennan, D. (1992). *Transforming company culture: Getting your company from where you are now to where you want to be.* London, UK: McGraw-Hill.

Dubnick, M. (2005). Accountability and the promise of performance: In search of the mechanisms. *Public Performance & Management Review, 28*(3), 376–417.

Duckworth, A. L. (2016). *Grit: The power of passion and perseverance.* New York, NY: Simon and Schuster.

Duckworth, A. L., Eichstaedt, J. C., & Ungar, L. H. (2015). The mechanics of human achievement. *Social and Personality Psychology Compass, 9*(7), 359–369.

Duckworth, A. L., Grant, H., Loew, B., Oettingen, G., & Gollwitzer, P. M. (2011a). Self-regulation strategies improve self-discipline in adolescents: Benefits of mental contrasting and implementation intentions. *Educational Psychology, 31*(1), 17–26.

Duckworth, A. L., Kirby, T. A., Tsukayama, E., Berstein, H., & Ericsson, K. A. (2011b). Deliberate practice spells success: Why grittier competitors triumph at the National Spelling Bee. *Social Psychological and Personality Science, 2*(2), 174–181.

Duckworth, A. L., Peterson, C., Matthews, M. D., & Kelly, D. R. (2007). Grit: Perseverance and passion for long-term goals. *Journal of Personality and Social Psychology, 92*(6), 1087.

Duff, D. C. (2010). *The relationship between behavioral intention, self-efficacy and health behavior: A meta-analysis of meta-analyses.* East Lansing: MI: Michigan State University Press.

Dunlap, E., Golub, A., Johnson, B. D., & Benoit, E. (2009). Normalization of violence: Experiences of childhood abuse by inner-city crack users. *Journal of Ethnicity in Substance Abuse, 8*(1), 15–34.

Dweck, C. S. (2008). *Mindset: The new psychology of success.* New York, NY: Random House.

Dweck, C. S. (2014). *The power of believing that you can improve* [Video file]. Retrieved from https://www.ted.com/talks/carol_dweck_the_power_of_believing _that_you_can_improve?language=en#t-386248

Dweck, C. S., & Leggett, E. L. (1988). A social-cognitive approach to motivation and personality. *Psychological Review, 95*(2), 256–273.

Dweck, C. S., & Reppucci, N. D. (1973). Learned helplessness and reinforcement responsibility in children. *Journal of Personality and Social Psychology, 25*(1), 109–116.

Easterlin, R. A., McVey, L. A., Switek, M., Sawangfa, O., & Zweig, J. S. (2010). The happiness-income paradox revisited. *Proceedings of the National Academy of Sciences, 107*(52), 22463–22468.

Elkind, D. (2007). *The power of play: How spontaneous imaginative activities lead to happier, healthier children.* Da Capo Press.

Elliott, E. S., & Dweck, C. S. (1988). Goals: An approach to motivation and achievement. *Journal of Personality and Social Psychology, 54*(1), 5–13.

Emmons, R. A. (2000). Is spirituality an intelligence? Motivation, cognition, and the psychology of ultimate concern. *The International Journal for the Psychology of Religion, 10*(1), 3–26.

Emmons, R. A. (2007). *Thanks!: How the new science of gratitude can make you happier.* Boston, MA: Houghton Mifflin Harcourt.

Ericsson, K. A. (2006). The influence of experience and deliberate practice on the development of superior expert performance. In K. A. Ericsson, N. Charness, P. J. Feltovich, & R. R. Hoffman (Eds.), *Cambridge handbook of expertise and expert performance* (pp. 685–706). Cambridge, UK: Cambridge University Press.

Ericsson, K. A. (2014). Why expert performance is special and cannot be extrapolated from studies of performance in the general population: A response to criticisms. *Intelligence, 45,* 81–103.

Ericsson, K. A., & Pool, R. (2016a). *Peak: Secrets from the new science of expertise.* New York, NY: Houghton Mifflin Harcourt.

Ericsson, K. A., & Pool, R. (2016b, April 10). *Malcolm Gladwell got us wrong: Our research was key to the 10,000-hour rule, but here's what got oversimplified.* Retrieved from http://bit.ly/1S3LiCK

Ericsson, K. A., & Pool, R. (2016c, April 21). *Not all practice makes perfect: Moving from naive to purposeful practice can dramatically increase performance.* Retrieved from http://nautil.us/issue/35/boundaries/not-all-practice-makes-perfect

Ericsson, K. A., Krampe, R. T., & Tesch-Romer, C. (1993). The role of deliberate practice in the acquisition of expert performance. *Psychological Review, 100*(3), 363–406.

Feinberg, J. (1966). Duties, rights, and claims. *American Philosophical Quarterly, 3*(2), 137–144.

Felitti, V. J., Anda, R. F., Nordenberg, D., Williamson, D. F., Spitz, A. M., Edwards, V., . . . & Marks, J. S. (1998). Relationship of childhood abuse and household dysfunction to many of the leading causes of death in adults: The Adverse Childhood Experiences (ACE) Study. *American Journal of Preventive Medicine, 14*(4), 245–258.

Flynn, F. J., & Bohns, V. K. (2012). Underestimating one's influence in help-seeking. In D. T. Kenrick, N. J. Goldstein, & S. L. Braver (Eds.) *Six degrees of social influence: Science, application, and the psychology of Robert Cialdini* (pp. 14–26). Oxford, UK: Oxford University Press.

Flynn, J. R. (1987). Massive IQ gains in 14 nations: What IQ tests really measure. *Psychological Bulletin, 101,* 171–191.

Flynn, J. R. (2012). *Are we getting smarter? Rising IQ in the Twenty-first Century.* Cambridge, UK: Cambridge University Press.

Flynn, J. R., & Rossi-Casé, L. (2012). IQ gains in Argentina between 1964 and 1998. *Intelligence, 40*(2), 145–150.

Foley, T. E., & Fleshner, M. (2008). Neuroplasticity of dopamine circuits after exercise: Implications for central fatigue. *Neuromolecular Medicine, 10*(2), 67–80.

Forward, J., & Zander, A. (1971). Choice of unattainable group goals and effects on performance. *Organizational Behavior and Human Performance, 6*(2), 184–199.

Fowler, J. H., & Christakis, N. A. (2010). Cooperative behavior cascades in human social networks. *Proceedings of the National Academy of Sciences, 107*(12), 5334–5338. doi:10.1073/pnas.0913149107

Fredrickson, B. (2004). The broaden-and-build theory of positive emotions. *Philosophical Transactions of the Royal Society B, 359*(1449), 1367–1378.

Frink, D. D., & Ferris, G. R. (1998). Accountability, impression management, and goal setting in the performance evaluation process. *Human relations, 51*(10), 1259–1283.

Frost, R. O., & Henderson, K. J. (1991). Perfectionism and reactions to athletic competition. *Journal of Sport and Exercise Psychology, 13,* 323–335.

Fuligni, A. J. (2001). Family obligation and the academic motivation of adolescents from Asian, Latin American, and European backgrounds. *New Directions for Child and Adolescent Development, 2001*(94), 61–76.

Gagné, F. (1985). Giftedness and talent: Reexamining a reexamination of the definitions. *Gifted Child Quarterly, 29*(3), 103–112.

Gandy, W. M., Coberley, C., Pope, J. E., Wells, A., & Rula, E. Y. (2014). Comparing the contributions of well-being and disease status to employee productivity. *Journal of Occupational and Environmental Medicine, 56*(3), 252–257.

Garrett, G., Benden, M., Mehta, R., Pickens, A., Peres, C., & Zhao, H. (2016). Call center productivity over 6 months following a standing desk intervention. *IIE Transactions on Occupational Ergonomics and Human Factors, 4*(23), 188–195.

Gentry, W. A., Gilmore, D. C., Shuffler, M. L., & Leslie, J. B. (2012). Political skill as an indicator of promotability among multiple rater sources. *Journal of Organizational Behavior, 33*(1), 89–104.

Ghaemi, N. (2011). *A first-rate madness: Uncovering the links between leadership and mental illness.* New York, NY: Penguin.

Ghosh, S., Laxmi, T. R., & Chattarji, S. (2013). Functional connectivity from the amygdala to the hippocampus grows stronger after stress. *Journal of Neuroscience, 33*(17), 7234–7244.

Gil, E. (2012). *The healing power of play: Working with abused children.* New York, NY: Guilford Press.

Giorgi, S., Lockwood, C., & Glynn, M. A. (2015). The many faces of culture: Making sense of 30 years of research on culture in organization studies. *Academy of Management Annals, 9*(1), 1–54.

Goleman, D. (1998). *Working with emotional intelligence.* New York, NY: Bantam.

Goleman, D. (2007). *Social intelligence.* New York, NY: Random House.

Goleman, D., Boyatzis, R., & McKee, A. (2001). Primal leadership: The hidden driver of great performance. *Harvard Business Review, 79*(11), 42–53.

Goleman, D., Boyatzis, R., & McKee, A. (2013). *Primal leadership: Unleashing the power of emotional intelligence.* Boston, MA: Harvard Business Press.

Gollwitzer, P. M. (1999). Implementation intentions: Strong effects of simple plans. *American Psychologist, 54*(7), 493.

Gollwitzer, P. M., & Brandstätter, V. (1997). Implementation intentions and effective goal pursuit. *Journal of Personality and Social Psychology, 73*(1), 186.

Gollwitzer, P. M., & Oettingen, G. (2016). Planning promotes goal striving. In K. D. Vohs & R. F. Baumeister (Eds.), *Handbook of self-regulation: Research, theory, and applications* (3rd ed., pp. 223–244). New York, NY: Guilford.

Gottfredson, L. S. (1997). Why g matters: The complexity of everyday life. *Intelligence, 24*(1), 79–132.

Gottfredson, L. S. (1998, Winter). The general intelligence factor. *The Scientific American Presents, 9*(4), 24–29.

Gottman, J., & Silver, N. (1995). *Why marriages succeed or fail: And how you can make yours last.* New York, NY: Simon and Schuster.

Gottman, J., & Silver, N. (2015). *The seven principles for making marriage work: A practical guide from the country's foremost relationship expert.* New York, NY: Harmony.

Gould, S. J. (1996). *The mismeasure of man.* New York, NY: W. W. Norton.

Grabner, R. H., Stern, E., & Neubauer, A. C. (2007). Individual differences in chess expertise: A psychometric investigation. *Acta Psychologica, 124*(3), 398–420.

Grant, A. (2013). *Give and take: Why helping others drives our success.* New York, NY: Penguin.

Grant, A. M., & Gino, F. (2010). A little thanks goes a long way: Explaining why gratitude expressions motivate prosocial behavior. *Journal of Personality and Social Psychology, 98*(6), 946–955.

Grawitch, M. J., Gottschalk, M., & Munz, D. C. (2006). The path to a healthy workplace: A critical review linking healthy workplace practices, employee well-being, and organizational improvements. *Consulting Psychology Journal: Practice and Research, 58*(3), 129.

Grossman, P., Niemann, L., Schmidt, S., & Walach, H. (2004). Mindfulness-based stress reduction and health benefits: A meta-analysis. *Journal of Psychosomatic Research, 57*(1), 35–43.

Grugulis, I., Holmes, C., & Mayhew, K. (2017). The economic and social benefits of skills. In J. Buchanan, D. Finegold, K. Mayhew, & C. Warhurst (Eds.), *The Oxford Handbook of Skills and Training* (p. 372). Oxford, UK: Oxford University Press.

Grzegorek, J., Slaney, R. B., Franze, S., & Rice, K. G. (2004). Self-criticism, dependency, self-esteem, and grade point average satisfaction among clusters of perfectionists and nonperfectionists. *Journal of Counseling Psychology, 51,* 192–200. doi:10.1037/0022-0167.51.2.192

Haeffel, G. J., & Hames, J. L. (2013). Cognitive vulnerability to depression can be contagious. *Clinical Psychological Science, 2*(1), 75–85.

Hampson, S. E., & Goldberg, L. R. (2006). A first large cohort study of personality trait stability over the 40 years between elementary school and midlife. *Journal of Personality and Social Psychology, 91*(4), 763.

Hanson, R. (2013). *Hardwiring happiness: The new brain science of contentment, calm, and confidence.* New York, NY: Harmony.

Harkin, B., Webb, T. L., Chang, B. P., Prestwich, A., Conner, M., Kellar, I., & Sheeran, P. (2016). Does monitoring goal progress promote goal attainment? A meta-analysis of the experimental evidence. *Psychological Bulletin, 142*(2), 198.

Harris, M. A., Brett, C. E., Johnson, W., & Deary, I. J. (2016). Personality stability from age 14 to age 77 years. *Psychology and Aging, 31*(8), 862.

Hart, B., & Risley, T. R. (2003). The early catastrophe: The 30 million word gap by age 3. *American Educator, 27*(1), 4-9.

Harter, J. K., Schmidt, F. L., & Keyes, C. L. (2003). Well-being in the workplace and its relationship to business outcomes: A review of the Gallup studies. *Flourishing: Positive Psychology and the Life Well-Lived, 2,* 205–224.

Hasenkamp, W., & Barsalou, L. W. (2012). Effects of meditation experience on functional connectivity of distributed brain networks. *Frontiers in Human Neuroscience, 6,* 38.

Heatherton, T. F., & Weinberger, J. L. E. (1994). *Can personality change?* Washington, DC: American Psychological Association.

Hefferon, K., Grealy, M., & Mutrie, N. (2009). Post-traumatic growth and life threatening physical illness: A systematic review of the qualitative literature. *British Journal of Health Psychology, 14*(2), 343–378.

Heilman, M. E., & Wallen, A. S. (2010). Wimpy and undeserving of respect: Penalties for men's gender-inconsistent success. *Journal of Experimental Social Psychology, 46*(4), 664–667.

Hertenstein, M. J., Holmes, R., McCullough, M., & Keltner, D. (2009). The communication of emotion via touch. *Emotion, 9*(4), 566.

Herzberg, F., Mausner, B., & Snyderman, B. (1969). *The motivation to work.* Hoboken, NJ: John Wiley & Sons.

Hewitt, P. L., & Flett, G. L. (2002). Perfectionism and stress in psychopathology. In G. L. Flett & P. L. Hewitt (Eds.), *Perfectionism: Theory, research, and treatment* (pp. 255–284). Washington, DC: American Psychological Association.

Hoddinott, J., Maluccio, J. A., Behrman, J. R., Flores, R., & Martorell, R. (2008). Effect of a nutrition intervention during early childhood on economic productivity in Guatemalan adults. *The Lancet, 371*(9610), 411–416.

Horan, R. (2009). The neuropsychological connection between creativity and meditation. *Creativity Research Journal, 21*(23), 199–222.

Howe, M. J., Davidson, J. W., & Sloboda, J. A. (1998). Innate talents: Reality or myth? *Behavioral and Brain Sciences, 21*(3), 399–407.

Hume, D. (1970). *Enquiries concerning the human understanding and concerning the principles of morals: Reprinted from the posthumous edition of 1777.* Oxford, UK: Clarendon Press.

Humphreys, M. S., & Revelle, W. (1984). Personality, motivation, and performance: A theory of the relationship between individual differences and information processing. *Psychological Review, 91*(2), 153.

Hyde, J. S. (2005). The gender similarities hypothesis. *American Psychologist, 60*(6), 581–592.

Immordino-Yang, M. H., Christodoulou, J. A., & Singh, V. (2012). Rest is not idleness: Implications of the brain's default mode for human development and education. *Perspectives on Psychological Science, 7*(4), 352–364.

Isen, A. M., & Levin, P. F. (1972). Effect of feeling good on helping: Cookies and kindness. *Journal of Personality and Social Psychology 21*(3), 384–388.

Isen, A. M., Clark, M., & Schwartz, M. F. (1976). Duration of the effect of good mood on helping: "Footprints on the sands of time." *Journal of Personality and Social Psychology 34*(3), 385–393.

Isen, A. M., Rosenzweig, A. S., & Young, M. J. (1991). The influence of positive affect on clinical problem solving. *Medical Decision Making, 11*(3), 221–227.

Isovich, E., Mijnster, M. J., Flügge, G., & Fuchs, E. (2000). Chronic psychosocial stress reduces the density of dopamine transporters. *European Journal of Neuroscience, 12*(3), 1071–1078.

Issa, G., Wilson, C., Terry, A. V., & Pillai, A. (2010). An inverse relationship between cortisol and BDNF levels in schizophrenia: Data from human postmortem and animal studies. *Neurobiology of Disease, 39*(3), 327–333.

Jacobs, B. L. (1994). Serotonin, motor activity and depression-related disorders. *American Scientist, 82*(5), 456-463.

Jacobs, B. L., & Azmitia, E. C. (1992). Structure and function of the brain serotonin system. *Physiol Rev, 72*(1), 165-229.

Jain, S., Shapiro, S. L., Swanick, S., Roesch, S. C., Mills, P. J., Bell, I., & Schwartz, G. E. (2007). A randomized controlled trial of mindfulness meditation versus relaxation training: Effects on distress, positive states of mind, rumination, and distraction. *Annals of Behavioral Medicine, 33*(1), 11–21.

Jecker, J., & Landy, D. (1969). Liking a person as a function of doing him a favour. *Human Relations, 22*(4), 371–378.

Jensen, A. (1969). How much can we boost IQ and scholastic achievement? *Harvard Educational Review, 39*(1), 1–123.

Jensen, A. R. (1982). Reaction time and psychometric g. In H. J. Eysenk (Ed.), *A model for intelligence* (pp. 93–132). Berlin, Germany: Springer Berlin Heidelberg.

Judge, T. A., Thoresen, C. J., Bono, J. E., & Patton, G. K. (2001). The job satisfaction–job performance relationship: A qualitative and quantitative review. *Psychological Bulletin, 127*(3), 376–407.

Jung, R. E., Mead, B. S., Carrasco, J., & Flores, R. A. (2013). The structure of creative cognition in the human brain. *Frontiers in Human Neuroscience, 7,* 330.

Kahneman, D., & Deaton, A. (2010). High income improves evaluation of life but not emotional well-being. *Proceedings of the National Academy of Sciences, 107*(38), 16489–16493.

Kant, I. (1997). *Lectures on ethics.* Cambridge, UK: Cambridge University Press.

Kanter, R. M. (1999). The enduring skills of change leaders. *Leader to Leader, 1999*(13), 15–22.

Kashdan, T. (2017, April 13). How I learned about the perils of grit: Rethinking simple explanations for complicated problems. *Psychology Today.* Retrieved from https://www.psychologytoday.com/blog/curious/201704/how-i-learned -about-the-perils-grit

Kaufman, S. (2015). *Ungifted: Intelligence redefined.* New York, NY: Basic Books.

Kaufman, S. B., Quilty, L. C., Grazioplene, R. G., Hirsh, J. B., Gray, J. R., Peterson, J. B., & DeYoung, C. G. (2015). Openness to experience and intellect differentially predict creative achievement in the arts and sciences. *Journal of Personality, 82,* 248–258.

King, L., & Hicks, J. (2009). Detecting and constructing meaning in life events. *Journal of Positive Psychology, 4*(5), 317–330.

Kleinginna, P. R., & Kleinginna, A. M. (1981). A categorized list of emotion definitions, with suggestions for a consensual definition. *Motivation and Emotion, 5*(4), 345–379.

Koball, H. L., Moiduddin, E., Henderson, J., Goesling, B., & Besculides, M. (2010). What do we know about the link between marriage and health? *Journal of Family Issues 31*(8): 1019–1040.

Koblin, J. (2016, June 30). How much do we love TV? Let us count the ways. *The New York Times.* Retrieved from https://www.nytimes.com/2016/07/01/business/media/nielsen-survey-media-viewing.html

Koestner, R., Losier, G. F., Vallerand, R. J., & Carducci, D. (1996). Identified and introjected forms of political internalization: Extending self-determination theory. *Journal of Personality and Social Psychology, 70*(5), 1025.

Kouzes, J. M., & Posner, B. Z. (2011). *Credibility: How leaders gain and lose it, why people demand it.* Hoboken, NJ: John Wiley & Sons.

Kramer, A. F., & Hillman, C. H. (2006). Aging, physical activity, and neurocognitive function. In E. Acevado & P. Ekkekakis (Eds.), *Psychobiology of exercise and sport* (pp. 45–59). Champaign, IL: Human Kinetics.

Kristof, N. (2016, October 28). 3 TVs and no food: Growing up poor in America. *The New York Times.* Retrieved from http://www.nytimes.com/2016/10/30/opinion/sunday/3-tvs-and-no-food-growing-up-poor-in-america.html

Kross, E., Bruehlman-Senecal, E., Park, J., Burson, A., Dougherty, A., Shablack, H., . . . & Ayduk, O. (2014). Self-talk as a regulatory mechanism: How you do it matters. *Journal of Personality and Social Psychology, 106*(2), 304.

Kruse, E., Chancellor, J., Ruberton, P. M., & Lyubomirsky, S. (2014). An upward spiral between gratitude and humility. *Social Psychological and Personality Science, 5*(7), 805–814.

Ladd, H. A., & Fiske, E. B. (Eds.). (2015). *Handbook of Research in Education Finance and Policy* (2nd ed.). New York, NY: Routledge.

Lambert, N. M., Stillman, T. F., Baumeister, R. F., Fincham, F. D., Hicks, J. A., & Graham, S. M. (2010). Family as a salient source of meaning in young adulthood. *The Journal of Positive Psychology, 5*(5), 367–376.

Lang, P. J. (2010). Emotion and motivation: Toward consensus definitions and a common research purpose. *Emotion Review, 6*(2), 93–99.

Lavie, N. (2010). Attention, distraction, and cognitive control under load. *Current Directions in Psychological Science, 19*(3), 143–148.

Law, K. S., Wong, C. S., Huang, G. H., & Li, X. (2008). The effects of emotional intelligence on job performance and life satisfaction for the research and development scientists in China. *Asia Pacific Journal of Management, 25*(1), 51–69.

Lee, T. (2016, October 20). The city: prison's grip on the black family: The spirals of poverty and mass incarceration upend urban communities. *MSNBC.* Retrieved from http://www.nbcnews.com/specials/geographyofpoverty-big-city

Lemonick, M. D. (2005, January 9). The biology of joy: Scientists know plenty about depression. Now they are starting to understand the roots of positive emotions. *TIME: Special Mind and Body Issue.* Retrieved from http://bit .ly/2mPoVcG

Lerner, J. S., & Tetlock, P. E. (1999). Accounting for the effects of accountability. *Psychological Bulletin, 125*(2), 255.

Leroy, S. (2009). Why is it so hard to do my work? The challenge of attention residue when switching between work tasks. *Organizational Behavior and Human Decision Processes, 109*(2), 168–181.

Levitin, D. J. (2014). *The organized mind: Thinking straight in the age of information overload.* New York, NY: Penguin.

Lewis, K., Lange, D., & Gillis, L. (2005). Transactive memory systems, learning, and learning transfer. *Organization Science, 16*(6), 581–598.

Lewis, M., Haviland-Jones, J. M., & Barrett, L. F. (Eds.). (2010). *Handbook of emotions.* New York, NY: Guilford Press.

LexisNexis (2010, October 20). New survey reveals extent, impact of information overload on workers; from Boston to Beijing, professionals feel overwhelmed, demoralized. [News release]. Retrieved from http://www.lexisnexis .com/en-us/about-us/media/press-release.page?id=128751276114739

Linley, P. A., & Joseph, S. (2004). Positive change following trauma and adversity: A review. *Journal of Traumatic Stress, 17*(1), 11–21.

Lipari, R. N., Park-Lee, E., & Van Horn, S. (2016, September 29). *America's need for and receipt of substance use treatment in 2015.* (The CBHSQ Report.) Retrieved from Substance Abuse and Mental Health Services Administration website: http://bit.ly/2mPrRGl

Locke, E. A., & Latham, G. P. (1990). *A theory of goal setting and task performance.* Englewood Cliffs, NJ: Prentice-Hall.

Locke, E. A., & Latham, G. P. (2002). Building a practically useful theory of goal setting and task motivation: A 35-year odyssey. *American Psychologist, 57*(9), 705.

Lykken, D. (2000). *Happiness: The nature and nurture of joy and contentment.* New York, NY: Picador.

Lyubomirsky, S., King, L., & Diener, E. (2005). The benefits of frequent positive affect: Does happiness lead to success? *Psychological Bulletin, 131*(6), 803–855.

MacKenzie, M. J., & Baumeister, R. F. (2014). Meaning in life: Nature, needs, and myths. In P. Russo-Netzer & A. Batthyany (Eds.), *Meaning in positive and existential psychology* (pp. 25–37). New York, NY: Springer.

Macmillan, T., & Rachman, S. (1988). Fearlessness and courage in paratroopers undergoing training. *Personality and Individual Differences, 9,* 373–378. doi:10.1016/0191-8869(88)90100-6

Macnamara, B. N., Hambrick, D. Z., & Oswald, F. L. (2014). Deliberate practice and performance in music, games, sports, education, and professions: A meta-analysis. *Psychological Science, 25*(8), 1608–1618.

Mahncke, H. W., Connor, B. B., Appelman, J., Ahsanuddin, O. N., Hardy, J. L., Wood, R. A., . . . & Merzenich, M. M. (2006). Memory enhancement in healthy older adults using a brain plasticity based training program: A randomized, controlled study. *Proceedings of the National Academy of Sciences, 103*(33), 12523–12528.

Marano, H. E. (1999). The power of play. *Psychology Today, 32*(4), 36.

Mark, G., Gonzalez, V. M., & Harris, J. (2005, April). *No task left behind? Examining the nature of fragmented work.* Paper presented at the Conference on Human Factors in Computing Systems, Portland, OR.

Markman, K. D., Proulx, T. E., & Lindberg, M. J. (2013). *The psychology of meaning.* Washington, DC: American Psychological Association.

Marquardt, M. J. (2011). *Leading with questions: How leaders find the right solutions by knowing what to ask.* Hoboken, NJ: John Wiley & Sons.

Martela, F., & Steger, M. F. (2016). The three meanings of meaning in life: Distinguishing coherence, purpose, and significance. *Journal of Positive Psychology, 11*(5), 531–545.

Masicampo, E. J., & Baumeister, R. F. (2011). Consider it done! Plan making can eliminate the cognitive effects of unfulfilled goals. *Journal of Personality and Social Psychology, 101*(4), 667.

Maslow, A. (1962). *Towards a psychology of being.* Princeton, NJ: Van Nostrand.

Maslow, A. (1971). *The farther reaches of human nature.* New York, NY: Viking Press.

McAdams, D. P. (1994). Can personality change? Levels of stability and growth in personality across the life span. In D. P. McAdams, J. L. Weinberger, & J. Lee (Eds.), *Can personality change?* (pp. 299–313). Washington, DC: American Psychological Association.

McCrory, M. A., Suen, V. M., & Roberts, S. B. (2002). Biobehavioral influences on energy intake and adult weight gain. *Journal of Nutrition, 132*(12), 3830S–3834S.

McDermott, R., Fowler, J., & Christakis, N. (2013). Breaking up is hard to do, unless everyone else is doing it too: Social network effects on divorce in a longitudinal sample. *Social Forces, 92*(2), 491.

Mednick, S. C., Christakis, N. A., & Fowler J. H. (2010). The spread of sleep loss influences drug use in adolescent social networks. *Public Library of Science One, 5*(3), e9775.

Merzenich, M. M. (2013). *Soft-wired: How the new science of brain plasticity can change your life.* San Francisco, CA: Parnassus.

Michaels, E., Handfield-Jones, H., & Axelrod, B. (2001). *The war for talent.* Boston, MA: Harvard Business Press.

Miller, G. E., & Wrosch, C. (2007). You've gotta know when to fold 'em: Goal disengagement and systemic inflammation in adolescence. *Psychological Science, 18*(9), 773–777.

Miller, J. (2016). The well-being and productivity link: A significant opportunity for research-into-practice. *Journal of Organizational Effectiveness: People and Performance, 3*(3), 289311.

Miller, J. J., Fletcher, K., & Kabat-Zinn, J. (1995). Three-year follow-up and clinical implications of a mindfulness meditation-based stress reduction intervention in the treatment of anxiety disorders. *General Hospital Psychiatry, 17*(3), 192–200.

Morgeson, F. P., Campion, M. A., Dipboye, R. L., Hollenbeck, J. R., Murphy, K., & Schmitt, N. (2007). Are we getting fooled again? Coming to terms with limitations in the use of personality tests for personnel selection. *Personnel Psychology, 60*(4), 1029-1049.

Munyon, T. P., Summers, J. K., Thompson, K. M., & Ferris, G. R. (2015). Political skill and work outcomes: A theoretical extension, meta-analytic investigation, and agenda for the future. *Personnel Psychology, 68*(1), 143–184.

Nanus, B. (1992). *Visionary leadership: Creating a compelling sense of direction for your organization.* San Francisco, CA: Jossey-Bass.

National Institute on Drug Abuse (2012). Principles of drug addiction treatment: A research-based guide (3rd ed.). Retrieved from https://www.drugabuse.gov/publications/principles-drug-addiction-treatment-research-based-guide-third-edition/preface

Newport, C. (2016). *Deep work: Rules for focused success in a distracted world.* New York, NY: Hachette.

Nickerson, R. S. (1998). Confirmation bias: A ubiquitous phenomenon in many guises. *Review of General Psychology, 2*(2), 175–220.

Nisbett, R. E. (2009). *Intelligence and how to get it: Why schools and cultures count.* New York, NY: W. W. Norton.

Nisbett, R. E., Aronson, J., Blair, C., Dickens, W., Flynn, J., Halpern, D. F., & Turkheimer, E. (2012). Intelligence: New findings and theoretical developments. *American Psychologist, 67*(2), 130.

Norton, P. J., & Weiss, B. J. (2009). The role of courage on behavioral approach in a fear-eliciting situation: A proof-of-concept pilot study. *Journal of Anxiety Disorders, 23*(2), 212–217.

Nuñez, M. (2015, June 18). Does money buy happiness? The link between salary and employee satisfaction. [Web log post]. Retrieved from https://www.glassdoor.com/research/does-money-buy-happiness-the-link-between-salary-and-employee-satisfaction/

O'Boyle, E. (2016). Does culture matter in economic behaviour? *Social and Education History, 5*(1), 52–82. doi:10.17583/hse.2016.1796

Oettingen, G., Pak, H. J., & Schnetter, K. (2001). Self-regulation of goal-setting: Turning free fantasies about the future into binding goals. *Journal of Personality and Social Psychology, 80*(5), 736.

Ogden, C. L., Carroll, M. D., Fryar, C. D., & Flegal, K. M. (2015). Prevalence of obesity among adults and youth: United States, 2011–2014. *National Center for Health Statistics Data Brief, 219,* 1–8. Retrieved from http://c.ymcdn.com/sites/www.acutept.org/resource/resmgr/Critical_EdgEmail/0216-prevalence-of-obesity.pdf

Pachucki, M. A., Jacques, P. F., & Christakis, N. A. (2011). Social network concordance in food choice among spouses, friends, and siblings. *American Journal of Public Health, 101*(11), 2170–2177.

Penninx, B. W., Rejeski, W. J., Pandya, J., Miller, M. E., Di Bari, M., Applegate, W. B., & Pahor, M. (2002). Exercise and depressive symptoms: A comparison of aerobic and resistance exercise effects on emotional and physical function in older persons with high and low depressive symptomatology. *Journals of Gerontology Series B: Psychological Sciences and Social Sciences, 57*(2), P124–P132.

Pilcher, J. J., & Huffcutt, A. J. (1996). Effects of sleep deprivation on performance: A meta-analysis. *Sleep: Journal of Sleep Research & Sleep Medicine, 19*(4), 318–326.

Pink, D. H. (2011). *Drive: The surprising truth about what motivates us.* New York, NY: Penguin.

Plomin, R., & Deary, I. J. (2015). Genetics and intelligence differences: Five special findings. *Molecular Psychiatry, 20*(1), 98–108.

Pury, C. L., & Hensel, A. D. (2010). Are courageous actions successful actions? *Journal of Positive Psychology, 5*(1), 62–72.

Pury, C. L., & Kowalski, R. M. (2007). Human strengths, courageous actions, and general and personal courage. *The Journal of Positive Psychology, 2*(2), 120-128.

Pury, C. L., & Lopez, S. J. (Eds.). (2010). *The psychology of courage: Modern research on an ancient virtue.* Washington, DC: American Psychological Association.

Pury, C. L., & Starkey, C. B. (2010). Is courage an accolade or a process? A fundamental question for courage research. In Pury, C. L., & Lopez, S. J. (Eds.), *The psychology of courage: Modern research on an ancient virtue* (pp. 67–87). Washington, DC: American Psychological Association.

Pury, C. L., Kowalski, R. M., & Spearman, J. (2007). Distinctions between general and personal courage. *The Journal of Positive Psychology, 2*(2), 99–114.

Pury, C. L., Starkey, C. B., Kulik, R. E., Skjerning, K. L., & Sullivan, E. A. (2015). Is courage always a virtue? Suicide, killing, and bad courage. *The Journal of Positive Psychology, 10*(5), 383–388.

Quoidbach, J., Dunn, E. W., Petrides, K. V., & Mikolajczak, M. (2010). Money giveth, money taketh away: The dual effect of wealth on happiness. *Psychological Science, 21*(6), 759–763.

Rachman, S. (1990). *Fear and courage* (2nd ed.). New York, NY: Freeman.

Rachman, S. J. (2010). Courage: A psychological perspective. In C. L. Pury & S. J. Lopez (Eds.), *The psychology of courage: Modern research on an ancient virtue* (pp. 91–107). Washington, DC: American Psychological Association.

Rate, C. R., Clarke, J. A., Lindsay, D. R., & Sternberg, R. J. (2007). Implicit theories of courage. *Journal of Positive Psychology, 2*(2), 80–98.

Ratey, J. J., & Hagerman, E. (2008). *Spark: The revolutionary new science of exercise and the brain.* New York, NY: Little, Brown and Company.

Regan, D. T. (1971). Effects of a favor and liking on compliance. *Journal of Experimental Social Psychology, 7*(6), 627–639.

Reivich, K., & Shatté, A. (2002). *The resilience factor: 7 essential skills for overcoming life's inevitable obstacles.* New York, NY: Broadway Books.

Rethorst, C. D., Wipfli, B. M., & Landers, D. M. (2009). The antidepressive effects of exercise. *Sports Medicine, 39*(6), 491–511.

Rice, K. G., & Ashby, J. S. (2007). An efficient method for classifying perfectionists. Journal of *Counseling Psychology, 54,* 72–85. doi:10.1037/0022-0167.54.1.72

Rice, K. G., Bair, C., Castro, J., Cohen, B., & Hood, C. (2003). Meanings of perfectionism: A quantitative and qualitative analysis. *Journal of Cognitive Psychotherapy, 17,* 39–58. doi:10.1521/jscp.2005.24.4.580

Roberts, B. W., Luo, J., Brile, D. A., Chow, P. I., Su, R., & Hill P. L. (2017). A systematic review of personality trait change through intervention. *Psychological Bulletin, 143*(2), 117–141.

Roe, A. (1953a). *The making of a scientist.* New York: Dodd, Mead.

Roe, A. (1953b). A psychological study of eminent psychologists and anthropologists, and a comparison with biological and physical scientists. *Psychological Monographs: General and Applied, 67*(2), 1.

Rosenquist, J. N., Fowler, J. H., & Christakis, N. A. (2011). Social network determinants of depression. *Molecular Psychiatry, 16*(3), 273–281.

Rosso, B. D., Dekas, K. H., & Wrzesniewski, A. (2010). On the meaning of work: A theoretical integration and review. *Research in Organizational Behavior, 30,* 91–127.

Rozin, P., & Royzman, E. B. (2001). Negativity bias, negativity dominance, and contagion. *Personality and Social Psychology Review, 5*(4), 296–320.

Ruff, G., & Korchin, S. (1964). Psychological responses of the Mercury astronauts to stress. In G. Grosser, H. Wechsler, M. Greenblatt (Eds.), *The threat of impending disaster* (pp 46–57). Cambridge, MA: MIT Press.

Rummler, G. A., & Brache, A. P. (1995*). Improving performance: How to manage the white space on the organization chart* (2nd ed.). San Francisco, CA: Jossey-Bass.

Rushton, J. P., & Jensen, A. R. (2010). Race and IQ: A theory-based review of the research in Richard Nisbett's Intelligence and How to Get It. *Open Psychology Journal, 3*(1), 9–35.

Ruthsatz, J., Detterman, D. K., Griscom, W. S., & Cirullo, B. A. (2008). Becoming an expert in the musical domain: It takes more than just practice. *Intelligence, 36*(4), 330–338.

Ryan, R. M., & Deci, E. L. (2000a). Intrinsic and extrinsic motivations: Classic definitions and new directions. *Contemporary Educational Psychology, 25*(1), 54–67.

Ryan, R. M., & Deci, E. L. (2000b). Self-determination theory and the facilitation of intrinsic motivation, social development, and well-being. *American Psychologist, 55*(1), 68.

Ryff, C. D., & Singer, B. (1998). The contours of positive human health. *Psychological Inquiry, 9*(1), 1–28.

Safire, W. (2004). *Lend me your ears: Great speeches in history*. New York: NY: W.W. Norton & Company.

Samuels, C. (2009). Sleep, recovery, and performance: the new frontier in high-performance athletics. *Physical Medicine and Rehabilitation Clinics of North America, 20*(1), 149–159.

Savitsky, K., Epley, N., & Gilovich, T. (2001). Is it as bad as we fear? Overestimating the extremity of others' judgments. *Journal of Personality and Social Psychology, 81*(1), 44–56.

Schein, Edgar H. (2010). *Organizational culture and leadership* (4th ed.). San Francisco, CA: Jossey-Bass.

Schimel, J., Arndt, J., Banko, K. M., & Cook, A. (2004). Not all self-affirmations were created equal: The cognitive and social benefits of affirming the intrinsic (vs. extrinsic) self. *Social Cognition, 22*(1: Special Issue), 75–99.

Schirmer, A., Teh, K. S., Wang, S., Vijayakumar, R., Ching, A., Nithianantham, D., . . . & Cheok, A. D. (2011). Squeeze me, but don't tease me: Human and mechanical touch enhance visual attention and emotion discrimination. *Social Neuroscience, 6*(3), 219–230.

Schwartz, T., & McCarthy, C. (2007). Manage your energy, not your time. *Harvard Business Review, 85*(10), 63.

Scott, G., Leritz, L. E., & Mumford, M. D. (2004). The effectiveness of creativity training: A quantitative review. *Creativity Research Journal, 16*(4), 361–388.

Sedlmeier, P., Eberth, J., Schwarz, M., Zimmermann, D., Haarig, F., Jaeger, S., & Kunze, S. (2012). The psychological effects of meditation: A meta-analysis. *Psychological Bulletin, 138*(6), 1139.

Seidman, D. (2011). *How: Why how we do anything means everything.* Hoboken, NJ: John Wiley & Sons.

Seligman, M. E., Steen, T. A., Park, N., & Peterson, C. (2005). Positive psychology progress: Empirical validation of interventions. *American Psychologist, 60*(5), 410.

Seligman, M. E. P. (1990). *Learned optimism: The skill to conquer life's obstacles, large and small.* New York, NY: Pocket Books.

Seligman, M. E. P. (2012). *Flourish: A visionary new understanding of happiness and well-being.* New York, NY: Simon and Schuster.

Senécal, C., Koestner, R., & Vallerand, R. J. (1995). Self-regulation and academic procrastination. *Journal of Social Psychology, 135*(5), 607–619.

Seppala, E., & Cameron, K. (2015, December 1). Proof that positive work cultures are more productive. *Harvard Business Review.* Retrieved from https://hbr.org/2015/12/proof-that-positive-work-cultures-are-more-productive

Sgroi, D. (2015). *Happiness and productivity: Understanding the happy-productive worker.* (SMF-CAGE Global Perspectives Series Paper 4.) Retrieved from Social Market Foundation website: http://bit.ly/2ndmvFA

Shadyab, A. H., Macera, C. A., Shaffer, R. A., Jain, S., Gallo, L. C., LaMonte, M. J., . . . & Manini, T. M. (2017). Associations of accelerometer-measured and self-reported sedentary time with leukocyte telomere length in older women. *American Journal of Epidemiology, 185*(3), 172–184.

Sheldon, K. M., Jose, P. E., Kashdan, T. B., & Jarden, A. (2015). Personality, effective goal-striving, and enhanced well-being: Comparing 10 candidate personality strengths. *Personality and Social Psychology Bulletin.* doi:10.1177/0146167215573211

Shoji, K., Cieslak, R., Smoktunowicz, E., Rogala, A., Benight, C. C., & Luszczynska, A. (2016). Associations between job burnout and self-efficacy: a meta-analysis. *Anxiety, Stress, & Coping: An International Journal, 29*(4), 367–386.

Sibley, B. A., & Etnier, J. L. (2003). The relationship between physical activity and cognition in children: A meta-analysis. *Pediatric Exercise Science, 15*(3), 243–256.

Simonton, D. K. (1988). Creativity, leadership, and chance. In R. J. Sternberg (Ed.), *The nature of creativity: Contemporary psychological perspectives* (pp. 386–426). New York, NY: Cambridge University Press.

Sparling, P. B., Giuffrida, A., Piomelli, D., Rosskopf, L., & Dietrich, A. (2003). Exercise activates the endocannabinoid system. *Neuroreport, 14*(17), 2209-2211.

Spelke, Elizabeth S. (2005). Sex differences in intrinsic aptitude for mathematics and science? A critical review. *American Psychologist, 60*(9), 950–958.

Stajkovic, A. D., & Luthans, F. (1998). Self-efficacy and work-related performance: A meta-analysis. *Psychological Bulletin, 124*(2), 240–261.

Stavrou, N. A., Jackson, S. A., Zervos, Y., Karterolliotis, K. (2007). Flow experience and athletes' performance with reference to the orthogonal model of flow. *Sport Psychologist, 21,* 438–457.

Staw, B. M., & Barsade, S. G. (1993). Affect and managerial performance: A test of the sadder-but-wiser vs. happier-and-smarter hypothesis. *Administrative Science Quarterly, 38*(2), 304–331.

Steger, M. F., Frazier, P., Oishi, S., & Kaler, M. (2006). The meaning in life questionnaire: Assessing the presence of and search for meaning in life. *Journal of Counseling Psychology, 53*(1), 80.

Sternberg, R. J. (1999). *Handbook of creativity.* Cambridge, UK: Cambridge University Press.

Sternberg, R. J., & Frensch, P. A. (1992). On being an expert: A cost-benefit analysis. In R. R. Hoffman (Ed.), *The psychology of expertise: Cognitive research and empirical AI* (pp. 191–203). New York, NY: Springer.

Sternberg, R. J., & Grigorenko, E. L. (2003). *The psychology of abilities, competencies, and expertise.* Cambridge, UK: Cambridge University Press.

Stevenson, B., & Wolfers, J. (2013). Subjective well-being and income: Is there any evidence of satiation? *American Economic Review, 103*(3), 598–604.

Stillman, T. F., Baumeister, R. F., Lambert, N. M., Crescioni, A. W., DeWall, C. N., & Fincham, F. D. (2009). Alone and without purpose: Life loses meaning following social exclusion. *Journal of Experimental Social Psychology, 45*(4), 686–694.

Strauss, J., & Thomas, D. (1998). Health, nutrition, and economic development. *Journal of Economic Literature, 36*(2), 766–817.

Sulsky, L. M. (1999). Commitment in the workplace: Theory, research, and application. [Review of the book *Commitment in the workplace: Theory, research, and application*, by J. P. Meyer & N. J. Allen.] *Canadian Psychology, 40*(4), 383–385.

Sun, J., Kaufman, S. B., & Smillie, L. D. (2017). Unique associations between big five personality aspects and multiple dimensions of well-being. *Journal of Personality*. doi:10.1111/jopy.12301

Sy, T., Cote, S., & Saavedra, R. (2005). The contagious leader: Impact of the leader's mood on the mood of group members, group affective tone, and group process. *Journal of Applied Psychology, 90*(2), 295–305.

Tafet, G. E., Idoyaga-Vargas, V. P., Abulafia, D. P., Calandria, J. M., Roffman, S. S., Chiovetta, A., & Shinitzky, M. (2001). Correlation between cortisol level and serotonin uptake in patients with chronic stress and depression. *Cognitive, Affective, & Behavioral Neuroscience, 1*(4), 388–393.

Tangney, J. P., Baumeister, R. F., & Boone A. L. (2004). High self-control predicts good adjustment, less pathology, better grades, and interpersonal success. *Journal of Personality, 72*(2), 271–324.

Tedeschi, R. G., & Calhoun L. G. (2004). Posttraumatic growth: Conceptual foundations and empirical evidence. *Psychological Inquiry, 15*(1), 1–18.

Teixeira, P. J., Carraça, E. V., Marques, M. M., Rutter, H., Oppert, J. M., De Bourdeaudhuij, I., . . . & Brug, J. (2015). Successful behavior change in obesity interventions in adults: A systematic review of self-regulation mediators. *BMC Medicine, 13*(1), 84.

Tenenbaum, G., Yuval, R., Elbaz, G., Bar-Eli, M., & Weinberg, R. (1993). The relationship between cognitive characteristics and decision making. *Canadian Journal of Applied Physiology, 18*(1), 48–62.

Tetlock, P. E. (1992). The impact of accountability on judgment and choice: Toward a social contingency model. *Advances in Experimental Social Psychology, 25,* 331–376.

Thomas, D., & Frankenberg, E. (2002). Health, nutrition and prosperity: A microeconomic perspective. *Bulletin of the World Health Organization, 80*(2), 106–113.

Thompson, C. A., & Prottas, D. J. (2006). Relationships among organizational family support, job autonomy, perceived control, and employee well-being. *Journal of Occupational Health Psychology, 11*(1), 100.

Tognatta, N., Valerio, A., & Sanchez Puerta, M. L. (2016). *Do cognitive and noncognitive skills explain the gender wage gap in middle-income countries? An analysis using STEP data.* (World Bank Policy Research Working Paper No. 7878.) Retrieved from SSRN website: http://bit.ly/2nehVaf

Tomporowski, P. D. (2003). Effects of acute bouts of exercise on cognition. *Acta Psychologica, 112*(3), 297–324.

Torrance, E. P. (1983). The importance of falling in love with "something." *Creative Child & Adult Quarterly, 8*(2): 72–78.

Tracy, J. L., Cheng J. T., Robins, R. W., & Trzesniewski, K. H. (2009). Authentic and hubristic pride: The affective core of self-esteem and narcissism. *Self and Identity 8*(2–3), 196–213.

Treffert, D. A. (2010). *Islands of genius: The bountiful mind of the autistic, acquired and sudden savant.* London, UK: Jessica Kingsley.

Treffert, D. A. (2014). Accidental genius. *Scientific American, 311*(2), 52–57.

Trougakos, J. P., & Hideg, I. (2009). Momentary work recovery: The role of within-day work breaks. In P. Perrewé, D. Ganster, & S. Sonnentag (Eds.), *Research in occupational stress and wellbeing* (Vol. 7, pp. 37–84). West Yorkshire, UK: Emerald Group.

Trougakos, J. P., Beal, D. J., Green, S. G., & Weiss, H. M. (2008). Making the break count: An episodic examination of recovery activities, emotional experiences, and positive affective displays. *Academy of Management Journal, 51*(1), 131–146.

Trougakos, J. P., Hideg, I., Cheng, B. H., & Beal, D. J. (2014). Lunch breaks unpacked: The role of autonomy as a moderator of recovery during lunch. *Academy of Management Journal, 57*(2), 405–421.

US Department of Labor (2016, February 25). Volunteering in the United States, 2015. [News release.] Retrieved from https://www.bls.gov/news.release/volun.nr0.htm

Vaeyens, R., Lenoir, M., Williams, A. M., & Philippaerts, R. M. (2008). Talent identification and development programmes in sport. *Sports Medicine, 38*(9), 703–714.

Valentine, E. R., & Sweet, P. L. (1999). Meditation and attention: A comparison of the effects of concentrative and mindfulness meditation on sustained attention. *Mental Health, Religion & Culture, 2*(1), 59–70.

Wan, C. Y., & Huon, G. F. (2005). Performance degradation under pressure in music: An examination of attentional processes. *Psychology of Music, 33*(2), 155–172.

Wand, B. (1956). Hume's account of obligation. *The Philosophical Quarterly (1950–), 6*(23), 155–168.

Wang, G. J., Volkow, N. D., Logan, J., Pappas, N. R., Wong, C. T., Zhu, W., . . . & Fowler, J. S. (2001). Brain dopamine and obesity. *The Lancet, 357*(9253), 354–357.

Weaver, K., Garcia, S. M., Schwarz, N., & Miller, D. T. (2007). Inferring the popularity of an opinion from its familiarity: A repetitive voice can sound like a chorus. *Journal of Personality and Social Psychology, 92*(5), 821.

Weldon, E., & Weingart, L. R. (1993). Group goals and group performance. *British Journal of Social Psychology, 32*(4), 307–334.

Weldon, E., Jehn, K. A., & Pradhan, P. (1991). Processes that mediate the relationship between a group goal and improved group performance. *Journal of Personality and Social Psychology, 61*(4), 555.

Whittaker, S., Matthews, T., Cerruti, J., Badenes, H., & Tang, J. (2011, May). Am I wasting my time organizing email? A study of email refinding. In Proceedings of the Conference on Human Factors in Computing Systems (pp. 276–283). Retrieved from http://bit.ly/2nkpdGq

Wigfield, A., & Eccles, J. (2002). The development of competence beliefs, expectancies for success, and achievement values from childhood through adolescence. In A. Wigfield & J. Eccles (Eds.), *Development of achievement motivation* (pp. 91–120). San Diego, CA: Academic Press.

Wood, R., & Locke, E. (1990). Goal setting and strategy effects on complex tasks. In B. Staw & L. Cummings (Eds.), *Research in organizational behavior* (Vol. 12, pp. 73–109). Greenwich, CT: JAI Press.

Woodard, R. W., Pury, C. L. S. (2013). The construct of courage: Categorization management. *Consulting Psychology Journal: Practice and Research,* Vol 59, *(2),* 135-147

Wright, J. C., Nadelhoffer, T., Perini, T., Langville, A., Echols, M., & Venezia, K. (2017). The psychological significance of humility. *The Journal of Positive Psychology, 12*(1), 3–12.

Wright, T. A., & Cropanzano, R. (2000). Psychological well-being and job satisfaction as predictors of job performance. *Journal of Occupational Health Psychology, 5*(1), 84.

Wrzesniewski, A. (2003). Finding positive meaning in work. In K. S. Cameron, J. E. Dutton, & R. E. Quinn (Eds.), *Positive organizational scholarship: Foundations of a new discipline* (pp. 296–308). San Francisco, CA: Berrett-Koehler.

Young, W. T. (1971). The role of musical aptitude, intelligence, and academic achievement in predicting the musical attainment of elementary instrumental music students. *Journal of Research in Music Education, 19*(4), 385–398.

Yousef, D. A. (1998). Satisfaction with job security as a predictor of organizational commitment and job performance in a multicultural environment. *International Journal of Manpower, 19*(3), 184–194.

Yu, R. (2014). Choking under pressure: The neuropsychological mechanisms of incentive-induced performance decrements. *Frontiers in Behavioral Neuroscience, 9,* 19–19.